Closely Observed Children
The diary of a primary classroom
Michael Armstrong

Writers and Readers
in association with **Chameleon**

Writers and Readers Publishing Cooperative Society Ltd
144 Camden High Street London NW1 0NE
England

Published by Writers and Readers Publishing
Cooperative Society Ltd in association with
Chameleon Editorial Group 1980
Reprinted 1981, 1982

Printed in Great Britain
at the University Press, Oxford
Set in 10/11 Baskerville by Shanta Thawani
ISBN 0 906495 21 0 Paperback
Cased 0 906495 04 0

For Carol Norton
For Tony Kallet
and for Isobel, Thomas, Ursula and Stephen Armstrong.

"Neither Youth nor Childhood is Folly or Incapacity."
William Blake (in a letter to Dr Trusler, 23 August, 1799)

Contents

Preface

The origin of this book goes back to 1968 when I was invited to attend one of the Leicestershire Primary School Teachers' Workshops held every Easter during the late 1960s and early 1970s at Loughborough University. It was there, in 1968 and again in 1969 and 1970, that I began to develop the ideas which underlie the story written here, in conversation and workshop practice with Bill Browse and Tony Kallet, Allan Ahlberg and Byron Thomas, Bill Hull, David and Frances Hawkins, and Brenda Engel. My ideas took further shape at Countesthorpe College which opened in 1970 under the guidance and inspiration of Tim McMullen. I owe a very special debt to the students and teachers with whom I worked at Countesthorpe. The six years I taught there transformed my understanding of education and made me long to explore at greater leisure the nature of intellectual growth. For the opportunity to carry out a programme of teaching and research directed to that end I would like to thank in particular David Hawkins whose writings made me see what I wanted to find out, Gurth Higgin who helped me to formulate a research proposal and get it accepted, the members of Countesthorpe College who gave me generous leave of absence, Bill Browse and Byron Thomas who enabled me to find my way into the world of primary schools, Andrew Fairbairn whose support and encouragement kept my research going, Brian Simon who was unfailingly helpful to a project very different to his own research in primary education, the staff of the Mountain View Center at the University of Colorado who invited me to Boulder in the autumn of 1977 and explored with me there the implications of my research, and above all, the pupils and teachers of Sherard School. The 32 children in Stephen Rowland's class, Stephen Rowland himself, Mary Brown and Janet Harvey are the heroines and heroes of this book, my gratitude to them is incalculable.

This book has a threefold dedication: to Carol Norton, a student of mine at Countesthorpe College who first showed me how to look at and seek to describe a primary school classroom; to Tony Kallet whose critical and enthusiastic response inspired me to write the book; and to my family who have encouraged, confirmed, criticised, revived, extended and reconstructed my thought.

1 Introduction: the Setting

This book is about a class of 32 eight to nine year old children in an English primary school; about intellectual growth and intellectual achievement; about understanding the understanding of children. It is not a study of classroom life as a whole; for example, it contains little about the social life of the class or about the organisation of classroom activity. Its aim is to explore some of the ways in which the children learnt, within a classroom environment, as they sought to make sense of the world and to reflect upon their own experience of it. It examines the intellectual experience of children in one particular classroom for the light it may shed on intellectual growth in general.

The school is Sherard School, a large county primary school which stands at the top end of a modern private housing estate on the edge of a small town in the East Midlands. Sherard School opened in 1968 as two schools, infant and junior, with separate staffs, sharing a single building. Three years later, on the resignation of the junior school headteacher, it was reorganised as one school; Mary Brown, who was previously headteacher of the infants, became head of the whole school.

In 1976 there were some 500 children in the school, between five and eleven years old, and 18 teachers. Most of the children lived on the estate around the school; the rest came from across the main road that bounds the estate on one side, or from outlying villages and farms. Many of their parents worked in the large animal food factory at the bottom of the estate, beyond the river and the railway line. Others worked in shops and offices in the town, in the nearby city, in the army, in agriculture. A majority of the children's fathers were in clerical and skilled or semi-skilled manual occupations; a few were shopkeepers, teachers, farmers, sales representatives, or in business on their own account. Many of their mothers also had full time or part time jobs.

The school building is half open-plan, a compromise between the traditional school building with its corridors and classrooms, and the wide open spaces favoured in more recent schools built by the same local education authority. A few classrooms are joined by sliding panels which can be pulled back to make a large double classroom. All of them are without doors, opening out onto shared work areas lit by skylights. There are no corridors. It would be just possible for a class of thirty children to work entirely within their own classroom but most teachers find it more convenient to spread out into the shared areas if they can. These common spaces include a few special facilities: cooking bays, clay benches, small libraries. For the rest they are organised and furnished as the classes that share them decide from year to year. The distribution of space makes it comparatively easy for a class to withdraw into its own particular room if it wants to, while opening up each classroom to outside influences. Many of the teachers work in pairs, organising two classes more or less as one.

The atmosphere of Sherard School, its philosophical outlook and style, is best described through the work and play of the children whose experience provides the subject matter of the remaining chapters in this book, and only the briefest characterization is necessary here. The first impression which the school makes on a visitor is of a certain bustling informality. The walls and corners of classrooms are full of the children's paintings, writings, models and constructions; many different activities can be observed, as a rule, taking place side by side within the same classroom; there is an air of action, experiment and invention and a good deal of movement, intellectual as well as physical. But this initial impression may conceal from the visitor the many different ways in which the various teachers interpret informality according to their own particular philosophy and practice. As headteacher, Mary Brown welcomes and fosters this variety, which she regards as an essential condition of self-criticism and thus of growth. Nevertheless her own thought is broadly representative of what the Plowden Report in 1967 identified, mistakenly as it now appears,* as the 'quickening trend' in primary schools towards a freer and more self-directed style of work. Before she came to Sherard School, Mary Brown was headteacher of an infant school not far away and there she had written, with the head of the adjacent junior school, an account of their curriculum, which was organised in a manner known at that time as 'the integrated day' and strongly favoured by the Plowden Report

---

* To judge from the latest report on primary schools by Her Majesty's Inspectors, no more than a small minority of primary schools have followed this trend. See *Primary Education in England and Wales,* HMSO, 1978. See also *Inside the Primary Classroom,* Maurice Galton, Brian Simon, and Paul Croll, Routledge & Kegan Paul, 1980.

itself.* She belongs firmly within that tradition of early education which, as the American philosopher and educationalist David Hawkins once put it, has tried to bring about 'a major reorganisation of subject-matter into a common and coherent framework'. 'The sand and water and clay,' Hawkins continues, 'the painting and writing and reading, the cooking and building and calculation, the observing and nurture of plants and animals, are woven together into a complex social pattern which sustains romance as it extends a concern for detail and for generalisation . . . Teachers of the young are not usually regarded, by themselves or by others, as 'intellectual' . . . Yet the skilful among them are able to see order and number, geography and history, moral testing grounds and aesthetic qualities in all the encounters of young children with the furniture of a rich environment.'** When, once, I was discussing with Mary Brown the essay from which these words are taken she told me that they represented very much her own convictions. They might equally well be said to represent the aspirations of a majority of teachers at Sherard School, however fragmentary and incomplete the teachers may consider their present achievement of these aspirations to be.

I spent the school year 1976–1977 observing and teaching children in one particular classroom at Sherard School. For several years I had been looking for an opportunity to study the learning of children at greater leisure than the daily routine of classroom teaching afforded, yet without abandoning the teaching role. It seemed to me that the study of intellectual growth and its enabling conditions demanded a more intimate relationship between the activities of teaching and observation than has been common in educational research. In this I was much influenced by the work of David Hawkins. David Hawkins is Professor of Philosophy at the University of Colorado, a philosopher of science who in the early 1960s became closely involved in attempts to recast the subject matter of science so as to make it more diversely accessible and appealing to primary school children in American schools. In 1974 he published a fascinating but little known collection of essays on the practice and theory of education, especially at primary school level, under the title *The Informed Vision : essays on learning and human nature.**** One of their most persistent themes is the critical importance of linking teaching with observation and analysis in any sustained effort

---

* *The Integrated Day in the Primary School,* Mary Brown and Norman Precious, Ward Lock, 1968.
** *Two Sources of Learning,* David Hawkins, FORUM for the Discussion of New Trends in Education, Vol. 16, No. 1, Autumn 1973.
*** Agathon Press, 1974.

to develop what he calls 'a theory of the life of reason from the beginnings of learning'. In an essay on 'Childhood and the Education of Intellectuals' he outlines his position as follows: 'The truth is that there has been relatively little close and disciplined scientific observation of the learning behaviour of young children as related to their distinctively intellectual development. It helps to work by stages, as Piaget has done, but we need to see such development *in statu nascendi*. Nor is such observation likely to prove fruitful under short term, transient conditions arranged for the benefit of the psychologist or psychiatrist observer. A Lorenz swims with his goslings, a Schaller lives with mountain gorillas, ethnologists live the life of the peoples they would study. To expect more from the ethological study of young children, for a lesser effort, seems naive indeed. The time scale of such observations is very clearly not the day or the week. The transitions and transformations of intellectual development may be rapid indeed, but they are statistically rare and must be observed in context to be given significance.

'The most important area of control, for making the intellectual development of children more visible, happens to coincide with the major practical aim of educational reform: to provide both the material and social environment, and the adult guidance, under which the engagement of children with their world is most intrinsically satisfying and most conducive to the development we would study. Thus to be the best scientific observers we must be at once the best providers for and the best teachers of those whom we would study. If this seems too much to ask, we must then associate ourselves in teams which work harmoniously and with considerable overlapping of their various functions.'

Although the study of intellectual growth through a combination of teaching, observation and analysis, after the manner described by David Hawkins in this passage, was my aim, I was acutely conscious, through my own previous experience, that teaching and observation are not easy to reconcile. On the one hand, the pressures of classroom life make it exceptionally difficult for an individual teacher to describe the intellectual experience of his pupils at length, in detail and with a sufficient detachment. Conversely, as Hawkins implies, to observe a class of children without teaching them is to deprive oneself of a prime source of knowledge: the knowledge that comes from asking questions, engaging in conversations, discussing, informing, criticising, correcting and being corrected, demonstrating, interpreting, helping, instructing or collaborating — in short, from teaching. I decided that one way to resolve this dilemma might be to work as an auxiliary or assistant to another teacher. If two teachers were to assume joint, though not necessarily equal, responsibility for a single class of children it might be possible between the two of them to find sufficient time and space both for sustained observation and for sustained teaching. It was this solution that I was anxious to test.

The opportunity to test it arose in the summer of 1976 when the secondary school at which I was then teaching gave me leave of absence, with the support of the local education authority, to carry out a small pilot study in a primary school elsewhere in the county. I wanted to work in another school than my own and with children of a different age from those I was teaching, because at the time I felt it necessary to distance myself in some degree from preoccupations which had become too familiar during the previous six years. Friends and colleagues suggested Sherard School as one of several schools in the county that might welcome the study I had in mind. I visited the school twice in the spring of 1976 and found that Mary Brown and several other teachers were interested in taking part. It was the first school that I had visited and I was struck by the freedom of choice with which both teachers and children worked and which seemed to be favourable to the kind of inquiry I wanted to conduct. After the second visit I decided to look no further, and on September 1st the field work began.

The object of my inquiry was necessarily limited and tentative. I did not intend to assess in detail the children's attainment, nor to judge the effectiveness of particular teaching methods, nor to compare informal and formal classrooms. I wanted to study, within the context of one particular school, the character and quality of children's intellectual understanding: the insights which they display and the problems which they encounter, their inventiveness and originality and their intellectual dependence. I chose to concentrate on intellectual growth rather than social development, and on learning rather than teaching, without, I hope, ignoring the interdependence of each pair of terms.

At the start of the year I worked with two classes, Janet Harvey's class of seven to eight year olds, and Stephen Rowland's class of eight to nine year olds. I began the year in Janet's class and many of the strands of thought that developed during the course of the months that followed can be traced back to my early days in Janet's classroom. But in November Janet was granted maternity leave and when she returned to the school the following spring it was decided that she should teach a new class of infants. So for most of the year I worked in Stephen Rowland's classroom alone and it is around the life and work of the children in Stephen's class that this book revolves.

Stephen had been teaching at Sherard School for two years; it was his second teaching post, his fourth year as a full time teacher. The year before he had worked closely with another teacher in the school, the two of them organising their classes as a single unit. Now however, though he would still be working next door to his friend's class, he was intending to work more independently. He was to be the only regular teacher of his class, although from time to time other teachers became involved in the work of the class in one way or another.

There were 32 children in Stephen's class, 19 girls and 13 boys.*At the start of the year, their ages varied from 8 years 2 months to 9 years; two thirds of them had birthdays that fell between October and March. They were, as primary school teachers say, a class of second year juniors.

Stephen's classroom was in one corner of the school building: a light, airy room, opening out onto a verandah that ran along to the school's front entrance, overlooking the car park and the playing fields beyond. Beside the windows, and the glass door that led to the verandah, was a sink, the only permanent fixture in the room. The classroom was furnished and arranged as most other classrooms in the school, except perhaps for the unusual quantity of bric-à-brac and junk which Stephen collected for the children's use: a radiogram casing, a discarded spin dryer, two or three large tyres, a turntable, boxes of wood and metal scraps. One corner of the room was carpeted. Here the children gathered to hear a story, to be registered, to read or display their work to the rest of the class, to take part in a quiz or a discussion. It was a corner often used also for reading, either to a teacher or to oneself. The area around the sink was kept mostly for art and craft and included a woodwork bench as well as two large lino top tables. In the middle of the year, in response to demand, Stephen created, alongside the art area, a small screened-off space for the children's improvisations: a variation of the infant classroom's Wendy House. The rest of the room contained a variety of smaller tables, rectangular or trapezoidal in shape; a couple of pegboard screens; free-standing cupboards and shelves, filled with the children's personal trays and an assortment of classroom materials; and further shelves and a blackboard fixed to the wall. At times, when all the children were packed into it, the classroom could seem

---

* 2 of the 32 joined the class after the start of the year. 3 other children moved out of the class during the year, while one child came and left within one term.

very crowded, but often the activity of the children spilled out into the open area immediately outside the classroom which was shared with the two classrooms on either side and contained more tables and chairs.

The pattern of a school day was as follows. Stephen would assemble the whole class together perhaps as often as two or three times a day but rarely more than that. These were occasions for reading to the class, explaining his plans and intentions, giving instructions or introducing new themes and ideas to the class as a whole, encouraging children to read out or show their work to the class, watching an improvised play, running quizzes, games, talking things over with the class. At first Stephen always assembled the class at the start of the morning and afternoon to take the register but later in the year he began to take the register less formally, as the children settled down to their own individual tasks. Four times a week the class went down to the school hall for an assembly, or service, usually in the second session of the day, after morning play. (There were three sessions to the school day: 8.50 a.m. — 10.45 a.m., 11.00 a.m. — 12 a.m., and 1.25 p.m. — 3.30 p.m.) One morning a week began with a P.E. session in the hall, and the hall was also available at certain other times in the week if it was needed.

For most of the day however the children worked in small groups, in pairs, or on their own, while Stephen moved among them, teaching. Occasionally a group was formally timetabled; so it was with the maths groups, of eight children each, which met with Stephen once a week for the introduction and discussion of new topics and activities. But most groups were informal and irregular, improvised for particular purposes and occasions and usually, though not always, self-selected. About half of the children had one or two particular friends with whom, if other things were equal, they would most often choose to work; but there were many exceptions and frequent small shifts and disruptions in the pattern of friendships and the choice of working partners.

From the very first day that I spent with Stephen's class, I found myself teaching as well as observing, and it soon became clear that teaching and observation would prove even more inextricable than I had supposed. The pattern that emerged was simple enough. During the school day I taught alongside Stephen, following the plans and procedures that he devised from day to day and week to week, and taking my lead from him. Sometimes I took charge of the whole class or of one particular group within it but for the most part I moved freely around the classroom, working with children in ones, twos or threes as the occasion demanded. My freedom of movement was considerably greater than Stephen's inasmuch as his own activity was necessarily constrained by his responsibility for the class as a whole. Although we never attempted to draw a clear distinction between our respective roles in the classroom, the children were in no doubt as to the difference between us. On my first appearance in the classroom, on the first Friday of the school year, Stephen had explained to the children that I was going to teach with him, and also to write about the work which the children were doing. From that day on, Stephen was their 'teacher' and I was his 'helper', or, as some put it, his 'student', and the children treated us accordingly.

At the end of each school day Stephen and I used to talk about it, sometimes for a few minutes, often for an hour or more. As time passed these conversations became the occasion not only for recalling the day's events but for formulating and elaborating our ideas about the children's learning. In the evenings Stephen had preparations to make for the following day, children's work to look at, records to keep, the daily round of out of school tasks to attend to. Occasionally I helped in these tasks but usually I spent my evenings writing about the day. I never wrote fewer than three times a week and often it was four or five times. The diaries or notebooks that I kept were the heart of our research; in them I recorded what seemed to me on reflection to have been the most significant events of the day, together with my observations, interpretations and speculations on these events. Sometimes I wrote down as much as I could recall of the day; more often I would choose to describe particular incidents, children, pieces of work: whatever seemed to bear most directly on the character of the children's learning. Although I tried to make my notes detailed and objective, I did not seek to avoid subjective impression or judgement.

Every week I showed Stephen what I had written and he read through my notes, adding his own comments and corrections on interleaved pages. In time I began to incorporate into my notes many of the ideas and impressions which we had exchanged in conversation at the end of the day. By the end of the year the daily notes represented less my own independent judgement than a common viewpoint established in our seemingly endless conversations. ('Do you two ever stop?', we were asked in the staffroom one day.) Stephen wrote notes of his own too, usually once a week, concentrating on particular incidents and activities in which I had not been directly involved. Every so often we would show our notes to Mary Brown who added fresh comments, often pointing to particular themes, suggested by the notes, which she thought it would be worthwhile to examine in greater detail. Gradually the three of us came to share each other's preoccupations, as the notes themselves bear witness.

By the end of the school year I had completed ten volumes of notes amounting to some 300,000 words, while Stephen and Mary between them had written a further 30,000 words or so. We had also assembled a large quantity of the children's writings, paintings, models, charts, plans, designs and notebooks, including as many as possible of the examples of work that were discussed in the notes themselves. It is these notes, and the samples of work that accompany them, that compose the material on which this book is based.

The chapters that follow describe the thought and action of children in Stephen Rowland's class as displayed in their work and play within the intellectual, social and physical environment of the classroom. Because my purpose is to draw closer to an understanding of the understanding of children, I have mostly chosen to concentrate attention on moments of intellectual absorption: those occasions on which the children were engrossed in the subject matter of their activity and evidently concerned with the significance of what they were saying, writing, painting, making, experimenting with, calculating, designing or inventing. Although productive learning is obviously not confined to moments of absorption, I believe that such moments are of critical importance both for the course of learning itself, and for thinking about the course of learning. For these are the moments at which children are most in earnest, however playfully, and it is then, in my view, that they reveal most about themselves: about the quality of their thought, about their own intellectual competence, and about their capacity for sustained intellectual growth. I begin by describing the children's writing because it was in relation to their writing that Stephen, Mary and I first began to develop the argument that is central to this book. Next I consider aspects of the children's art and mathematics. Then follows a study of one child's sustained absorption in subject matter and its consequences for intellectual growth. Finally I consider the intellectual significance of the children's play, as shown by the models and toys which they made.

2 The Literary Art of Children

Anyone who comes into contact with young children's writing for the first time is likely to be impressed by the apparent discrepancy between the liveliness and fluency of their conversation and the flatness and awkwardness of their writing. It seemed almost painfully obvious on my first morning at Sherard School. As Janet's old class gathered around her chair at the start of the morning everyone seemed to have stories to tell about the holidays. One boy told how his family's car had exploded while they were travelling to their holiday; another informed us of the £250 his family had been given; there was much talk of new dresses, new shoes, a new caravan. Later that morning, partly to fill in time before the children moved off to their new classes, — for only half of them were to stay in the same class — Janet asked those children who were staying in her class to get out their old writing books and turn to the first clean double page. They were to put the words 'Autumn Term 1976' at the top — she wrote the words out and pinned them to the wall for the children to copy — and then write just a little about anything they had done during the holiday. Despite, or perhaps because of, the conventional theme, everyone seemed to settle down to write readily enough; and then the troubles began. As I wrote in my notes at the end of the day:

'Most children could only manage a few stiff sentences and several couldn't really think of anything special that had happened to them in the holidays. (Or perhaps it's that everything is special and how, after all, is one to select.) Writing it is not like telling it anyway, especially not if you're only at the beginning of learning to write. So the boy who had been so keen at the start of the day to let Janet know that his family had been given £250, now said that, well, it wasn't really all that interesting a thing to write about. How then, in these early days, so important no doubt for the future development of writing, to arouse excitement in the art, to give children a sense of something worth saying in writing, or, more than that, of something worth saying that can *only* be said in writing?'

At first I scarcely understood the significance of the question I had asked. I identified the problem as one of helping children to reproduce in writing the vivacity of their talk, as if it were simply a matter of copying onto the page what they had said aloud. As time went on, however, and I grew more familiar with children's writing, I began to see that this was to misunderstand both their intentions and their achievements. The way in which the children with whom I worked set about writing suggested that they were strongly impressed by the contrast between the improvisatory quality of conversation, where meaning depends not on the words alone but on the gestures, expressions and tones of voice accompanying them, on the immediate and direct response between teller and listener, and the relative permanence and isolation of written words on the page. It seemed as if the children identified their problem not as how to reproduce in writing the expressiveness of their speech but as how to distil the experiences of which they had spoken in new and different ways appropriate to the distinctive medium of writing. It is hardly surprising that children should be impressed by the conflicting requirements of speech and writing in view of the manifold problems which the art of writing presents to them: problems of handwriting, spelling and punctuation, of grammar and syntax, of vocabulary, length of composition, style, appropriate form and content. Yet the more closely I studied what the children wrote the clearer it became that they did not regard these problems simply as so many barriers to significant expression; rather, they made use of the problems, expressively, as devices for liberating and controlling the imagination. Time and again the children managed to turn to their own advantage the very constraints which at first seemed so severe.

I want to examine first a group of writings which deal with just those kinds of experiences and events, such as the holiday anecdotes of the first morning of the school year, which the children were so ready to talk about and seemed to find so hard to set down in words on the page. Consider how Debra, an eight year old girl in Stephen Rowland's class, tackled such a problem early in October.

'Monday, October 11th.

After Stephen had finished another chapter of the book he is reading to the class, I settled down with three children who were engaged on writing: Simon, William and Debra. Simon was continuing a story he had begun about a rabbit. He suggested the same idea to William but William preferred to write about the wires he had been experimenting with a week ago. Debra chose to write about going mushroom picking on Saturday, having already told the story excitedly to Stephen and me and several others — how she'd gathered over 4 pounds of mushrooms (she'd told Mary Brown the exact weight, 4 lb. 6 oz.) while her brother's group had found no more than ten mushrooms all told.

Whether or not Debra would have chosen to record this incident in writing had writing not been suggested to her that morning I don't know. She may or may not have had a spontaneous urge to write about her experience. But once the idea of writing *something* was mooted she had no doubt about what it was that she wanted to write. She had been full of the Saturday's mushroom picking from the moment she arrived at school; now she wanted to record the events she'd regaled us with. Throughout the hour or so between the end of Stephen's reading and morning break she sat and wrote and sometimes spoke and stopped writing and thought or daydreamed — and by the end she had written some 15 lines. And then she turned to me and said, "Can I have a rest now?" It was hard, she said, adding that she'd only got up to the point at which they were about to set off on the mushrooming itself. What, I wondered, had been hard? Not, I think, the process of writing itself since Debra is usually a pretty confident writer. I think it was, rather, the whole business of remembering just what had happened — she kept on going over for me the various complex comings and goings between her gran's and her great gran's that had preceded the mushrooming — and then getting it into a succinct enough shape to write down: this is what had been hard. As Stephen pointed out at morning break, Debra was so captivated by her experience that she was determined to get it down just right, just as it had happened. And then, having begun to reflect back on it, she'd realised how much there was to say even before she got to the crux of it all, the mushrooming. By the end of the hour she may well have been saying to herself, "Oh dear, all this thinking and remembering and writing and I've still hardly started. I've still got all the exciting bit to come".'

This is what Debra had written:

'On Saturday

On Saturday me and my brother went to our grandma's. When we got there my grandad asked us if we wanted to go up and see my great grandma. So we went up there and my Uncle Cecil asked me if I wanted to go mushrooming after dinner. I said yes please so we went back to have dinner. After dinner I got my wellingtons on and my coat on and said good bye but my brother wanted to come so my grandad told Adam that he would take (him)* and we could see who could get the most.'

The problem of narrative preliminaries plagued many children in the class from time to time. Often they would begin a story or reminiscence boldly enough, recording the opening events in considerable detail and with a certain descriptive verve, only to find that by the time they had finished the introduction they had already exhausted their narrative energy and were at a loss how to continue. Or else, as Debra seemed to, they would worry about the time and the length it would require to complete the story in as much detail as they had begun it with. In Debra's case it may also have been that she had started to write before she had given herself sufficient time to order the experience in her mind in an appropriate form for writing. At any rate she wrote no more that day and my notes record that she had still not finished the piece on the Tuesday.

'Tuesday, October 12th.

I asked her if she had had time to finish her mushrooming account. Not yet she hadn't, she said, but she would. "Don't leave it too late", I cautioned. She's still bound up in it however, to judge by the way in which she took the opportunity of Mary Brown's presence in the classroom first thing in the morning to mention it to her too. And of course the episode was reverberating through the work she'd begun on fungi and on corals.'

Later that week, however, Debra did finish her account. When I first read the complete account, some time afterwards, I was disappointed by it. The elaborate sequence of events with which her story had begun had led me to expect, as maybe Debra had at first herself intended, a lengthy description of the mushroom picking itself, rich in incident. Instead I found that she had condensed the whole of the rest of the adventure into some ten lines, compared with the fifteen lines which she had devoted to the preliminaries. Once

---

* The bracketed word has been added by me. I have regularised spelling and punctuation in this and most other quotations from children's writings. Words themselves, however, have not been omitted, added or altered in any way without specific indications, as here.

again I had the feeling that the excitement of her spoken account had been dissipated by the struggle to write; and it may indeed be that the brevity of the climax of her story owes something to the fact that she had spent too long on the preliminaries. A closer reading, however, suggests a quite different judgement. The story ended as follows:

> 'So I set off. I ran as fast as I could. I soon got there. My uncle was waiting for me so we set off. We went in no end of fields and we walked about three miles. We took a bread bag. It got so full that the mushrooms kept falling out. When we got back we weighed all of them. We had got 4 lb. 6 oz.'

The climax is certainly brief but consider how deftly and economically Debra has succeeded in distilling the essence of her excitement in the shortest of narratives. From the moment she sets off after dinner every detail counts: running as fast as she can, her uncle waiting, going in 'no end of fields', walking 'about three miles' as if to confirm the 'no end', and above all the bread bag that 'got so full that the mushrooms kept falling out'. That one observation, together with the weighing that follows and the exact weight with which the story closes, is sufficient to convey the enthusiasm with which at the beginning of the week Debra had recounted her adventure. Without imitating the way in which she had spoken of it, without the help of those gestures, expressions and tones of voice that had earlier conveyed so much of her excitement, she had nevertheless managed to incorporate into her written account enough significant detail to recapture, in a new form, the quality and cause of her excitement. The selection and ordering of the incidents to describe and of the words in which to describe them seem impeccable within the limitations of Debra's literary experience at that time. Perhaps the space between the first and second stage of the writing had given her the time she needed to clarify the literary form her experience seemed to require. Certainly that was true of other instances of similar writing within the class, as I will show. In any case Debra had found a way of transforming her experience into the distinctive medium of literary expression. The story had not petered out, as I had at first supposed; the economy of its climax surpasses the circumstantial detail of its opening.

It is interesting to compare this early piece of writing of Debra's with a second account of a visit to her grandparents which she wrote towards the end of the school year. During the previous two terms she had demonstrated her agility as a writer in several different genres:

satire, bawdy, adventure, reportage, fairy tale. Occasionally she had written again about her own experiences out of school, at home or during weekends, though without ever quite recapturing the intensity of her description of mushroom picking. Then, one Monday in May, she came to school full of another visit to her grandad's.

'Monday, 9th May.

Debra went out again at the weekend with her grandad, looking for birds and birds' nests. She was talking a lot about it this morning, as is her habit after such weekend experiences, and decided to write about it. I spoke to her once as she was writing and formed the impression that she was a little at a loss for what to say or how to say it — and a bit uninspired. But by the end of the piece she was quite pleased with the way it had turned out and decided to go on to some kind of illustration, which she plans to begin tomorrow. My final impression was that the writing had grown on her as she proceeded. This is what she wrote:-

"Birds Nesting.

On Saturday we went to see our grandma and grandad. We arrived at about half past nine. I went shopping with my grandma and my brother went with my grandad to fix some tiles. My grandad got back at dinner time so we had dinner and washed up. We went for a walk. We went up the Rotherby Road and found a wren's nest with one broken egg in. Then we got in the field to find the hedge sparrow's nest we found the other week. My grandad found it first. He said 'there's no eggs in'. Then I look in and there was five little baby chicks. They had got tiny feathers which looked like little hairs and you could see their skin, it was orange. Then we moved on. Then my grandad found a goldfinch's nest with three eggs in. Then we walked right down to a big pond and we saw a water hen's nest in the middle of the pond and one in the reeds. Then we went into the spinney to look for a robin's nest I found the other week. We looked everywhere but we couldn't find it but as I walked past a clump of nettles a bird flew out, it nearly hit me in the face. We had a look in. There was still five eggs in. So we got out of the spinney and went home and told my grandma, my mum and dad about it.'"

This second account of a visit to her grandad's, besides being longer than Debra's first, is more ingenious in construction and more elaborate in syntax. It is perhaps more coherent as a whole, even if it lacks the intensity of the climax to her description of mushroom picking. I had first glanced at the writing at the point when the wren's nest was found, and my initial impression that Debra was finding it hard to get involved probably reflects no more than the fact that at this point she had barely begun the adventure proper. On this occasion, however, the balance between narrative preliminaries and narrative crux is smoother and the adventure itself takes up the bulk of the story. It is a story that is told with considerable skill. Debra is particularly successful at managing the surprise and excitement of the discovery of the hedge sparrow chicks and the rediscovery of the robin's nest. On the first occasion she is careful to preserve the deliberate ambiguity of her grandad's remark 'there's no eggs in', following it by the simplest revelation of what his words had concealed: 'then I look in and there was five little baby chicks'. The drama of the discovery is enhanced by the directness of the narrative means. The rediscovery of the robin's nest is handled in the same dramatic way, the bird, not identified explicitly as the robin, flying out of the clump of nettles only after the apparent finality of the words 'we looked everywhere but couldn't find it'. The added qualification, 'it nearly hit me in the face' increases the excitement which is resolved once again in a simple statement of subsequent action, 'we had a look in, there was still five eggs in'. Even at this point it is left to the reader to identify this, from the narrative context, as the rediscovered robin's nest.

It is interesting to see how Debra reserves her most elaborate descriptive detail for the high point of the adventure, the discovery of the chicks: 'they had got tiny feathers which looked like little hairs and you could see their skin, it was orange'. It is interesting, too, to watch how she manipulates the syntax of her account. At first reading it may seem that she has included too many unnecessary 'thens', 'buts' or 'ands', but a closer inspection suggests that there is a good deal of care in her choice of conjunctions. Thus, the succession of 'thens' in the middle of the piece reflects the rapid succession of events at that point in the story; the 'thens' stop once the final search for the robin's nest begins. After the nest is discovered, instead of '*Then* we got out of the spinney' Debra writes '*So* we got out of the spinney', as if in recognition that now the adventure is at an end. Earlier she uses 'but' rather than 'then' — ('*but* as I walked past a clump of nettles a bird flew out') — where the word 'but' suggests more appropriately than the word 'then' the contrast between the apparent failure of the search and the subsequent discovery. Where Debra avoids an opening conjunction, that too seems to reflect more than a casual intention. Thus the decisive break between 'so we had dinner and washed up' and the sentence that follows, 'we went for a walk', marks the end of the preliminaries and the start of the adventure proper. Like all young writers Debra has a limited repertory of means for linking sentences, phrases and clauses; those at her disposal however do not seem to be used haphazardly, but, often at least, with a view to their particular expressiveness within a given context.

Debra was a relatively fluent writer but the same concern for appropriate form was apparent in the work of children whose writing was technically less assured. Consider, for example, *'My Go Cart'*, written by Paul, a boy whose reading and writing were much less advanced than Debra's. While Debra was already reading children's novels Paul was struggling with his early 'readers'. At the start of the year he was still at the stage of dictating what he wanted to write to the teacher and then copying from the teacher's writing. By the time he wrote *'My Go Cart'* he was writing for himself but only with difficulty.

Like the two pieces of Debra's, Paul's was an account of personal experience. It resembled the writings which had seemed to cause the children in Janet's class such difficulty on the first morning of the school year, in being an account of something that had happened to Paul during the holidays, on this occasion, the Christmas holiday. Like those earlier pieces, too, it was written, in part at least, in response to a request from the teacher for an account of some aspect of the holiday.

'Tuesday, January 11th.

Yesterday morning, the first day back at school, Paul wrote about the go cart he'd had for Christmas, his first rides on it and its rapid breakdown. Stephen had suggested that everyone begin the day quietly with writing or reading, and he'd given the holiday as a possible subject to write about. (Stephen had been dissatisfied with this suggestion at the end of the day and had found himself wondering whether there had been any point to any of that first day's activity or whether its only point had been to keep everyone occupied. I had not felt this myself although I *had* felt myself somewhat lacking in initiative — perhaps the effects of Christmas!) A good many children were reluctant to write about the holiday although they were all anxious to talk about it, with Stephen or me or each other. Several took up, instead, themes, or titles, or half finished stories, from the end of last term. By contrast, Paul, after telling me about his go cart adventures, was keen to commit them to writing and settled down to the task with his usual concentration, by turns earnest, pensive, pained, listless, and sometimes all in one. It took him all morning and the last sentence I had to write for him, as his scribe, but the thought and language were entirely his own. The piece that emerged was more assured than much of Paul's writing despite the limits of length which his present technical ability imposes on his pieces. Stephen noticed this too and asked me later in the day if I'd helped Paul with the language, but I hadn't, not at all.'

Paul wrote as follows:-

'*My Go Cart*.

At Christmas I had a go cart. When I had my first ride on my go cart I was amazed that I could drive the go cart. The next morning I got up and went down the road and when I came to the end of the road and the go cart stopped and I tried to start the go cart I couldn't start it. I ran home to tell my dad. My dad came down with the trailer. Dad picked the go cart up and took the go cart and put the go cart in the garage and the next morning Kevin came up and Kevin said it is broken. The next morning Kevin mended it.'

Paul's writing here, like Debra's, is notable for the very quality which, at the beginning of the school year, I had failed to notice in the children's writing, the fitting expression of felt incident by means of the written as opposed to the spoken word. The incident of the first breakdown of his go cart, so directly and baldly expressed, enables Paul to convey in a few simple sentences the excitement and exasperation his Christmas present had occasioned. Notice how effectively the word 'amazed', a word I had to help Paul to spell, is used at the beginning. Notice also, how elaborate is the sentence that follows with its long delayed main clause and the sense it conveys of a single sustained burst of activity ending in misfortune. Although the technical means at his disposal are more limited than Debra's, Paul is no less successful at distilling a personal experience in narrative form.

I have implied that in order to distil an experience in writing, so permanent and isolated in character by comparison with talking, it is necessary first to order it in the mind, to reconsider and rearrange it in a form appropriate to the written word. Sometimes the children found it hard to order their experience with sufficient clarity to write about it, often, it seemed, because of their closeness to the experience itself. On these occasions even the best of intentions would go awry, as happened with a piece which Chris wrote in the middle of the Spring Term.

'Monday, February 14th. St. Valentine's Day.

Chris had spent much of Sunday round at Robbie's where the big event had been Chris accidentally pushing Robbie off a haystack and Robbie falling on his head, his feet bent back so that his head almost touched them, giving him quite a pain in the back. [The following day as I recorded in my notes Chris confided to me that Robbie hadn't told his dad about this, implying that he would have had every right to do so and that it was good of him, when all was said and done, not to have done. Perhaps I should add that Robbie had a damaged leg and wore a caliper at that time.]*

Chris told me that he would like to draw a picture of Robbie falling off the haystack and a little later he added that he would like to write about it too. Even before Stephen had announced that it was to be a quiet opening session with writing as a favoured activity, Chris had chosen to write and decided what to write. I was pleased and looked forward to a fine piece, Chris being so full of Sunday's events. As it happened, however, the writing proved a disappointment. As soon as Robbie and Chris had settled down together and Chris had written the title for his piece he began to feel that he didn't know what to write and wanted to give up. It was as if the desire to write, the motivation provided by the incidents of Sunday which he so much wanted to describe, vanished the instant he began. I kept on urging him to continue and as soon as I started asking him what had happened he would become very lively again while he and Robbie recalled and recounted the day's events.

Chris told me he'd asked his mum and dad if he could go over to Robbie's and at first they'd said they didn't think he should but finally they'd agreed as long as it was only for two hours. But as it was, he told me with eyes opening wide in mock serious astonishment, he had stayed for five hours. They'd had dinner there. 'What was it' asked Chris; 'curry' said Robbie 'and rice'; 'yes' said Chris who had obviously found the food a little strange. He told me about

* Square brackets indicate a new addition to the note.

Robbie's bathroom; 'it's huge', he said, comparing it, I guess, with his own. Together they told me how they'd been in the land rover, how they'd helped Robbie's brother Adrian, how they'd played in the haystack, just how it was arranged, how it was that Robbie had fallen, the pile of mud he'd fallen into, and so on.

But then, when once more, at my insistence, Chris turned to write, he fussed and bothered and wasn't really interested and the excitement seemed to be frittered away. One difficulty, I think, was the problem of how to include everything, of the time it would take, the number of words, the amount of writing, the trouble of getting it all down on the page — as, sometimes, I feel myself, as I sit down at night to write these notes. While he was thinking about what had happened, talking about it, considering how he would like to write it, the experience was all, in a sense, simultaneously present in his mind, clear and exciting in the memory. Writing, by contrast, was a detached and dispassionate activity which no longer partook of the glow of the remembered incidents. It had a linear quality which somehow contradicted the richness of the experience, narrowing it down to a mere succession of events.

It is tempting perhaps to conclude that writing was not appropriate to the situation, and that it would have been better to have encouraged Chris to talk over his experience and then move on to other things, or at most to tape-record with Robbie his impressions of the day. But I do not find that conclusion altogether satisfying. I think perhaps Chris *did* have something he wished to put into writing only he was unable to find a way of doing so that really engaged him, and I was unable to help him.

This was what he wrote.

"Me and Robbie in the haystack.

Yesterday was Sunday and I went up to Robbie's house. Then we went upstairs and we played with the train set and the tank. Then we packed it up and then we got a sleeping bag and then we put it on the stairs, then one of us got in, then we slid down the stairs to the bottom. Then we packed that up. Then we went outside into the farm. Then Robbie went to get a little push chair. Then we went round. Then it was dinner time. We had our dinner. Then we went to help Adrian put the pig trailer (on the Land Rover). Then we got in the Land Rover. Then we went down Cold Overton." '

The stammering succession of brief sentences, each with its accompanying 'then', confirms Chris's inability, on this occasion, to translate the richness of his impressions into appropriate written form. The contrast between the liveliness of his spoken recollections and these flat, broken sentences was so striking that his own frustration with his writing could readily be understood. It was as if when he tried to write, all the impressions presented themselves to his mind in undifferentiated confusion. How was he to select, order and phrase this rich, complex, many-layered image? At that moment the task seemed beyond his capacity.

Chris wrote no more that day and it was not until late in the afternoon that he seemed to recover his poise, by making a valentine card for his mum and dad, which, though roughly drawn, possessed the very warmth and clarity of feeling which his account of Sunday's adventure had seemed to lack.

That, however, was not the end of the affair. The following day Chris asked me to help him make a model of the barn in which he and Robbie had played, while Robbie was modelling a Ploughmaster tractor which his father had just hired.* Once again, as we worked, Chris talked about the Sunday which was still very much on his mind. Then, on the Wednesday, he returned to his unfinished account.

'Wednesday, February 16th.

At the start of the day Chris and Robbie wanted to carry on with Chris's barn but Stephen had planned a quiet session and after some more or less ritual griping, as it seemed to me, Chris settled down to write. During the course of the first half morning he described to me one or two more incidents from Sunday but I saw nothing of the writing itself until it was finished. Stephen spoke to him from time to time about it, but only, Stephen later told me, to say "Get on with your work". When Chris had finished he came over, keen to show me how much he had written, almost three more pages. He pinned them together and gave them to me, at my request, to bring home tonight.

How is it that this morning he wrote so much when the day before yesterday he had found it so hard? Was it a conviction on his part, born in part perhaps out of Stephen's insistence, that now was the time for writing rather than anything else? Was it that with yesterday's successful modelling behind him, writing

* See Chapter 6.

was now more acceptable? Or was it simply that having once settled down to write, without perhaps worrying over how long he would have to go on or how much he had to say, the words flowed more freely and the story came alive for him. Here, at any rate, is what he wrote, following straight on from where he had left off on Monday:-

"Then we stopped at someone's house. They were about to have their dinner so we sat down on the settee until they finished. When they finished we went out to play on the haystack, and we were playing on it, then Robbie got his leg stuck down a hole, then he pulled it out, then I got hold of his jumper, then I chucked him down off the haystack, then I was about to jump down but I tripped over a piece of string, it was tied round the bales, but I landed safely. So we got up and went to see Robbie's dad about the pigs but when we got there he was not there, his shoes were off, so we went to find him. We went round the corner and his dad was there. We asked the other man that was with his dad if the water in the trough was clean. He said yes so we had a drink of it. It was very nice water. Then we got an old long metal gate, then we put it on the corner of the door and the pig trailer. We got all of the pigs, then we shut it up. Then we went off home. When we got home we went out to play again with the push chair but Robbie's mum said I had to go home now so she took me home." '

This second half of Chris's account is strikingly different from the first. There is still a certain breathlessness about the succession of phrases and events but the syntax is more elaborate, the sentences more varied, and the content richer. On this occasion Chris has shown a much keener eye for significant detail: the sequence of incident on the haystack, the shoes that were left where Robbie's father had been, the 'old long metal gate' used to help chivvy the pigs into the trailer. The tone is no longer matter of fact but enlivened by the variety of sentence constructions and the reflective asides: 'then I was about to jump down but I tripped over a piece of string, it was tied round the bales, but I landed safely.'

Although even the second half of the account is hardly the work of a confident writer it possesses an assurance that was lacking in Chris's opening sentences. His pleasure in the finished account was amply justified. It seemed that the intervening day, accompanied by the experience of modelling the barn and talking still more about the adventure, had given Chris the space and time he needed to reconstruct his experience in written words that might reflect at least part of the vivacity of his original impressions. In a comment written shortly afterwards Stephen summarised the process as follows:-

'I think there is a sense in which children, like adults, have to "objectify" a personal experience before they can write about it. Often "stimuli for writing", such as walks through the snow,[we had tried this out a week or two before] are excellent stimuli but not for writing — the experience is too immediate and subjective. After an exciting experience we do perhaps go through a process of sorting it out, after which we can write about it. Two days later, Chris wrote extremely well about this experience. Had the modelling made his experience in some way objective so that he could then write about it? The success of his piece of writing, and I believe it was for Chris a considerable success, depended not upon the teacher's intervention at the time, except inasmuch as this may have provided the right environment for writing, but rather upon a series of previous events → the experience → talking → expression through modelling → writing. Perhaps writing is naturally the last of these modes of expression, both psychologically and historically.'

One way in which the children imposed order on the experiences they wrote about was by choosing to describe no more than a single incident or impression, a significant moment rather than a sustained sequence of events. It was easier then to keep within the limits of their own technical skill in respect of vocabulary, syntax, length of composition, spelling and handwriting. Whereas Chris, like Debra, had struggled to compress a welter of incident into an account of a whole day's activity, Paul, in describing his go cart, had concentrated on one event alone, the breakdown of the cart, which served to encapsulate much of the complexity of his feelings about his present. Often a piece of writing was confined to no more than a fragment of experience, described in a few short lines. On such occasions I was sometimes tempted to ignore the wholeness of the reconstructed experience and to assume that the account was incomplete, as fragmentary as the experience to which it appeared to relate. It was as if I felt that the writing was too brief to be whole.

Here, for example, is a note which I wrote in February, concerning a brief account by Neil of something that happened to him one morning, before coming to school.

'Friday, February 11th.

At the start of the morning Neil had been talking to me about it
being his dad's birthday on Monday. His dad is home for the
weekend and Neil is obviously delighted. He told me how his
dad would be 34; how he'd told his mum that his dad was very
old then; how his mum was making his dad a cake with a
Manchester United footballer on top; how he'd been showing his
dad his newly acquired cards of footballers this morning in his
bedroom; how his dad had built a new wardrobe in his, Neil's
room, which he shares with his brother, and was going to raise
their beds up in the air on stilts of some sort to give them more
room; and so on. So when it came to thinking of something to
write, and Neil couldn't quite think what, I suggested that he
might write about his dad's forthcoming birthday. Often Neil
rejects my suggestions for writing but this time he accepted the
idea without demur, asked for a large sheet of lined paper, and,
using his new fountain pen, "just to try it out" as he told me
later, wrote in one short burst the following piece:-

"My Dad's birthday.

On 13th February it's my Dad's birthday. He is going to be 34.
At breakfast today I said to mum 'Dad's very old'. And my mum
said to me 'don't be cheeky'. When I was upstairs in my dad's
bedroom I was showing him my cards. So was my little brother
Ian and my sister Sharon. When me and Sharon were ready for
school my mum went upstairs and she told my dad what I said
and he started to laugh. Then I went to school."

I liked the piece as soon as I read it some twenty minutes
later. It was different from how he'd described the incident to me
first thing in the morning, omitting certain details and adding
others such as his dad's laughing. But the feeling in it was the
same, a sense of natural, uncontrived enjoyment in an incident of
family life. However, my first, unregenerate, teacher's reaction
was to think that this was hardly enough for a morning's writing.
It had taken no more than quarter of an hour or so, was no
longer than a dozen lines, surely there was more to be said. I
asked Neil whether he couldn't add a bit about the coming
birthday, the cake that was being prepared, the present he was
giving his dad, and so on. "I don't want to do that" Neil replied
and his tone, though friendly and uncomplaining, had that
decisive edge to it which alerts one to the fact that there's little

point in pressing the matter further. Which, after all, was just as well. The piece was complete, addition was superfluous, the day's writing was done.'

Neil's piece reminded me, at the time, of a similar experience I had had a week before in relation to a very short piece of writing by Sarah, one of a number of pieces written at this time, early in the spring term, which strengthened my impression of the integrity of many of the children's apparently fragmentary writings and of the deliberation and artistry of their writing as a whole.

'Thursday, February 3rd.

Early in the morning Sarah came to me, wanting to write but worried as ever about what to write. Not a story, she thought. Perhaps a poem, I suggested, reminding her of the poem about rain she had written last term, which at first she had some difficulty in remembering. Yes, she said, in that dreamy way she has, quite an idea, but then, looking at Philip's pegboard*, she thought that perhaps she would like to do something like that. Philip hinted that maybe she could use the pegboard but she felt that wouldn't be right, it would spoil his work. But, I went on, she could always write about how she had made her tape recordings yesterday. Yes, she mused, but she didn't seem keen and we returned to the idea of writing a poem. We went over to the bookshelves to look at one or two poems and then, I'm not sure why now, I started talking to her about whether she ever used to find thoughts passing through her mind just before she went to sleep. Yes, she said, she'd see through her curtains which were pinkish purple and think she saw a man there looking in and it was rather scary. We talked a little more about this and about last night when she had been fed up, she said, with her mother because her mum and dad had gone out and so she'd been staying up late with her sister but then they'd come back and she'd had to go off in a hurry to bed. And about how there was a building site opposite her home, and the shapes of the girders could be seen through the curtains and how, when it was wet and had been raining, you could hear the footsteps of people walking past very clearly and they made, as she put it, "a sort of hollow sound". Later, when she was in the middle of writing and stuck, and I reminded her again of how she had said she imagined a man outside her window and how she had said it was

* See Chapter 4.

scary, she told me it was "a bit scary" just listening to me saying it.

She began to write but found it hard to keep at it, to sit quiet and still and just go on writing. Not that she wanted to get up, drift off, chatter. But, as so often before, she fussed over her writing, losing her drift and letting her mind wander. I kept her near me so as to make sure that she got something finished, having been delighted with all she had talked about and her obvious pleasure in telling it. By ten minutes before play she had written this.

"On looking through my bedroom curtains when I go to bed (the title I had written for her).
When I go to bed I look through my bedroom curtains.
I think I see a man looking in my window.
It makes me a bit frightened
But when I put my head under my blanket I normally fall asleep."

Now that I have copied it out I find myself touched by it. At the time, though, I was disappointed that there was no mention of the colour of the curtains, the shapes of the girders, the sound of passing footsteps in the rain. I explained my disappointment and asked Sarah if she couldn't add a little more about the other sights and sounds she had talked of. She said she didn't see how the colour of the curtains had anything to do with it. But she remembered again the girders and sounds and added a few words about each as follows:-

"and when I look through my window and I see the girders of the new houses (she asked me for the word for what she called the "tubes" and I suggested "girders" which she thought was right) and when it is wet I hear the footsteps of people and they sound sort of scary and hollow. (This final phrase was written by me to Sarah's dictation, it now being the middle of playtime and I anxious that the piece be completed there and then.)"

On the whole I felt that this last part had not added much to the original — (I explained to Sarah the need to get rid of at least one of those 'ands') — and it was then that I began to feel that perhaps the original had been self-sufficient. I had, perhaps, been misled by a desire that she should get down in writing all the detail of her conversation. But she had concentrated on only the first thing she had told me, adding to what she had said by including the detail about putting her head under the blanket and normally falling asleep. And at that, the piece was complete.'

Sarah's remark, that she didn't see how the colour of the curtains had anything to do with it, is clear evidence of the deliberateness of what she wrote, her understanding of the requirements of writing and its difference from talking. In her four short sentences she was trying to express the essence of her experience. So many words were necessary and no more. She was no longer simply chatting.

The writings I have examined so far, accounts of personal experience, represent only one among several literary genres practised by the children in Stephen's class during the year. Sarah's piece 'On looking through my bedroom curtains when I go to bed' is itself an example of another genre, that of the brief evocative description or reflection, often written as an accompaniment to a painting or drawing. The best of these poetic miniatures were remarkable for the clarity with which, in a very few words, the children managed to capture a particular mood, scene or vision. Some of their effects were at least in part accidental, the fortunate consequences of a kind of word play, but there was ample evidence, also, of the children's deliberation, as Sarah's rejection of an irrelevant detail has already shown.

Several children in Stephen's class handled this particular genre with greater confidence than other genres. One such child was Louise. Although she wrote many stories they were often confused, as if the plot were clear in her mind but only half stated on the written page. By contrast her poetic miniatures were often strikingly successful in evoking a mood or a scene with some precision. An early example is this description of a wet day, written in December. The division into lines follows a suggestion of Stephen's when he first read her description, after which she revised and rewrote it, eliminating several conjunctions and arranging it in lines as in a poem.

'A wet day
people asleep
making their beds
making hot tea˙
sitting by the fire
raining hard
people are very sad
wet grass
children at school
girls and boys play
lights on
I am sad because it's raining.'

Early in the summer term I described in my notes another of Louise's miniatures, written on this occasion to accompany a landscape she had painted, one of a series of imposing landscape pictures which Louise painted during the spring and summer.

'Friday, April 29th

Louise asked me early on what she should write about. I remembered that on Tuesday Stephen had encouraged her to write a piece associated in some way or other with her recent painting. She hadn't though, as she now told me, so I suggested it again, and we talked briefly about the painting itself. She decided to write a poem to accompany the picture. Her conception of such poems — she's written in similar vein before — is that they should describe a scene through a series of phrases, mostly governed by a present participle. The technique is reminiscent of certain of the texts that accompany large picture books for children, for example, John Burningham's *Seasons,* and perhaps it is derived from such examples, though it also reflects the way in which in previous classes as well as in ours children are encouraged to write brief descriptions alongside their drawings. [It is common practice at Sherard School for teachers to encourage children, in the earliest stages of writing, to draw or paint and then to write, or at first to dictate to the teacher a few brief words, phrases or sentences to accompany their picture.] She wrote as follows, the division into separated lines occurring in a neat copy written after I'd suggested such a division to her.

"people eating their picnic in the sunny grass
boys and girls climbing trees
boys and girls running around the trees
flowers growing, people picking them
the house far away in the distance
trees blowing side by side." '

The last two lines were added after I had suggested that Louise should say something about the house on the hill in her picture and the trees in the foreground. Although these lines are evocative they are not essential and they reflect my own determination that the poem should describe the whole of the picture rather than Louise's original intentions. She had taken the picture itself, in which the few pencilled picnickers were the least dramatic feature, as no more than a theme on which her four short lines elaborated. The simple phrases and images capture the mood of a summer's picnic very well. They would have been an appropriate expression of the class's own summer picnic later that term in a large wood a few miles from the school.

Some weeks later Louise returned to a similar theme, this time in advance of another landscape painting the subject of which was suggested by the poem.

'Tuesday, May 17th.

Louise began yesterday by writing another of her poems, as she sees them, brief phrases of evocative description which are still much the best of her writings, without the strange omissions and confusions which often seem to characterise her longer pieces, especially her stories. She wrote:

"*A tree on a windy day.*
On a windy day the wind blows in and out of the trees, the leaves fall down and go into the grass, the branches snap, the workman saws the trees down."
It is a precise picture, envisaging not only the windy day but its consequences — the trees that, their branches snapped, have to be sawn down. Note the prepositions, the wind blowing "in and out of" the trees, the leaves falling down and going "into" the grass. Note also the word "snap" for the breaking branches.'

'A tree on a windy day' is a little different from the other two pieces by Louise which I have quoted. The participles are replaced by present tenses, the broken phrases of 'A Wet Day' disappear, the writing is perhaps more carefully articulated and unified. Her choice of prepositions here enhances the clarity of Louise's vision of the day, a vision further elaborated in the painting which followed and which marked the climax of Louise's series of landscapes.

I have spoken of the artistry evident in the children's writing, the careful and deliberate, if uncertain, skill with which they sought to express their ideas in appropriate literary form, within the limitations of their present experience of life, of language and of literature. Nowhere was the artistry displayed more ambitiously than in their stories. For many children the stories they wrote, the best of them, represented the high point of their literary achievement and they regarded a successful story with particular pride. As with other kinds of writing, it took me a while to learn how to read these stories which could at first seem strangely inconsequential or fragmentary. Consider, for example, an early story of Simon's.

'Monday, October 11th.

The third writer was Simon whom I hadn't worked with before. I found out today that he is sometimes dubbed Professor W. although at first glance his writing appears somewhat to belie the professorial image. He wrote his story very slowly, partly because of his considerable problems with spelling but partly, too, because of a deliberation in the process of working out the plot and the sequence of ideas. He didn't ask for help with his spelling but went on puzzling it out for himself with painstaking care, so that a word like "ckarat" (carrot) or "axeddentilie" (accidentally) seemed to represent quite an achievement, as if he had devised a wholly personal but rational system of spelling out of his efforts to render his own pronunciation into coherent lettered form.

The first sentence and the title of the story, "I'm a rabbit", had already been written by the time I arrived, the main character "Tufty, the snow rabbit" already chosen. (Stephen tells me that Simon has a rabbit of his own at home.) After almost every sentence or incident in the story he would stop and say that he didn't know how to go on. I kept on making suggestions, hoping I might be helping. Eventually Simon turned to me and said, in a gentle, matter of fact tone, "I can think better if somebody's not helping me". (I wrote his exact words down at the time to be sure of remembering them.) I stayed near him though and he continued from time to time to inform me as to what was to come, how the snow rabbit would meet another rabbit and how they would both meet Simon himself, but not the narrator of the story who was the snow rabbit. Simon would take them home and befriend them and eventually they would have babies.

By the end of the morning Simon had taken the story as far as the middle of its first page, the point at which Tufty hurts his "little foot". He had got stuck as to what should happen next but had thought his way through to the general idea I've mentioned, as he explained it to me. At the start of the afternoon I found him beginning to make a new, neat copy of what he had already written on the other side of the page he'd been writing on. I felt this might be a mistake; I could imagine him spending all his time copying up and correcting what he had written and never getting onto the rest of the story. (I daresay I felt this because it is a weakness of my own.) So I thought it was time to intervene. A pity, I suggested to Simon, to go back and rewrite rather than go on. He seemed uncertain though, as if really he did still want to rewrite what he'd done so far before continuing. There were parts he wanted to change, the title for instance which was no longer to be "I'm a rabbit" but "my rabbit's adventures". However I still felt that if he wrote the whole piece out again he would lose interest in it, remembering how slowly he wrote, how painfully he had to work out his idiosyncratic spellings. So I suggested that I should act as his scribe, writing out a fair copy as he dictated to me what he'd already written. After a minute or two for me to explain more clearly what I meant, he seemed attracted to this idea and so we continued; Simon told me what he had written, reading it out very clearly without pausing or stumbling over his own handwriting or spelling, and I wrote it out again. At one point he corrected a confusion in what he had written; at another he told me to make sure to include an exclamation mark after the word shot gun. (In his own text he had two exclamation marks, one after shot! and the other after gun!) When I had finished copying out what he'd written he continued the story in rough and later I copied out the rest of his day's writing. On this occasion he made one significant addition to the text. In the original draft, the character Simon in the story says to the black rabbit "Got yourself a friend?". When he read it back to me he told me I should add after the word "friend", the word "then". The final word seems to me to make the remark that much more realistically observed, "Got yourself a friend, then?" Perhaps it was his reading back to me aloud that suggested to Simon this small but crucial addition.

At the start of the afternoon Simon had told me that he intended to write a whole book of adventures about his rabbit, of which this was to be the first, entitled "Lost in a Cave". I remembered how Neil had said the same after two stories he had written about an old man with a walking stick and I began to wonder if this might be a common desire — to invent one or more characters capable of sustaining a whole collection of stories. [In the event, Simon never did write another story about Tufty; neither did Neil about the old man. It seems to me more likely, now, that to conceive of a story as the first of many is a way of reconciling oneself to the limitations of the story's scale, an indication perhaps that the story is to be read as if it were one small episode among many. Or perhaps children like Simon are reluctant, naturally enough, to abandon a framework that might provide the material for many stories.]'

It was not until the following morning that Simon finished his story and then, as he explained to me, he had to force himself to finish it. It was hard to concentrate, he said. 'I have to keep snapping myself out of it.' My first reaction to the finished story was mixed, as I explained in my notes.

'Tuesday, October 12th.

I felt that in some respects, the end of Simon's piece, written today, lacked something of the quality of yesterday's writing. It seemed to end more quickly and suddenly than Simon had intended yesterday although when I asked him whether he'd really come to the end he was emphatic that he had. Later, however, when I read the story a second time, I felt more convinced by its ending.

   The story ran as follows.

"My rabbit's adventures.

I'm Tufty the snow rabbit and I'll tell you the adventure I had one winter's morning last year when I was collecting carrots. I saw Farmer Brown walking down the field with his shotgun! I was so scared I picked up all my carrots and ran into a cave. I accidentally ran through a passageway and tripped over and hurt my little foot, but luckily another rabbit came hopping up, a black rabbit, and he said "I'm Simon's rabbit". I said "Who's Simon?". "Simon W," Messy said. Just then I heard footsteps. "Don't be afraid" Messy said, "it's only Simon." I said "Let's go and meet him then." Simon said "Got yourself a friend, then?" "What a shame, you've hurt your little paw" he said and took a handkerchief from his pocket and wrapped it round my paw and tightened it so it wouldn't fall off. "We better get going. I've got a trolley with a box of hay on." He picked my carrots up and put them in the box, then he picked me up and put me in the box, then he picked Messy up and put him in with me, and we all went home." '

The more I thought about it the more Simon's story intrigued me. I had not expected it to end as and when it did but on reflection the ending was both natural and necessary. For the most striking feature of the story is the way in which Simon manages to convey so much in so little space, a complete adventure in a bare 200 words. As Simon had suggested when describing to me the plot, the story is about making friends. It is told by a rabbit but its concern is with human feelings and human relationships. After introducing his narrator he sets the scene with a simple, exact detail, 'one winter's morning last year when I was collecting carrots'. The panic flight follows, its cause made more dramatic by the device of punctuating the word shot gun with an exclamation mark, originally two marks. One thing leads to another in quick succession, the flight to the fall, the fall to the chance encounter with the black rabbit and thereby to the introduction to Simon whose kindness is at once confirmed by the care with which he binds up the damaged paw with his handkerchief. It is a sign of Simon, the author's, attention to detail that at this point he should add that Simon, the character in the story, 'tightened' the hand-kerchief 'so it wouldn't fall off', a detail which succinctly expresses the character's tender concern. That is the end of the adventure, the act of bandaging signifying the establishment of friendship. All that remains is for the three characters to return home together, a resolution which Simon achieves neatly in the long, slow final sentence with its cumulative 'thens' and 'ands'.

I do not wish to overstate Simon's achievement. The story was slight, yet it was also skilful and its skill was not accidental or unaccountable. Simon pondered the story as he wrote; its form and its language reflect the care with which he composed it.

Simon's story was one of the earliest stories that impressed on me the narrative skill and judgement with which many of the children could write. This impression was confirmed by two unusual stories of Sarah's written shortly afterwards. I have already mentioned Sarah as the girl who wrote about looking through her bedroom curtains before she went to sleep. Like Simon she was a diffident writer, easily distracted and frequently dissatisfied. Some of her difficulties arose out of a certain fastidiousness. She would worry over an inexact word or a flaw in the plot of a story until her writing bored her. Then she would give up in dismay or find an excuse for starting on something new. Her writings were usually no more than a few lines long yet the best of them were notable for the directness of their vision and the sensitivity of their language.

The first story of hers that I read was about an elf. Whether because of the triteness of its opening or its extreme brevity I paid little attention to it and it was not until I came across it again, several months later, that I realised how curious and sinister it was.

'The Little Elf

Once upon a time there was a little elf. Its name was Elfred. One day Elfred decided to go for a walk. He had not got very far until he came to a toy shop. In the window there was a little elf. Elfred was very jealous because the other elf was prettier so he went into the shop and bought it. He took it home and took all of the clothes off him and put them on, and then he broke the model elf and threw it in the bin.' The next of her stories I came across I read more carefully.

'Tuesday, November 16th.

Yesterday Sarah came to show me a story she had written, pointing out to me that she was now writing rather longer pieces, trying, at Stephen's suggestion, to complete a whole page rather than a few lines. The piece she showed me, begun in pen and finished in pencil, for which she excused herself, was exactly a page long and I had the impression that she had finished it, come what may, at the bottom of the page although in fairness I should add that it did indeed come to a conclusion at that point. I was impressed once again (as with other children's stories) by the strange, inconsequential story, in part conventional, in part imitative of certain elements in stories written for very young children, in part unique to Sarah and her particular imagination.

"Once upon a time there was two little children, Peter and Sally. One day Peter and Sally asked their mummy if they could go for a walk. Mummy said "yes, alright, I'll get you some food, what do you want." "I don't mind" they said, so they set off. It was a bit cold but they did not mind much. A little while later they came to a little old house. It was very dirty but very pretty too. Peter said "Let's go and have a look inside." Sally said "no, I'm not." "All right" said Peter "I am going." Peter opened the door. In the corner there was a box. Peter opened the box. Inside the box was another box and inside there was another box and inside the last box a rabbit jumped out. "Sally" said Peter, "try and catch that rabbit." "No, look at your watch, it is 4 o'clock, we are late for tea already, let's run.' "

Notice the realistic details: the children's mother preparing food, their not minding the cold "much", Sally looking at her watch and realising, fortunately no doubt from her own viewpoint, that they were late for tea, the house dirty but pretty.

Notice also how the story is reduced to its essentials and yet how sufficient they are to suggest an entire world and an entire adventure.'

Like Simon, Sarah had managed to tell a story in the simplest and fewest of words. The variety of descriptive detail she had contrived to introduce into her narrative was one of the marks of her achievement. Equally impressive is the way in which she succeeds, simply by means of dialogue and the action that follows the dialogue, in expressing the psychological and moral contrast between Sally's responsible caution and Peter's irrepressible boldness. The story's syntax is noteworthy, too, particularly at the narrative climax. 'Peter opened the door. In the corner there was a box. Peter opened the box. Inside the box was another box and inside there was another box and inside the last box a rabbit jumped out.' The repetition of words and phrases establishes a sense of suspense which continues until the final 'inside the last box' at which point Sarah springs her surprise. One might have expected her to write 'there was a rabbit'; instead the sequence of phrases is suddenly broken and the sentence ends with dramatic, though barely grammatical, effect: 'a rabbit jumped out'. The resolution that follows is as sharp and sudden as the resolution of Simon's story was slow and measured. One small detail is missing in the printed form of the ending. The two children's shouts, Peter's 'Sally' and Sally's 'no', are surrounded, in Sarah's original manuscript, with radiating lines intended to signify their exclamatory character, an expressive form of punctuation practised by many children in their stories.

Like her previous story, the adventure of Peter and Sally begins in the most severely conventional manner, with the 'one day', 'once upon a time', when the principal character decides 'to go for a walk'. The same convention was followed in the next story Sarah wrote, soon afterwards. On this occasion, however, the convention was transformed by a singular change of expression.

'Monday, November 22nd.

Sarah returned to the class today after being away for two days at the end of last week. . . . This afternoon she began another story. She wrote no more than the opening sentence and a half, the story's introduction. She seemed to be back to her old ways of beginning something and then relaxing or drifting away or day dreaming. But that's not what interested me, and certainly she began the story with real attack again, as she often does in all her work. What I want to note now is how she came up to me and said, "Mr Armstrong, how do you spell 'bounce'?" I told her and looked at her story; she'd written "Once upon a time there was a rabbit, it was not very big at all. One day the rabbit decided to go for a". "For a what?" I asked her. Perhaps I half expected the answer she gave me, or perhaps I asked her because I couldn't see why she was asking me to spell "bounce" when it looked as though she was about to write "walk". "Bounce", she replied, "because rabbits can't go for a walk really." '

Sarah completed her story the following day.

'Tuesday, November 23rd.

Today Sarah finished the story about the rabbit, which she had begun yesterday. It was not till quite late in the afternoon that she completed it and then she came up to me and asked if she could read it to me. She had considerable difficulty reading it, stumbling over the words much as if she was reading from her reader. It was a sad story, she told me, the rabbit died.

"Once upon a time there was a rabbit, it was not very big at all. One day the rabbit decided to go for a bounce in the town. He had not got very far before he came to a big door, at the play school. It said "no animals allowed here". The rabbit was very sad. "No animals allowed, that's not fair at all." So he pushed the door open. Lots of children were running around in the playground, it was so exciting there. But, bang, a ball had hit the rabbit's head, he was dead. All the children ran to the rabbit, he was dead for sure. One of the little girls started to cry and then another and then another. It was very sad. You will be hearing more of the rabbit story another day."

Sarah explained to me that she was going to write more rabbit stories, hence the ending. "But the rabbit's dead now," I said. Well perhaps it had a baby, she replied, and later she added that she might write about the rabbit earlier, before it had been killed.

The end is a little flat but until that last sentence, — and I am still wondering why she added it* — the story matches her last in its vigour and precision and also in its strangeness. This time it's the rabbit's sad fate that is so surprising, and even shocking, and

---

* Later, a friend of mine, reading through my notes, suggested to me that perhaps Sarah just did not trust her reader to have grasped the full impact of the story.

Sarah was very conscious of its sadness, although when she told me how the poor rabbit died it seemed almost as if she was describing something which was independent of her will. (There was perhaps a trace of self-consciousness about Sarah's tone, as she spoke, and yet I am almost certain that yesterday when she began the story, Sarah had not intended that the rabbit should die. It seemed that the story had taken hold of her imagination and imposed its own conclusion on her, despite herself.) Once again the language is vivid and subtle, for example in expressing the rabbit's indignation, "that's not fair *at all*"; or the children's sad confirmation of the rabbit's death, "he was dead *for sure*"; or the slowly spreading ritual of sorrow, "one of the little girls started to cry and then another and then another, it was very sad"; as well as in her now famous phrase, "going for a bounce" The clarity with which the scene in the playground is imagined seems to me remarkable and despite, or perhaps just because of, the conventional opening and the conventional character of the little rabbit, the story is deeply human. There are also certain signs of Sarah's own distinctive character, for example in the way she describes the rabbit's size — "it was not very big at all": somehow that seems very like Sarah and her manner and style.

Stephen and I talked about Sarah's writing at the end of the day, about her growing confidence and about the time she takes to write — a day over this one short page. The pauses, the leaving it and returning to it, the ebb and flow of writing, even of writing just a page — which however for Sarah represents a sizeable effort considering all the individual words whose spelling she has to figure out besides unravelling her plot and choosing her language — all this seems to be a necessary part of writing for Sarah and something which she must be given space and time to indulge. Yesterday I wrote that perhaps Sarah hadn't really done enough in the afternoon, spending so long on one and a half sentences. Now I think my judgement was premature.'

The tale of a rabbit's death was Sarah's finest story of the year and demonstrated many of the qualities inherent in the children's earliest narratives. It demonstrated, for example, the moral and metaphysical concerns that ran through their stories, concerns which are often present, of course, in stories written for children by adults, but which seemed to acquire a new resonance in the best of the children's own work. The story deals with the unfairness, but perhaps also the necessity, of prohibitions, with excitement transformed into tragedy, with death and sorrow. It demonstrated, also, the children's ability to explore and to express their view of life through the vivid account of particular moments in particular lives, dramatised in Sarah's story in such details as the closed door that is pushed open in defiance of its warning notice, the 'bang' that shatters the playground's excitement, the succession of crying that marks the children's sorrow. And finally, the story demonstrated the children's concern for form, for telling a story in carefully ordered prose, however tentative. The tension that is created and resolved in Sarah's story reflects her own selection and ordering of the narrative material, of plot, syntax and vocabulary.

The narrative imagination, so evident in these early stories of Simon's and Sarah's, recurred again and again in the children's writing throughout the year. Their stories embraced many different themes and treatments, and it was not only the best, or most sophisticated, writing that gave evidence of a writer's powers. Few stories lacked at least some detail, however slight, that pointed to their author's concern for the form and substance of the story being told. Here for example is a comic story by David, derived from stories about mad professors which were popular in the class at the time he wrote his own. David had written little at the start of the year but in due course he began writing more regularly and often with some enthusiasm. This story was one of three concerning a certain Professor Wrongly, and his friend and adversary, Rightly (spelt by David 'Wrightly'). He wrote them in the summer term and once, rather surprisingly, he chose to stay behind in the classroom to get on with them rather than go down to the river with the rest of the class. This is the second of the three stories, entitled 'Professor Wrongly meets Professor Rightly".

'Professor Wrongly meets Professor Rightly .

Professor Wrongly was trying to make tea without putting tea bags in. He was just about to put a bit of soup in when he heard a knock at the door. He said "come in" but the man said "I can't, the door's locked". So the professor opened it and said "what do you want?"; and the man said "I'm Professor Rightly and I live next door to you and I thought you would need some help." Professor Wrongly said "I'm trying to make tea without tea bags." Professor Rightly said "can I help?" "Alright then, you could get me the things I want." But he said "I am meant for working, not for fetching so there" and with that he knocked Professor Wrongly's experiment over and it spilt all over the floor. Professor Wrongly called him back but he just went on to his house and shut the door with a bang and had a cup of tea. Then he went upstairs and started to make his own experiment and two days later he came out of the house with a smile on his face and he went straight to Professor Wrongly's house and said "I've made the experiment." But Professor Wrongly said "I haven't, because you knocked it over and it was all your fault." "No, it wasn't. You told me to fetch things, but I didn't want to so I knocked your experiment over and banged the door, so there." '

The story is less eloquent and economical than those I have already quoted, but it has considerable comic gusto, and, in several places, a subtlety of phrasing that enlivens the plot, underlining the rapid and sudden shifts of emotion on which the story depends: *'he was just about to* put a bit of soup in *when* he heard a knock' ; *'and with that* he knocked Professor Wrongly's experiment over '; 'shut the door *with a bang' ;* 'came out of his home *with a smile on his face* '; 'went *straight to* Professor Wrongly's home '. And then, of course, it contains the superbly indignant line "I am made for working, not for fetching ', the words 'working not for ', in the original manuscript, enlarged in size as if David had imagined the professor's voice swelling with indignation as he exlaimed them.

Comic stories like David's were common; less frequent were sad stories such as Sarah's. Here however is one more example of a story, this time by Karen, which ends in sadness, a sadness that is more bitter and unrelieved than in Sarah's story.

'The Little Cat.

One night an old man called Mr Jockys put his little cat out because he hadn't any money to feed it. The cat's name was Chap. Then the old man went back into his shop. And went to bed. In the morning the old man realised what he had done, then he decided to go and look for his cat. The cat had been found by a little girl called Merry, because she was merry. The old man had travelled all over the world but he could not find it. Merry had lots of friends but she had a nasty friend as well and her name was Nasty, because she is. She was jealous because Merry had a cat and she hadn't. So she went to Merry's house and said "Can I have a look at your cat" and Merry said "yes, you can". Then, when she saw the cat she said "I found that cat on Monday" and Merry said "Oh no you never," "Oh yes I did," and when they stopped the cat was dead and Merry said "now look what you have done". And they both started to cry. And the old man died when he was looking for the cat.'

My first contact with this story had been when Karen came to ask me how to spell the word 'realised'. I was struck by her choice of word and asked her what her story was about. At that, she outlined the entire plot, with a detailed assurance that was unusual in many until they were well into the middle of the writing. Her account of the plot had an unfortunate effect however on my first impression of the finished story, which seemed too attenuated. I felt that, like many of the children's stories, it had not quite lived up to the expectations aroused by its opening. In outlining the plot, for example, Karen had explained to me that the two girls who squabbled over the cat kept on snatching it from each other as they argued and so killed it; but this did not seem clear from the story as written. Karen seemed in part to share my dissatisfaction, for she told me that she was not altogether pleased with the way the story had worked out. Nevertheless, at the end of the day when I took the story home along with some of her earlier stories she advised me to take no notice of her first few pieces, implying that there was no real comparison between what she was writing at the beginning of the year and a story like the one she had just finished.

As it was, I was much more impressed by the story when I read it a second time. I was no longer so worried by the apparent lacuna in Karen's account of the girls' squabble. The context makes it more or less clear what must have happened, as clear perhaps as is necessary to the story, while the sudden starkness of the dialogue and its shocking consequence — ' Merry said "Oh no you never," "Oh yes I did," and when they stopped the cat was dead ' — heightens the sensationalism of the event. The opening of the story, too, is wonderfully dramatic and direct. Above all, however, I am impressed now by the moral force of the narrative. 'In the morning the old man realised what he had done ': that is perhaps the most important sentence in the story, which traces the irreparable consequences of the old man's action, and, later, in parallel, of the actions of the two girls, describing with considerable clarity, for all the sketchiness of the narrative, a world in which actions and intentions go awry and lead only to misfortune and misery. Originally Karen ended the story at the words 'and they both started to cry '. She had intended to go on to describe the old man returning and discovering his cat's sad fate but she finally decided to close the story with the accidental killing of the cat. Later however she added the final sentence as if to confirm her story's gloomy vision.

There were a few themes that recurred many times in the children's stories. One of the most frequent was that of friendship, the theme explored in Simon's story about the snow rabbit Tufty. Simon's characters were animals although his treatment of them was wholly human. Louise tackled the same theme, later in the year, within a more realistic setting.

'*At School*

One morning as I was going to school Ann said "are you having a club on Monday". "Yes, I am," but Ann had gone. When I got to school Sarah said that Ann was coming to your club, she told me in the shop. Then Ann came in. "Did someone say my name?" "No," said Sarah. At home time, when I went home, Ann went by me and I said "you cannot come to my club." She ran off. I got home and mum said that Ann was coming for tea and "there went the door"* said mum, "she is going to sleep the night." Then Ann came in and they had tea and they had a big cake. At 9 o'clock they went to bed. Then daddy came home and went up to bed, then mum did, and me and Ann went to sleep.'

I have already quoted three of Louise's descriptive miniatures and suggested that they were considerably in advance of her stories. This story however was among her best, and my attention was particularly drawn to it because I was aware of the difficulty Louise was herself experiencing at the time in making friends.

'Thursday, June 2nd.

Louise's stories have often suffered from a curious habit she has of leaving out so much of the story that what is left scarcely makes sense, as if she has the whole thing in her mind but has neglected to set important parts of it down on paper at all. However the inconsequential aspect of this particular story is the inconsequence of life itself which the story reflects in simple form. Louise often seems rather lonely, finding it hard not so much to make friends as to keep them. More than once during the year she has been in tears about this and although she recovers quickly and has much self-possession, and growing self-confidence, she remains a girl who is subject to periods of withdrawal and isolation, often not of her own seeking. And this character seems to be reflected in her story, in the shifting, unstable relationship between the three girls and in the longed for friendship with which the story seems to end. A very personal world of feeling and relationship is compressed into these few lines with their strange twists and turns.'

The story describes a pattern of misunderstanding, secretiveness, and indignant squabbling suddenly resolved by the mother's unexpected act which brings about an ending as comforting in its language as in

---

* I have punctuated the story here in accordance with Louise's explanation when I read the story out loud to her.

its sentiment. The resolution may be sentimental but the story is also true to a child's experience, and illustrates how a girl like Louise can make use of narrative to reflect upon a problem which looms large in her own life.

The same theme found expression in a very different form in a nursery tale written by Sally earlier in the year. Sally was one of several children who were particularly successful at exploiting the conventions of the nursery story. It is, of course, a form which would have been very familiar to them from their own nursery experience, or from stories they had listened to in their early days at school. The best of the children's own nursery stories seemed more than a match for the stories likely to have been read to them in the past even if their plots were commonplace enough. Sally's story 'The Secret of the Red Ball' was somewhat different, however, not exactly like any other story written during the year.

'The Secret of the Red Ball.

There was once a little boy named Matthew. He was a very funny little boy because everywhere he went he carried a big red ball, but no one seemed to notice it. He had no friends at all, only one, and that was his big red ball, at least a kind of friend anyway, because Matthew talks to it and plays with it, he even takes it to bed with him, he really does love it. One day as Matthew was playing on the swings with his ball he was thinking "it is a bit sil.y not having a name even though it is a ball". So Matthew thought and thought, but he could not think of a name. So he went and asked his mummy but his mummy was too busy so he went and asked his daddy and his daddy said "Well is it a boy or a girl?" "Oh", said Matthew, "I don't know". "Well let's call it Joe because that is a boy's name and a girl's name", said his daddy. "Thank you" said Matthew, and from that day the ball was called Joe.'

Sally, as we will see in a later chapter,* was a girl with a tendency to speculate about ideas, events, objects. Her story, with its ingenious puzzles and reflections, is characteristic of her frame of mind. In part it is a story about the relationship of people to things, about naming and identity: does an object have a gender? does a thing require a name to be a friend? It is also, in a less personal way than Louise's story, about being alone and coping, a theme that is made explicit by Sally's reflective aside on the justification of calling the ball a friend: 'he had no friends at all, only one, and that was his big red ball, at least a kind of friend anyway because Matthew talks to it and plays

* Chapter 4.

with it, he even takes it to bed with him, he really does love it '. It is interesting to observe how Sally marks this narrative interjection by changing from past to present tense, a device which she used occasionally in other stories also and which seems to have been a quite deliberate exploitation of tense.

Of the many fine story tellers in Stephen Rowland's class, Louise Ann was perhaps the most accomplished. For all that she would occasionally complain that she never seemed to do anything but write, writing was her favourite activity and absorbed her as nothing else did. Her chosen style was a very personal combination of enthusiasm and drama with a certain ironic detachment. It could be seen in all her writing, whether fiction or fact, poetry or prose. The particular quality of her work can be seen in one of her compara- tively rare attempts to write directly about her own experience, an account of an incident in which she and a friend had been involved one afternoon near her home. She described it as a "true story" and it provides a notable example of how a young writer contrives to turn a disturbing personal experience into a clear and direct narrative, both simple and stylish.

'*The Kidnapper.*

This is a true story that I am just going to tell you. It all started when my friend Alison came to play with me, and my brother Paul had got one of his friends to play with him. Alison had to go home at 5.30. The afternoon went fast. She likes me to go up to Martins with her so I did and when we were going through the Jitty a man came up to us and said "Which is the heaviest out of you two". We didn't say anything because he was a stranger to us. He looked horrible, he had brown curly hair, a red jumper and dark brown trousers. We thought he was going to lift one of us up and run away with her so we ran our fastest up to Martins. The man followed us. I said goodbye to Alison. We were rather scared. The man followed Alison but he went into a sweet shop near Alison's house. When I got home Paul's friend was still there. I told mummy about the man. When Paul's friend went home he told his daddy and he rang the police and at night a policeman came and knocked on the door. I was in the bath at the time. I had to go down with a towel round me. He asked me what he looked like and what he was wearing. I told him and he went to Alison's house. She was in the bath too. I don't know if they caught him but that is my story of the kidnapper.'

Louise Ann's chief delight, however, was in fiction rather than fact. She wrote fictions of many kinds: fairy tales, comic satires, adventure stories, moral parables, a long tragi-comic crime story about a burglar who turned out to be a policeman, and, at the end of the year, an ambitious story of a shipwreck, divided into three chapters. Her favourite stories were rounded off with the flourish of her full signature. She was always delighted with a successful story and fretful if a story failed. Her stories were in many respects the most comprehensive literary achievement of any writer in the class and I want to make use of two representative examples of her story-telling as a final illustration of narrative imagination and literary skill in the work of eight and nine year old children. The two stories were composed within a few weeks of each other towards the end of the school year and are related in theme though very different in complexity and length.

The first story, entitled 'Lost in a Wood', represents Louise Ann's version of one of the children's favourite plots, a plot that was treated in a wide variety of ways by different children at different times in the year.

'Tuesday, May 17th.

Louise Ann wrote a story today, her first settled piece of writing for more than a week, which is unusual for Louise Ann (though of no particular account in itself). I hadn't been involved in her decision to write but both she and Gwyneth [her closest classroom friend at that time], having for several days rejected any thought of writing, chose it today for themselves. She came to me with what she had written, after the end of her first page, at the point when the two children fall into a doze under the oak tree. She wanted to know how to go on. Had she no idea what was to come, I asked. No, she said. How about the children waking up after some time, trying to go home and finding themselves going further into the wood and getting lost, I suggested, unoriginally. Ah yes, she said, with a little smile of recognition, and then what? Ah well, that's for you to decide I said, sliding away from committing myself, and so, with a cheerful tutting at me, and a mock scowl, off Louise Ann went, having received, as it seemed, the impetus she needed to carry on with the story. Later she brought it to me finished and I was surprised how quickly she had completed it. Well, she said, she'd decided at the start that it would be just a little story. She didn't want anything that would go on too long.

Throughout our exchanges about the story, Louise Ann had adopted a cheerful but quite casual manner, as if to indicate that this was not a story to be taken too seriously, although I think she was pleased with it. And indeed when I read it, agreeable as it is, I felt that it was the kind of story she can spin off whenever she chooses, now, happily enough and without too much exertion — though Louise Ann is a child whose work is often strenuous. The writing seemed almost effortless, though skilful and fluent. It's a lovely story however, for, after all, thought doesn't have to be strenuous to be successful.

"Lost in the Wood.

"Oh for god's sake go and do something, you're getting on my nerves" shouted Jane's mum. "You have been hanging around all day. You have a bedroom full of toys, why not use them, or you can watch TV, there are loads of things you can do if you think about it." Jane went into the living room and turned on the TV. There was nothing on except the stuff all about Jesus and Jane wasn't very religious. "I know" she thought, "I can go for a walk in the wood and pick wild strawberries, that would be fab. I will go and call for Jemma and we can go together." "Mum, I am going to pick wild strawberries in the wood with Jemma." "Alright, anything to get rid of you." "I hate you" whispered Jane to herself. Jemma didn't live very far away so they were soon in the wood. It was lovely, the sun shone down and the breeze blew the trees. They found some strawberries, they were lovely and sweet. "Let's sit down and have a doze, I feel very sleepy", so they settled down under a big oak tree and they fell fast asleep. When they awoke the sun was setting behind the hills. They set off for home but the further they walked the deeper they went into the wood. "I think we are lost" said Jane at last. "I am very tired, we will have to stay here for the night and find our way home tomorrow." So they settled down once more and went to sleep, dreaming that they were in their own beds at home. Meanwhile at home their mums and dads had rung the police up. The police were trying to calm the ladies down but they were in vain. They had search parties everywhere in the wood. Suddenly one of the policemen found the two children under a holly bush. He blew his police whistle, that was a sign to say that he had found them. He carried the two sleepy heads home and the ladies made a great fuss. They never stirred until the morning." '

The story's strength and charm lies as much in its elegant form as in its vigorous mixture of realism and fancy. The opening is magnificently direct and particular, at the opposite extreme from the conventional formality of 'once upon a time'. The mother's exasperation and the child's response to it are conveyed with skilful realism. And then, with the beginning of the walk in the wood, the story moves into an altogether more fanciful world and its mood dramatically changes. The sometimes burdensome world of parents and home and boredom disappears; the language becomes dreamy, easeful and idyllic: 'they were soon in the wood, it was lovely, the sun shone down, and the breeze blew the trees. They found some strawberries, they were lovely and sweet. "Let's sit down and have a doze, I feel so sleepy" so they settled down under a big oak tree and they fell fast asleep.' Even the knowledge that they are lost and will have to spend the night in the wood does little to disturb the children's idyll, and it is only with the return of parents and home that anxiety appears, a change of mood and scene neatly introduced by the opening conjunction: 'Meanwhile at home '. Finally the two worlds are reunited, as it were, the quarrelsomeness forgotten in the 'great fuss' made by 'the ladies' and the children returning to the beds in which they had dreamt that they were sleeping where, now, 'they never stirred until the morning'. These final words show how keen a sense of an ending Louise Ann possessed, a quality that was evident in many of the children's writings, a sense of the appropriate mood, or gesture or incident with which to bring their stories to a close.

Five weeks later Louise Ann composed what was her longest and finest story of the year, a complex and a elaborate narrative that stretched to three tightly written chapters. It was a story in which she set out to explore further the relationship between writer and reader, something which had engaged her attention already in some of her earlier stories. Before she began to write, she discussed the proposed story with Stephen whose notes record the gist of their conversation.

'Before Louise Ann started writing this story she came to me to ask if I had any ideas of what to write about. Rather off the cuff I suggested a number of themes, including one about being in a spaceship about to take off. To this suggestion she replied "But that's the sort of thing boys write about, I don't want to write about that". When I later suggested a shipwreck theme, and she seemed attracted to the idea, I asked her if that wasn't also really a "boys'" subject. She replied "Oh no, I'm not a sissy you know, I don't want to write about flowers and things".

Having chosen the theme we didn't talk about the plot. I did say that it would be interesting if she could try to write about it in a different way. I had in mind (and I think I mentioned this) that she might concentrate on the description of the rescue itself. While she took the theme in quite a different way she did return to me on several occasions during the writing to say that her story was quite different from previous writings of hers.'

Here is the story.

'*The Desert Island.*

Chapter 1. The Wreck

A lot of people were having boat rides right out at sea and back again. On the last trip they had a great deal of people on board. It was a lovely sunny day but all of a sudden a big cloud came over them. There was going to be a storm, they had nowhere to go to safety. The big waves pounded against the side of the ship. Every one was in a panic and didn't know what to do. They got the dinghies in the water and made every one jump into them. They had to throw the babies and children down. There was an island about 6 miles ahead, they tried to reach it but in vain, a big wave turned the dinghies over and every one fell out into the rough water helplessly. They all gave up after a while. The next morning the sea was calm and you wouldn't have known there had been a storm that night. The first person to awake from her shock was a teenage girl, her name was Mary Smith. She had fair hair and blue eyes. She looked around her to see if she could see where she was, but she couldn't get her mind to think. She got up and walked along on the sand. Soon she came to something that surprised her, a whole lot more people lying on the sand, eyes shut. She went over to a lady and shook her. She awoke from her day dream and looked up at the blue sky. "Where am I?" "I don't know" said Mary, "I think we were ship wrecked and got washed up on this island." The lady sat up and looked around. Then she shouted out aloud "Oh where are my baby twins, I must have them with me." "Oh dear," thought Mary, "what are we going to do?" The lady's name was Mrs. Red. "Er, Mrs. Red, could you help me wake all these people up and then the more people we have awake the better because there will be more people to help you look." So Mrs. Red agreed, Mary helped her to her feet, but they weren't the only ones awake, oh no, there were two gleaming eyes looking at them from behind a bush.

Chapter 2. Exploring

Soon everyone was exploring the island, even the children were playing about. They were happy on the outside, but very sad on the inside. They all went into the trees and picked fruit and coconuts to get milk. The two eyes still watched carefully, gleaming bright at people. There were old people and young. Soon when everyone was back on the beach the captain of the ship told everyone to look for the missing twins, their names are Kerry and Gwyneth Red. Everyone took a gasp of astonishment, two twins missing, Gosh. Look everywhere that you can think of (by now the gleaming eyes had gone). Some went to look up every tree to see if there was any sign of the babies, some went and looked in pools to see if the babies had gone for a drink, they went everywhere but one place that they didn't see, it was where the mysterious eyes lived. Everyone crowded to their place that they met last time. They all looked as worried as Mrs. Red did. "Now then, don't look so worried, cheer up a bit, I know it's very sad, but we have done everything we can," said the captain, "so just cheer up and try to forget it." But it was impossible to forget. Darkness fell upon them. Everyone settled down on the sand and hoped they wouldn't be cold. Soon everyone was fast asleep and everything was quiet except the sea. The next morning everyone awoke with the same feeling that their children had gone, but there they were by the sides of their mothers and fathers, safe and sound. Later everyone was up and about picking coconuts. Some men were making rafts to try and get home.

Chapter 3. A discovery

The babies weren't found so no-one worried about them any more. They weren't quite forgotten, oh no, some one still looked after them, ho ho, yes, someone did, and they did it kindly (but I am not going to tell you who it is). They gave the babies milk and treated them as if they were their own. Everyone went around doing jobs, some cooking breakfast and making drinks out of the grapes and the berries. Some were even trying to build a tree house to live in but it kept on collapsing on them so they soon got fed up with it. The days went by slowly. One day a little boy about 4 went for a little walk by himself. Soon he came upon the cave where the mysterious eyes lived. He went in, looking around him as he went in, he saw a big fat ape sitting in the corner with two babies in its arms. The boy was very surprised, he turned around and ran back to his mother and told her but she didn't believe him and gave him a spanking for telling lies.

They saw a lot of ships at sea, they tried to signal to them but it was impossible, the boat was so far away. But one day they had a bit of luck, a big ship came close to the island. They set their fire going and the flames sprang up high. The ship saw the signal and hooted to say he had seen their signal and was coming to rescue them. They all jumped about with joy. The boat got as far as it could to shore. Just as the people were getting on board the mysterious eyes came plodding along with two baby humans in its arms, it was Kerry and Gwyneth. Mrs. Red screamed with joy to have her babies back. She rushed toward the ape to get her babies and to her surprise the ape gave the babies gently back to Mrs. Red. Everyone burst out laughing at the sight of it. Mrs. Red ran back to the ship with her babies in her arms. She waved to the ape until he was out of sight.'

In the introduction to her essay on the novel, *The Appropriate Form*, Barbara Hardy defines a novelist's task as follows: 'The novelist, whoever he is and whenever he is writing, is giving form to a story, giving form to his moral and metaphysical views, and giving form to his particular experience of sensations, people, places and society.'* Each one of these criteria, as I hope my examples have shown, is as germane to the stories written by the eight and nine year old children in Stephen Rowland's class as to the work of mature adult writers, and it is worth examining how in Desert Island, the most elaborate story written by any child all year, Louise Ann has exhibited them.

Consider first how Louise Ann exploits the form of her story. To a large extent this particular story was a formal experiment in the relationship of writer to reader. While she was writing it Louise Ann was very conscious of the differences between her own knowledge of the outcome, that of her readers, and that of the characters in the story. As Stephen explained in his notes:

'Throughout the writing of the story Louise Ann knew what had really happened to the twins and so she was not anxious about them. (The plot was not worked out as it went along, as often happens in the children's writing; Louise Ann already knew it.) On two occasions during the writing when Louise Ann asked me to read what she had so far written, she was eager to point out that the babies were "alright really". Where she writes about the other characters' anxiety for the twins she is writing a kind of double fiction — it's only a story and even *in* the story the twins are really alright. It is as if the fears of the characters in the story are twice removed from reality, once because it's a story and again because Louise Ann knows all along that the twins are in the safe hands of the kindly ape. Thus it is not surprising that Louise Ann sometimes finds it difficult to portray to the full her

* *The Appropriate Form*, Barbara Hardy, Athlone, 1964.

characters' anxieties.'

In the event Louise Ann has shown considerable ingenuity in the manner in which she withholds the story's secret while signalling its existence to her readers and relieving them of any anxiety as to the twins' fate. The secret is first mentioned at the end of the first chapter, after the shock of the twins' disappearance, when Louise Ann writes: 'Mary helped her to her feet but they weren't the only ones awake, oh no, there were two gleaming eyes looking at them from behind a bush.' Almost immediately the secret is mentioned a second time, as if to make sure that the reader doesn't forget it: 'the two eyes still watched carefully, gleaming bright at people' . Later, at the very moment when, if the eyes were still there, the secret would be out for everyone to know, Louise Ann includes the first of two significant parentheses: 'Look everywhere you can think of (by now the gleaming eyes had gone.)' I can think of few more appropriate occasions for a parenthesis; in her use of brackets here and later, Louise Ann demonstrates an understanding of the effectiveness of punctuation which might at first seem somewhat surprising in view of her common reluctance to add full stops at the end of her sentences. It recalls the use of exclamation marks in Simon's story and indicates the particular concern that children often show for punctuation when the occasion most clearly appears to demand it.

The first parenthesis is followed shortly by a further hint to the reader of the twins' whereabouts: 'but one place that they didn't see, it was where the mysterious eyes lived' . And then, finally, the reader, though not yet of course the characters in the story, is taken into the narrator's confidence, just at the point at which the twins are being forgotten by the rest of the castaways: 'they weren't quite forgotten, oh no, someone still looked after them, ho ho, yes, someone did, and they did it kindly (but I am not going to tell you who it is).' In this her second parenthesis, at the beginning of her final chapter, Louise Ann addresses the reader directly for the first, and only, time. Even now, though, the secret is not revealed; that happens later in the chapter and when it does it is not the narrator who gives away the secret but the four year old boy who wanders into the cave where the mysterious eyes live and sees 'a big fat ape sitting in the corner with two babies in its arms' . That it should be the boy and not the narrator who finally reveals to the reader whom the mysterious eyes belong to demonstrates the ingenuity of the story's construction, as does the sequel. Thus, Louise Ann continues to preserve a trace of the secret after it has been discovered to the reader, and when at last the ape emerges, babes in arms, it is recalled: 'just as the people were getting on board, the mysterious eyes came plodding along with two baby humans in its arms '. The narrative conceit of the plodding eyes completes the effect that Louise Ann has sought in concealing from reader and character alike the secret she alone has known all along: in this final trick of language even the ungrammatical "its" is irreplaceable.

Louise Ann's story is equally successful in articulating a vision of the world, a world of contrary feelings — anxiety and relief, mis- understanding and gratitude — and a world of moral sensations — of human weakness and strength. The moral world which she describes and explores is not a world of make-believe, for all the fanciful elements in her story. It reflects a clear understanding of particular human experience, especially the experience of emotion. Louise Ann shows a strong empathy with her characters and their predicament. She describes the confusion of the castaways as they wake up on the island: 'She looked around her to see if she could see where she was but she couldn't get her mind to think'. She observes the sudden onset of panic: 'She awoke from her day dream and looked up at the blue sky. "Where am I?" "I don't know" said Mary. "I think we were ship wrecked and got washed up on this island." The lady sat up and looked around. Then she shouted out loud "Oh where are my baby twins, I must have them with me." ' She notes the contrast between outward calm and inner anxiety: 'Soon everyone was exploring the island, even the children were playing about. They were happy on the outside, but very sad on the inside'. The reassurance which the captain seeks to offer is unsuccessful: ' "Now then, don't look so worried, cheer up a bit, I know it's very sad but we have done everything we can," said the captain, "so just cheer up and try to forget it." But it was impossible to forget.' The impossibility of forgetting is evoked in a haunting description of the first night and the following morning: 'Darkness fell upon them. Everyone settled down on the sand and hoped they wouldn't be cold. Soon everyone was fast asleep and everything was quiet except the sea. The next morning everyone awoke with the same feeling that their children had gone, but there they were by the sides of their mothers and fathers, safe and sound.'

Louise Ann's story, however, is comic rather than sad and along with sympathy for her characters' fear and confusion she displays again her keen sense of irony, for example in her account of the small boy who discovered the twins: 'he turned around and ran back to his mother and told her but she didn't believe him and gave him a spanking for telling lies.' There is irony in the ending too, in the comic transformation of emotion as Mrs. Red screams with joy and rushes towards the ape only to be brought up short in surprise as the ape hands the twins gently back. Notice the emotional contrast between 'screamed with joy' and 'burst out laughing', or between the words 'rushed toward the ape to get her babies' and 'ran back to the ship with her babies in her arms'.

I do not wish to minimise the story's limitations: the weakness in Louise Ann's treatment of time, for example, or the too rapid transitions, as at the start of the third chapter: 'The babies weren't found so no one worried about them any more.' Yet even the obvious weaknesses are in part a product of the story's exceptional ambition as to length, complexity of form, breadth of treatment and human scope. More than any other single piece of writing in Stephen Rowland's class, this remarkable story served to demonstrate the expressive concerns of young writers and the careful skill with which they sought to embody their ideas in appropriate literary form within the constraints of their as yet limited experience of life and language. In this respect Desert Island was much more than a model story; it was a model of the vitality and richness of children's thought in many different spheres of activity, as appropriate to art, or science or mathematics, as to literature, as we shall see.

3   Art and Representation

The previous chapter was concerned with children's literary thought and expression; this chapter and the next examine certain aspects of their art and of their mathematics. In each chapter my aim is to draw attention to the deliberation, skill, judgement and expressive concern which are inherent in the children's thought and action within the admittedly severe, but not necessarily inhibiting, limits set by their own immaturity. The present chapter concentrates on the art of three children in Stephen's class, Paul, Robert and Julie, and in particular on some of their representational paintings and drawings. The next chapter examines a different kind of art, the making of patterns and designs, relating it to mathematics, to logical ordering, and to the children's scientific and philosophical speculations.

I want to consider first a group of paintings which Paul composed towards the end of the Autumn term. The earliest of them was painted shortly after I had returned to Stephen Rowland's class after a fortnight spent in Janet Harvey's class of seven year olds. That fortnight had been especially rich in art. I had seen how the children interpreted, in a remarkable series of portraits in paint and collage, their experience of a puppet show presented to the school by a small professional group at the start of the fortnight; I had worked with a group who were cutting up wallpapers and rearranging them into new formal designs or into representational pictures; I had watched the class working, with paint, home made stencils, and cutout paper, on studies of leaves, trees, the field around the school, and various autumnal scenes. In the aftermath of this experience I was disappointed by the painting I found in progress in Stephen's class on my return to it. The children had only recently begun to mix their own paints and, as might have been expected, the early results were somewhat drab. I found it hard, during the first few days of my return, to take these paintings seriously; that is, until I came across the first of Paul's paintings of birds.

Fig. 1

'Thursday, November 18th.

I was a little disappointed with the painting yesterday . . .
Today, however, out of a large handful of paintings of richly
varying quality emerged one quite exceptional work — by Paul
(see fig 1). It had been begun two days ago and at the start of
today had been simply a harbour wall, beautifully textured —
green and mauve brush strokes on a background of black — with
a lighthouse on top, a greenish yellow sun in the corner, to which
Paul later added a red centre and red rays, and, beyond the wall,
taking up most of the sheet of brown sugar paper on which he
was painting, a blue sky above a strip of deeper blue sea on
which sailed a crudely drawn red and green ship. Sometime in
the early morning Stephen suggested to Paul that he might do
something about the large unfilled space beyond the lighthouse
wall which made the picture seem rather bare. Paul responded
by painting in the middle of the bare sky a large gull with black
and white body and red beak, using an illustration in a book of
birds as his guide. He was dissatisfied with it; "rubbish" he said
to me when, perhaps too casually, I praised it. ["Rubbish" was
Paul's favourite expression of dissatisfaction, both weak and
strong.] He was dissatisfied in part because the bird seemed to
him too big and in part because he had drawn it at rest, as in the

illustration, whereas he'd really wanted it to be in flight. When Stephen saw the picture he noticed the problem of the bird's position but said nothing to Paul about it. Later he returned to find that Paul had solved the problem for himself by painting a branch beneath the bird, part of a tree which now jutted out across the sea from the edge of the lighthouse wall, in thick, bold, black lines. In their stark clarity of outline Paul's branches formed quite a contrast with the more tentative trees drawn by the group of children in Janet's class whom I took on that frosty walk last week. I thought that was the end of Paul's painting and liked its effect though I felt it to be a little bleak. However I returned to Paul a minute or two later to find that he'd added a mass of yellow green catkins to his tree, and the picture was utterly changed. The catkins, like the branches, were painted impressionistically, the thick brush strokes squiggling down from the black branches. They composed the picture beautifully, as if precisely what it had required, although I think they had been added as an afterthought.

Stephen admired the picture and showed it to the rest of the class. He thought Paul was proud of it, in a quiet way. After dinner Paul added to it again, this time less fortunately I thought, painting a large brown nest in the tree, in the top right corner of the picture, with two thin black lines emerging from it — the chicks, he told me. I felt the nest muddied the composition though Paul liked it.'

It was the clarity of line and intensity of colour in this, the first of Paul's many fine paintings during the year, that marked it out at that time as exceptional. Its significance lay as much, however, in the manner of its composition as in its finished form. The picture grew out of the interplay between Paul's intentions and their various intended and unintended effects, effects which in turn generated new or revised intentions. The act of painting was marked by sustained deliberation and invention; it was the self-consciousness of his procedure that brought about a gradual transformation in the content and form of the composition. Thus the picture began as a brilliantly coloured variation on a conventional theme that was popular within the class at that time: a ship upon the sea. The first step in its subsequent transformation was taken in response to a spectator's, in particular a teacher's, implied criticism of the emptiness of the painted sky, which led Paul to paint in the middle of his sky a large seagull. But in choosing to model his bird on an illustration he had found in a book Paul made an unfortunate mistake, drawing the flying gull as if it were perched on land. It was his dissatisfaction with this result that produced his next and best invention; he took the bird, originally conceived of as flying over water, and first in thought, then in paint, transferred it to the branches of a tree. The bold shape of the overarching tree was determined in part by the space which it had to fill; Paul was not satisfied however by the bare black branches and, whether to relieve the starkness of the heavy black paint strokes or because the tree brought to mind a hanging willow or simply because he wanted his tree to be in leaf, he chose to add the lush green strokes, resembling catkins, enlivening both the tree itself and the whole of his composition. Last of all he added the nest, perhaps to strengthen the bond between bird and tree.

Two weeks after he had completed his picture Paul made it the subject of a second painting in which he varied the composition yet again but in a very different way.

'Thursday, December 2nd.

Paul's day was dominated by his second painting of harbour wall, lighthouse, sea, ship, bird and willow. It was yesterday or the day before that he decided to paint a second version of this picture. Today he told me the reason was that he was thinking of giving different versions to different relatives for Christmas. (I had the impression that this was perhaps a way of justifying the repainting rather than the chief reason.) At the start of the day the wall, bird and branches were more or less finished and during the day the sky was filled in. This time, wall, lighthouse and tree were brown and red and green whereas before they had been black and green and blue. The bird, black and white in the first painting, had now become green and yellow. The tree leant more gracefully but less palpably across the sea, its catkins long and arched and a large nest balanced precariously in the angle of one of its branches. This morning Paul began by painting a red and yellow sun in the opposite corner to the sun in the first picture, and a long red strip across the top of the sky which he told me was because it was sunset. We talked about how to colour in the rest of the sky and decided to make it yellow, to complete the sunset effect. Paul flecked the yellow with red, the red strokes streaking across the branches and catkins of the tree as well as the yellow sky. It was impossible to paint evenly around the already painted branches, catkins and bird, and this in part explains the difference between the rough strokes with which the sunset sky was painted and the even, overall blue of the sky in the first picture, in which the sky had been painted before the tree and bird. Given the difficulty, however, Paul used it to create a new effect. By the end of the day he had completed his 'copy' — a version very like the first in form and wholly different in colour and mood. Paul, who in painting it was continually beset, as before, by mumbled doubts as to the worth of his picture, especially liked this second painting when he stood a long way back from it and stared at it. Side by side on the wall, the two pictures make a fascinating pair, like a couple of Turner water colours of the same scene painted at midday and towards evening.'

Paul's next painting was a large portrait of an imagined seagull, or sea bird, which gave further evidence of the deliberation of his methods, in part playful and in part pained, and of the particular expressive quality of his achievement.

'Sunday, December 12th.

Last Tuesday Paul painted a large bird on a thick tree stump: a seagull (see fig 2). The origin of this painting lay in the circumstances surrounding his previous paintings of birds beside a harbour wall. Whether he chose this subject because of the way his previous work had been praised or whether the idea formed in his mind as he was engaged on the second painting I am not sure, but I think the latter is more likely. At any rate, almost immediately the sunset version was finished Paul was saying that now he intended to paint a large picture of a bird. He said it as if he saw this as the logical extension of his previous painting, the next step in an orderly sequence of work, a clear and proper succession of ideas. He chose to paint on a large sheet of old green sugar paper and he painted a large bird with yellow and white body, blue eyes with red pupils, thin brown legs and feet, and a long red beak, perched on a stump (thinner at first than in the finished picture). The brown stump rose from the bottom of the paper with the bird on top. I saw the picture before dinner, when Paul seemed to think it was finished, and I liked it, but because the green paper on which he had painted was grubby and torn I suggested to him that I should cut round the picture

Fig. 2

itself and mount it on another sheet of paper before putting it up on the classroom wall. Paul agreed, a little reluctantly. I cut carefully around the bird and stump, leaving a thin strip of unpainted green paper all round the picture; then I mounted it on a large sheet of blue sugar paper, since there was no more green. It stood out against the backing paper like a portrait bust.

After dinner Paul looked at his picture on the wall and saw that it must be added to. He was most dissatisfied with the way in which, now, the stump rose out of the middle of the paper. He did not appreciate the backing paper as just that, nor did he consider the portrait of bird on stump to be self-sufficient. He wanted to fix the bird and stump within an appropriate painted landscape, incorporating the backing paper into the painting itself. So we took the picture down from the wall and Paul spent much of the afternoon painting on. He turned the bottom of the paper into a sea out of which the brown stump rose with the bird upon it. Above the bird, in the top left corner, he painted a spiky yellow sun with green eyes and mouth. After he had retouched the bird here and there, we put the painting back on the wall. I had discouraged Paul from trying to paint out the green strip of paper that surrounded the bird. He had painted out the strip on either side of the stump simply by widening the stump itself but he could not do the same to the bird without destroying its shape. But I think he was already dissatisfied with this green halo around the bird, as also with the as yet unpainted blue backing paper above the painted sea. I'd suggested that the unpainted blue paper would do just as well for sky as painting it over; I was worried again, that in painting the sky Paul might spoil his delicately painted bird.

During the afternoon I noticed how careful Paul was over his painting, how deliberate and almost "professional" in the way he would stand back to look at it, retouching it here and there — looking, adding, reflecting. I noticed too how, once more, he would mutter to himself, now that it was rubbish, now that it was really quite good. At the end of the afternoon, taking a final look at it from a distance now that it was up on the wall again, he told me how the stump almost looked as if it really was standing out of the water because of the way he'd painted the sea coming up above the base of the stump on either side and disappearing behind it. (It was plain that he was commenting on a depth effect he had noticed in the painting but I doubt whether he had intended the effect while he was painting; it was a quality he recognised and appreciated in the painting now that it was finished and could be critically inspected.)

From Tuesday to Friday the painting stayed in its allotted place above Paul's two previous paintings, standing out on the opposite wall as one entered the classroom. Then on Friday Paul asked me to take it down so that he could work on it yet again. He just didn't like the green strip around the bird and between its legs. He'd decided to paint in the sky in order to cover up both the green strip and the surrounding blue backing paper. And so he did, as slowly and deliberately as ever, taking the added opportunity to retouch the bird again, its face, breast and beak. By the end of the morning the painting was finally complete, every square inch of the paper now painted, and ready to return to the wall. Before it went back, as he was adding the finishing touches, Paul suddenly said, "I wish I lived in a painting house". Then, he said, he could paint all day and every day.'

Early in the course of the painting Mary Brown had asked Paul whether the seagull's beak wasn't perhaps unrealistically long. Paul looked at her, his face assuming the quizzical, puzzled smile that was to become so characteristic of him, and answered something like 'ah yes, well . . . ', acknowledging nonetheless that the bird was indeed intended to be a seagull of sorts. However, the painting is not a portrait of any actual bird, nor did Paul on this occasion, as far as I know, make use of a photograph or a drawing in a book to guide him. And yet, once the picture was finished and hung in its allotted place on the classroom wall, the bird looked unquestionably real, almost touchable, for all the extravagance of its beak. There was something else about it too, a quality that suggested that this bird had entered into Paul's imagination as he painted and taken possession of him. A similar impression was conveyed by Paul's final painting of the term, composed a few days later: the portrait of an eagle. On this occasion his painting did derive from a photograph, and yet the finished portrait seemed rather more than an attempted copy, as if in the act of copying, as well as his very limited technique allowed, he were also attempting to reinterpret the photograph in accordance with his own distinctive vision. The eagle he painted seemed haughtier than the bird in the photograph, its head thrust upwards, hook nosed rather than beaked. It had become an emblem, the emblem of an eagle, just as his previous portrait had been the emblem of a sea bird.

This emblematic quality was, for me, the most striking aspect of Paul's early paintings. It emerges in the palpability and concreteness of the pictorial images, the intensity of colour and outline, the combination of realism and fancy in the composition, and the transformation of his own ideas, as also of the illustrations he used to guide him, in the act of painting and its varied consequences. His paintings seem to celebrate the objects they depict, both in themselves as objects, and also as the repositories for his fancy. As time went on, Paul's attention turned more often to the representation of objects within his own direct and immediate experience but the sense of celebration in his paintings persisted all year, along with a strong sense of play, and a fondness for the extravagant gesture.

Consider, for example, the two pictures of his go cart which Paul painted at the beginning and near the end of the Spring Term. This go cart was the Christmas present which, as I have already described in the previous chapter, Paul had been so eager to talk and write about on the morning of the first day of the new term. He painted his first picture of it on the afternoon of the same day.

'Tuesday, January 11th.

In the afternoon of the first day back Paul began a large drawing of himself on the go cart. He spent a long time at the start of the afternoon searching in the library for a book which might contain a picture of an engine something like the one on his cart to remind him of how it looked. He was evidently reluctant to trust his unaided memory on this detail, although at first I urged him to. Eventually he found a picture of an engine that looked right, and began. It was only the engine he didn't trust himself to remember. The rest of the cart was drawn from memory, himself in the driving seat, a blanket behind him, which, as he told me, he used to prop himself up on the seat. He was particularly careful to get this blanket into the picture, one end of it sticking up above and behind the seat. That afternoon he only had time to begin painting the cart frame but yesterday when I returned to the class [after two days' absence] the painting was finished, painted all over like last term's bird pictures, no inch of paper left unpainted. It had been put up on the wall in place of the bird paintings which Paul had taken home with him at the end of the first day of term, having been persuaded to leave them up on the wall at the end of the previous term so that we would all have something bright to come back to on the first day. I had hoped that Paul might agree to let them stay up longer but no; almost first thing on the first day he'd told me he would be taking them home at the end of the day.

The painting of the go cart was different in character from the bird paintings, less intense in vision, more matter of fact. Or so, at least, it seemed at a glance, which is all as yet I've given it.'

This first picture of the go cart was not so much an emblem as a record, the recording in loving detail of a treasured possession. Towards the end of term, however, he painted a second picture of the go cart and this time the quality of emblem returned. It was the most flamboyant picture he had yet painted and confirmed his growing powers of observation and representation at the same time as it demonstrated his love of fancy and extravagance.

'Tuesday, March 15th.

Yesterday Paul began a drawing of his go cart smashed up against a tree. [In the two months since he had been given it, the go cart had become quite a handful. He had got it stuck in mud, he had run it into a tree, he had found it almost impossible to control. One day he even told me, half in jest, that he was thinking of getting rid of it. Such mishaps were very much a part of Paul's life. For him the world was as irremediably obtuse as it was absorbing, and his experiences were constantly confirming this perception of things.] The drawing seemed to have worked out quite well but this morning Paul had turned the paper over and was drawing a warship on the other side. I asked him why and he said that, well, the go cart picture was no good. He turned the paper over again to show me, explaining that the trouble was that he'd drawn a road which looked as if it was up in the sky. (The problem was that the scene he had drawn required a perspective he had been unable to achieve.) I said I thought it a pity, even so, that he had given up the go cart picture, and tried to encourage him to return to it. He agreed, but only in so far as he agreed to paint the go cart; he refused to paint it smashed up against the tree. He spent most of the day on the drawing and painting and this time all went well. Instead of the crashed cart he painted the go cart as if it were new, spread across the paper, large and dominant, himself sitting serenely at the wheel (see fig. 3). When he had painted the go cart in January he had used an illustration from a book to help him get the engine right. This time, after several weeks of careful, and sometimes painful, observation of the real thing, he didn't need a book and even so the engine was drawn with greater precision and detail, as indeed was the whole cart. The elaborately drawn and painted cart rested on a thin black strip of road, with a large tree at one side (a tree that was quite different from the tree Paul had drawn on the abortive picture of the crashed cart) and above

Fig. 3

the go cart he placed a large blue pond (possibly in part to cover up the traces of the warship he had drawn to begin with on this side of his paper). In the corner, incongruously, he painted a yellow sun, with yellow rays, black eyes, nose and mouth, and smoking a brown pipe! The sun with its face, however ridiculous, is for Paul like a kind of signature, it seems.'

When the painting was pinned on the wall several children drew attention to the blue pond which seemed to be, as they put it, 'up in the air'. Oddly enough Paul had landed himself, accidentally, in the same difficulty as in his abortive drawing of the crashed cart, requiring a command of perspective which was beyond his present technique. On this occasion, however, Paul himself seemed less worried by the absence of perspective than by the vagueness of the blue patch that stood for the pond. As it was, it was unrecognisable. A day or two later he added wavy white lines to it as if to signify more clearly what it represented; finally, still dissatisfied, he painted in the middle of the pond a large black shark, that being, as he told me, his favourite fish.

The juxtaposition of so many disparate elements in the finished picture was perhaps as much accidental as deliberate but the ingenuity with which Paul managed to combine them showed once more how effectively he could capitalise on accidents, incorporating them in new intentions. The final effect delighted him, and nothing more, he told me, than the sun smoking his pipe. The most impressive part of the painting, however, as far as Stephen and myself were concerned, was the go cart itself, in the clarity and precision of its detail, and in its spectacular presence across the paper. The image Paul has painted embodies both his knowledge of the go-cart and his feeling for it. It has the same emblematic quality as his paintings of birds but it also reflects a more thorough observation of reality. Above all, it seems to me to express more clearly than any of his previous paintings, his love of objects, of objects in general and of this particular object. The same quality of feeling had already been evident in the minute cardboard models of go carts constructed by Paul earlier in the Spring term* but it gained perhaps its most complete expression in this, his second picture of his go cart.

Paul's realism however was confined to the go cart itself. At first he set it in a very simple and rudimentary landscape defined by the thin black strip of road on which the cart rested, the bare blue patch of pond above it, and, to the side of the pond, the flat and somewhat formal tree to which the grass at its base, and the barely recognisable squirrel on its trunk, added a hint of depth. Next came the irreverent signature of the pipe smoking sun which seems almost to be poking fun at realism. Lastly, as much maybe for its extravagance as for anything, he included the fantastic fish. The picture was no longer a simple celebration of a cherished object; it had become a kind of game, a playful and decorative fancy superimposed on the careful realism of the drawing of the go cart itself.

This kind of metamorphosis was a common experience in Paul's art and was to lead to his most extraordinary picture of the year, late in the summer, when a delicately drawn rabbit skull was suddenly transformed into a monstrous sculpture.** However I do not intend to consider the later development of Paul's painting here. Instead I want to compare his paintings with those of another boy, Robert, whose representation of the world and of his own experience of it through art was less fanciful and less emblematic though equally intense in its own particular way. I first remarked on the apparent contrast between Paul's and Robert's artistic styles and intentions

* For an account of these miniature models, see Chapter 6.
**See Chapter 5.

when I was describing, in my notes, the effect of Paul's portrait of a seagull, described above.

'Sunday, December 12th.

It's interesting to compare Paul's painting [of the imagined seagull] with a painting of Robert's and Mark's last Friday. They had come up to me first thing in the morning to say that they thought it was about time they had a go at painting. [At that time their favourite activity was writing stories.] They wanted to paint ducks, and Stephen told me later that they made a great point of insisting to him that the ducks must be mallards. They found an illustration in a bird book which they used as a model. Their painting was very carefully observed, much attention being paid to the details of the birds' appearance and to their surroundings. It was a fine piece of work and they followed it up by starting work on a second bird painting, this time of two hawks. For Robert and Mark, however, in contrast with Paul, the task seemed to be to make their birds, and the environment in which they were placed, as like the real thing as possible (inasmuch as the illustration they were using was itself an accurate likeness). Accuracy of representation was all important to them. Perhaps this was part of Paul's intention too but I don't think it fanciful to suppose that he was seeking something else as well, and that in some way the bird he painted possessed his imagination in a way in which Robert's and Mark's birds did not and were not intended to.'

At first I was tempted to attribute the difference between Robert's paintings and Paul's to a difference in the depth of their feelings as well as in their respective intentions. In this I was mistaken. Robert's paintings were every bit as deeply felt as Paul's but they pursued a different theme. As his later work made clear, Robert's concern, in his most careful or most ambitious drawings and paintings, was to depict the natural world with as intense a precision as he could manage. He was not inclined to turn reality into fancy, nor overtly to dramatise or idealise it. He did not share Paul's love of emblem and gesture. In this respect there was a strong contrast between his relatively infrequent paintings and his many stories. His stories were for the most part fantastic adventures, science fictions with little regard for the world's constraints, often derived from television or children's books, though with a certain individual style. The paintings on the other hand depended on thorough and painstaking observation of the real world.

The distinctive quality of Robert's drawing and painting can be seen at its best in a series of sketches he made during the month of May, and in the paintings he based upon them. In the Summer term, Stephen's class made several visits to a river bank about a mile away from the school, occasions for the study of the river itself and its banks, but also an opportunity to work in a less confined environment than that of the classroom. It was on the second of these visits that Robert made his first sketch of the river, but it was not until our fourth visit some three weeks later that I described the sketch and subsequent painting in my notes, although Stephen and I had often talked about it in the meantime.

'Thursday, May 26th.

This is an appropriate moment to return to Robert's picture of reeds reflected in water, completed almost three weeks ago now. The story begins on May 4th when, as that day's notes record, we all went down to the river — it was our second visit — and Robert spent his time drawing the reeds by the water's edge. [Robert described his own experience in a short account of this visit, written a day or two later, which recalls the quiet absorption of his work that afternoon.

"Down by the river.

I was sitting on a big root of a tree drawing a picture of the rustling reeds. It was very quiet by the river. One or two birds were singing. I went to show Mr Rowland (my picture). He liked (it). So did Mrs Rowland and Mr Armstrong. I wondered where the river ends. I started another picture but it went wrong. Then I went to find Mark. I hope to go next week."]

The drawing was remarkable for the accuracy of its rendering of the reeds themselves and of their reflection in the water. As I wrote on May 4th "there was no doubt for a moment as to the object and its reflection". The following Monday Robert sat down to turn his sketch into a painting. (Maybe he started the painting before the Monday but it was then that he completed it.) I remembered coming across him just once while he was painting it and feeling that the picture might turn out disappointingly since the relative clumsiness of powder paint as applied with thick brush strokes to sugar paper seemed to have diminished the fine accuracy of his sketch. But I was wrong.

Fig. 4

(Unfortunately he threw the sketch away after finishing the painting so that I can no longer directly compare the two.) The reeds were painted bright green, both above the water and as reflected in it, and the surface of the water itself, which covered the entire background of the painting, was a deep blue, applied rather unevenly, perhaps in part by design but also because it was painted after the reeds themselves so that it was impossible to apply an even colour wash. Later Robert added a number of wavy black lines across the blue to indicate the rippling of the water surface. He also began to outline the reeds and their reflections with black charcoal following up the one hint which Stephen had offered him when he wanted a way of marking off the green reeds more strongly from the surrounding blue. He outlined the reeds first and then began on their reflections but he soon decided that the effect of reflection would be better achieved if only the actual reeds themselves were outlined in black while their reflections were left as they were, less sharply distinguished from the water. At the dividing line between reeds and reflection he painted a few half circles of black, around each reed, signifying the water surface faintly disturbed around the obtruding reeds. (I remember these semicircular ripples around the reeds being on the original drawing as well as the painting.) The reflections themselves are an almost perfect mirror of the reeds (see fig. 4). You can turn the picture upside down and barely recognise the difference. (But note that you CAN recognise it.) Robert explained to Stephen his concern that at one point the reflection didn't quite match the reality, a reed being broken in its reflection when it was really unbroken. He had been especially careful to get the reflections exact and the discrepancy disturbed him. In defence of the discrepancy Stephen pointed to the effects of rippling water on the regularity of reflections and Robert was then satisfied.'

Robert's beautiful painting is a comprehensive study, at once artistic and scientific, of the reflection of reeds in water. Consider the power of observation displayed in the careful shaping of the reeds, and in the marking of the movement of water around them. Consider how thoughtfully Robert examined the resemblance of the image to the reflected object, how concerned he was that the reflection of the reeds should be an exact, mirror image of the reeds themselves and yet distinguishable from them. (It is interesting to observe that the reeds in Robert's paintings are longer than their reflection. I am uncertain, however, whether or not this was a deliberate effect and I cannot now remember if there was the same variation of length on the original drawing.) Consider what pains he took to record in paint the effects which he had observed: the movement of water by adding wavy black lines across the blue background and half circles of black around each reed at water level, the difference in clarity between object and reflection by outlining, in charcoal, only the reeds themselves and not their reflections. Consider, finally, the formal precision of his painting. The colour is rich in contrast and was the product of considerable repainting, while the clarity and harmony of line show that Robert had as lively a regard for pictorial values as for careful observation and representation.

Two weeks after his first riverside sketch Robert returned to the river bank, along with most of the rest of his class, determined to sketch again. This time his friend Mark had decided to sit and write about whatever Robert was sketching. They spent all afternoon together, drawing, writing, and following the swan that was the object of their attention. Mark described the scene as follows in the account he finally composed from his original notes.

"The swan was pruning its feathers. It was standing in the water. The water was flowing very fast. Two ducks went past. The reeds rustled in the wind. The wind was very cold. The swan was a mute swan. The ducks swam very fast. They were swimming near the bank. We were sitting in a tree. Later the swan moved. We ran after it. We ran over the bridge to have a better look. We followed it until we were three feet away from it. Then it opened its wings and rustled its feathers and (went) further down the river. [Mark omitted the word 'went' but Robert included it in the copy he made for himself of Mark's account.] We went back over the bridge and back to school. The river is called the River Eye. We have done a painting of the swan. It is outside the classroom. We are going this week.'

On this occasion I was careful to preserve Robert's original sketch, as well as the painting he made from it later in the classroom. He drew the swan standing in shallow water beside the river bank, its neck arched forward as it pruned its breast, the wing feathers slightly ruffled on its back. The fast flowing water rippled around its one visible leg while thick and spiky reeds and grasses, too tightly packed to be reflected in the water, crowded against the crooked line that marked the river bank. The swan's head and neck were drawn with great care, the curve of the neck established in a series of soft pencil strokes, revised and redrawn here and there, the head detailed and exact, with bill, knob and eye. The back seemed to have caused Robert some difficulty and his first attempts to fix its proper line were rubbed out; the ruffled wing feathers were added later in a series of heavier pencilled notches drawn over and across the finally determined line. Below the swan a dense thicket of short V shaped pencil strokes distinguished the shorter grasses from the taller reeds. The reeds themselves, rising behind and over the grasses, were drawn individually and Robert took care to observe and record how they overlapped and interwove. The water flowing around the swan's leg was indicated by the same half circles that Robert had used in his sketch of reeds while a few wavy lines beside and above the swan suggested, once more, the movement of water down the stream. It is worth noting that, while the painted black lines which served to indicate the movement of water in the painting of reeds were drawn horizontally across the picture, the pencilled ripples in this sketch, with greater accuracy, were drawn vertically down the paper.

Fig. 5

The painting (see fig. 5) which Robert made from this sketch, with help from Mark, was less vivid than the sketch itself and did not quite match, as the sketch had done, the quality of its immediate predecessor, the painting of reflected reeds. Robert began by making a greatly enlarged drawing of his sketch. He stuck closely to the original except for leaving out part of the thicket of shorter grasses at the river's edge and reversing, for some reason, the swan itself. (I never found out why.) The enlarged drawing pleased him; it was when he and Mark came to paint it that they ran into difficulties, partly perhaps because of the quality of paper they had chosen to use. Robert was particularly worried by the painting of the shorter grasses at the bottom of the picture. He had left this part of the painting to Mark and felt that he had spoilt it. Eventually Stephen helped him to restore it to something like his original intention but he was still not altogether satisfied. Nevertheless it was a striking picture. The large, white, sinuous swan is set in the centre of the painting. It has an orange bill, deep black head and faint, white eye and it preens itself against a rich blue background, somewhat blotchy on account of the running of the paint, above a border trellis of pale green reeds. It is in its details rather than its overall effect that the painting is weaker than the sketch: in the absence of the ruffled feathers, the mass of grasses, and the ripples across the water. The enlarged drawing had included most of these details, though not quite as intricately drawn as in the sketch, but they had disappeared in the course of the painting, neither Robert nor Mark finding it easy to handle the powder paint as they wished to on this occasion. (Yet perhaps these details, rich though they were in the original sketch, were less appropriate to a painting. I recall that the sketch of reflected reeds was also richer in detail than the subsequent painting derived from it.)

The last of Robert's three river sketches was drawn just one week after the sketch of the swan preening itself. Robert was one of a small group who had chosen to return to the river bank once more, to collect water specimens or to sketch or to write or read. His original intention had been to draw the lily pads that were now beginning to spread out across the river but it was too windy where he was sitting and his paper kept blowing away. Frustrated by the wind, he wandered off with Mark up stream and there they came across the swan's nest, beside the bank on the other side of the river, with one swan sitting on the nest while the other stood alongside. They sat down opposite the nest and watched, and Robert decided to forget about the lily pads and sketch the nest and the swans, finding a rough piece of lined paper on which to draw. Mark wrote again while Robert sketched, describing the scene before him. The two of them were more relaxed than on their previous visit and worked less earnestly. As I put it in my notes 'they spent the afternoon sketching and writing but also teasing each other and lying down and enjoying the sun and the warmth of the river bank'. It was that kind of day, an easeful afternoon in early summer.

Mark's writing, completed back at school a day or two later, was tersely observant.

'*The Swan's nest.*

The female swan was sitting on her nest. The male was standing on guard. The nest is like an island. It is made of twigs and mud. The nest is under a bush. The male went to sleep. It bent its neck over its back. Then the female went to sleep. Then the male woke up again. Then we went back to school and made a model and a picture.'

Robert sketched what Mark described, the female swan sitting on its island nest of twigs and mud under a bush while the male stands guard among the reeds beside the ripples and lily pads of the river. The pencil drawing was rougher and more impressionistic than in the previous sketch of the swan preening itself, suggesting that Robert's

Fig. 6

concern on this particular afternoon was to convey the essence of the scene without elaborating its particulars so exactly or with such precision of line. The looser treatment was partly attributable, no doubt, to the relaxed atmosphere of the occasion but it may also reflect here, as in the work of other children, a new confidence in sketching.* At any rate, although it was less painstaking, this third sketch demonstrated as vividly as its companions had done Robert's skill and assurance in observing and recording the scene before him. The two swans were drawn with great conviction, especially the sitting swan which was viewed from behind in careful perspective, its neck outstretched inquisitively as it squatted on the nest. The nest was very clearly the island of twigs and mud described by Mark and alongside it a mass of loosely drawn branches, twigs and scattered leaves suggested the ragged confusion of the bush under which the nest sheltered. This time the reeds themselves were no more than rough scribbles fringing the water, as if Robert no longer felt the need

* See Chapter 5 for further examples.

to explore in detail their disposition or shape. At the bottom of the sketch half a dozen heart shaped lily pads floated among the ripples which were more frequent than in the previous sketch and composed once again of vertical rather than horizontal lines.

Robert did not begin his painting from this third sketch until he and Mark had made an ingenious cardboard model of a swan sailing on a river. They spent the greater part of a day working on this model which resembled a stage set from a Pollock's Theatre, and it was not until late in the afternoon that Robert began to think about his intended painting of the swan's nest. Whether for this reason or from some other cause Robert was never as involved in this third painting (see fig. 6) as in the previous two. He began as before with an enlarged drawing, this time on sugar paper, but once again the subsequent painting bothered him. This time it was the heads of the two swans that caused most trouble and the difficulty of deciding how to treat the background. Eventually he abandoned the painting, at first intending to return to it later but in the end deciding to leave it as it was. By that time he was involved in other things and this particular subject matter no longer commanded his attention.

This was the last of Robert's studies of the river and its banks. Although his final painting was less successful, certainly in his own opinion, than either of its predecessors, it was by no means inexpressive, even in its unfinished state, and it brought to a close a fascinating sequence of drawings and paintings. I have referred to them as studies in order to draw attention to the depth of their content and to the manner of their composition. The careful curiosity they exhibit is as much that of the naturalist as of the artist. Robert, like his friend Mark whose study found expression in writing rather than drawing, had examined the river intently, observing the effects of water, the nature of reflections, the character of reeds and grasses, the movement and gait of swans, the structure of a nest, the configuration of a tree. His sketches, and his subsequent paintings, record his reflective experience and attempt to represent it in the medium of pencil and paint. In his determination to draw just what he saw before him, as realistically and as distinctly as he could, he differed from Paul whose art, as we have seen, displayed an equal fondness for the fanciful as for the real. (Although Paul too, especially during the summer term, made of his drawing and painting an occasion for scientific or naturalistic inquiry and observation as well as for fantasy.*). Yet Robert's studies are in no sense drily academic

* See Chapter 5.

or technical; they are as expressive of his emotional as of his intellectual commitment to the subject matter of his inquiry, imbued with the same quality of feeling that finds expression in the few brief sentences he wrote on the occasion of his first sketch when he noticed how quiet it was except for the sound of reeds and "one or two birds" and when he wondered where the river ended. The several drawings and paintings are not uniformly successful but in one way or another each of them is evidently the work of a passionate observer, absorbed in the life of the river, in the act of recording it in line and paint, and in the problems and possibilities of form and expression in representational art.

Robert's and Paul's paintings and drawings, those of them I have described here, are instances of the alternative, though not mutually exclusive, ways in which different children in Stephen's class tackled the problems of representation and pictorial form. Julie's art work, a part of which I want to examine next, offers a third approach to these problems. Her painting shares something of the scientific or naturalistic realism of Robert's work and something of the emblematic, and even fanciful, realism that was characteristic of Paul, but it is distinct from either in the range of its concerns and in its expressive means, especially as regards the use of paint.

Most children considered Julie to be the best artist in the class, especially in figurative matters, and many of them would ask her help when it came to drawing animals, birds or other objects which they felt unable to manage on their own. Her figures were lifelike and charming, and drawn with considerable fluency of line, even if they seemed, to me at least, to reflect, on many occasions, less her own direct observation of nature than a familiarity with book illustrations, or perhaps with her father's pictures — for she came from an artistic family, to judge by the sketches of her father's which she would occasionally bring to school to show us. In any case, good though they were, her two dimensional figures were no match for her plasticine or clay models and sculptures, either in their realism or in their depth of feeling; and it was thus her three dimensional work that set the standard by which, at first, I tended to judge her art.

Her remarkable skill at modelling became clear in the first few weeks of the school year when she caused something of a sensation with two plasticine figures, one of them of a horse complete with saddle, bridle and stirrups, and the other of an old lady. Each model figure was exceptional by virtue of the combination of technical assurance with psychological conviction. A few weeks later Julie achieved an almost equal success when she modelled a hedgehog in clay, a medium she handled, in general, less confidently than plas-ticine. The occasion which gave rise to this last model was a walk which a group of girls had taken around the playing fields adjoining the school, during which they had discovered a dead hedgehog. This hedgehog was a source of much excitement and interest and a day or two later at Stephen's suggestion, the girls buried it so that they might dig up its skeleton later in the year. Julie's model seemed to be her own way of reflecting upon the discovery.

'Friday, December 3rd.

The girls who had been out walking, round the field, yesterday, and had later assembled a picture out of the leaves and berries they had brought with them — (we had tried without too much success to make rough dyes out of crushed berries and fungus) — went out again this morning in search of materials for a second collage. The walk also gave them an opportunity to visit once more the dead hedgehog they had found. Later, this afternoon, Julie asked if she could join the three girls who were working at the clay bench and when she got there she made a clay model of the hedgehog, a very precise sculpture, modelled with affection as well as care. She was most anxious that the figure should be lifelike and wanted to know if hedgehogs had tails and how exactly their feet were shaped. When she came to the spines she modelled each one separately, covering the back of her clay model with more than a score of tiny rolls of clay, making sure that each was firmly pressed in place. Her activity seemed to be as much a matter of natural history as of art, an attempt to recall the structure and appearance of a hedgehog's body and recreate it as best she could in clay. I had not suggested the model to her; instead I had suggested to the group that they might each try to write about their walk. That idea had come to nothing though, perhaps because it was too pat and too immediate, allowing no time for the experience of the walk to settle in their minds. It was later in the day, after she had had some time in which to absorb the experience, that she herself thought of modelling the hedgehog in clay.'

The finest of all Julie's sculptures was the plasticine model she made, near the start of the spring term, on the same subject as the last of Robert's three river sketches: a swan's nest.

'Friday, February 4th.

In the second half of the morning Julie came up to me in search of ideas for a model. [It was a day on which all but six or seven children in the class were absorbed by model making in one guise or another.*] I mentioned the plasticine horse and old lady which she had made last term and suggested that she make another plasticine model. I've kept on hoping that Julie would return to her work in plasticine but usually, when I've suggested it to her directly, she has rejected it. This time though, she didn't. Instead she began right away and by dinner time she had finished her first model, a swan made out of blue plasticine with a black bill and eyes, a carefully arched neck, and outstretched wings as if rising up out of the water. The swan's wings were stippled with tiny cuts in the smooth surface of the plasticine, representing the ruffled feathers. I was astonished how well observed the model was, how finely and accurately shaped.

In the afternoon Julie continued modelling. She found a spare piece of hardboard and painted it over, green and blue, to represent a lake and its surrounding banks. Then she made a plasticine nest of reeds with three eggs on it and a second swan, its wings somewhat upraised but not outstretched, which she placed on top of the eggs. In the water, beside the nest and the two large swans, she placed a third much smaller swan which she told me was a cygnet. As a final touch she added a few reeds along the banks and in the water, made out of plasticine and card.

I don't know how far Julie's knowledge of swans is derived from direct observation and how far from books and pictures but the verisimilitude of her model is remarkable. The scene shows the same power of observation and the same grasp of three dimensional form that I noticed last term in her clay hedgehog. And the same detail. Each swan is given stippled and carefully shaped wings, arched neck, and bill, knob and eyes of contrasting colour. Each reed or branch in the nest is separately made out of a thin spool of plasticine. The eggs too are separate and all oval.

When the model was finished she told Stephen that she would like to write something about making it and a poem to accompany it, so while the rest of the class were listening to each

* See Chapter 6.

other's work at the end of the day Julie sat outside the classroom in the library area, composing her account and her poem. They suggest something of the feeling that has gone into the beautiful model.

"About my three swans.

In my model I have done a daddy, mummy and a baby one. The mummy is sitting on a nest with some eggs inside it. They are near to a lake. The baby swans are called cygnets.

My three swans.

I saw three swans sailing by. One was big and one was small and one was in the middle. Every one of them had a yellow beak and gleaming white wings and two lovely blue eyes what was the same colour as the sky."*

Julie found it hard to reproduce in her paintings the liveliness of representation and the technical flair that characterised her three-dimensional work and it may have been in part a sense of dissatisfaction with her painting that led her in the middle of the spring term to experiment, very deliberately, with a new painting technique. I first noticed the change at the beginning of March when Julie set to work, one morning, on a large painting on the subject of 'Growing Things'.

'Monday, March 7th.

Julie, this morning, got involved in a painting. I suggested to her the subject of "growing things", remembering how she and Louise, last week, had brought in from the playing field a collection of branches and twigs that were now sprouting away in a bucket of sand in the classroom. They had brought the bucket up to me early in the day to show me what was happening. We talked a bit about growing things, listing some of them — "flowers", "leaves", "buds", "shoots", "lambs", "foals". Julie also suggested "houses being built", and "ploughing". She began drawing, quite readily and freely, somewhat to my surprise since this last week or two Julie has tended to reject art in favour of

* The colours of the poem are not the same as those of the model. Nor of course are cygnets white. The poem expresses Julie's feelings for her model and for swans, not the accuracy of her observation.

activities more suited to the "tomboy" image which she seems to
have chosen for herself, for the time being. (On the other hand,
last week was the week in which she made a superb model of a
fishing scene, out of moss, twigs, silver paper, water in a bottle
cap, polystyrene and plasticine, a model that she gave to Betty
Jeal [the deputy head] together with a two verse poem on Spring
composed as an accompaniment to the model by Debbie.) The
drawing was in a style much favoured by Julie, the large sheet of
sugar paper roughly divided into a number of separate areas each
of which was drawn in turn, a horse and foal in one area, sheep
in another, a house being built, a girl planting seeds, a tree with
a few leaves budding on it, a pond with duck and ducklings, a
tractor ploughing. Each of these smaller drawings inhabits its
own distinct space without much attempt being made to relate
the several drawings or areas of drawing to each other. The one
strong link is a large fence crossing the paper high up as if in the
background though the size of the fence somewhat contradicts its
background placing. Above the fence she drew a faint line of
gentle hills as in our surrounding countryside and this, too, helps
to link the various parts of the picture. The drawing was neat
and delicate and Julie was reasonably satisfied with it by the time
she had finished, having asked me from time to time what else
she might include in the scene. But I don't know that she was
really pleased with it. At present indeed she rarely is altogether
pleased with her painting, I think because she is searching for an
accuracy and conviction in her representation of things which she
knows she can achieve less effectively in her two dimensional than
in her three dimensional work. Still she was by no means
*dis*pleased.

And then came the painting. As I looked at the drawing, while it
was in progress, I grew anxious about the prospect of painting it.
Painting seemed likely to muddle if not to obliterate the delicate
detail of the drawing, granted the quality of the powder paint
and relatively thick brushes that Julie was going to use. [It did
not occur to me at the time to suggest alternatives and
afterwards, in view of what happened, I was glad, on the whole,
that I hadn't.] But Julie chose to paint in an unusual way —
unusual, I mean, within the class. She kept her paint very dry,
adding as little water as necessary, and she applied it in thick
short strokes, beginning with certain prominent parts of her
drawing: red for the body of the tractor; brown for the horse and

foal; yellow for the sheep's coats, their heads and legs being left unpainted; reddish brown for the half built house the windows of which were outlined thickly in black superimposed on the brown; brown and green for the tree; deep blue for the pond. The sky was filled with smudges of dark and light blue paint, and a little lower down the fence, also, was streaked with blue. Beside the pond Julie added an uneven line of thick green strokes of paint suggesting a hedge, although there was no such hedge on the original drawing. She scattered the unpainted hills between fence and sky with short strokes of green paint, and the ground below the fence with paler green and white strokes, mixing the colour herself to get the right shade of green. These final strokes of paint scattered across the background of the picture relieved the isolation of the several painted details, linking them together in the same sort of way in which the fence had linked together the separate elements in the original drawing.

Julie made no attempt to paint in the shapes outlined in her drawing, except for the pond which for this very reason seems to me to be perhaps the weakest part of the picture. Instead, she dabbed the paint across and over the drawing, half submerging its pencilled outlines in the rough brush strokes. In the process a number of details have disappeared altogether: a bird in the sky, a tree or two on the horizon of the hills. For the most part however the objects that composed the drawing have survived in the painting though some of them, the foal beside its mare for instance, are barely perceptible behind the paint. The effect is striking and self-conscious. The new technique seemed to fascinate her. She was using paint not as a way of "colouring in" her drawing but as a counterpoint to the drawing, an independent medium related to the pencilled drawing as one layer of activity to another.'

The novelty of Julie's experiment seemed to me to be confirmed by other children's reaction to it. I pinned the painting on the wall after she had finished it and the following day she told me that everyone in the class thought she had spoiled it when she painted it. I asked her what she thought herself and she confessed that she was not sure. If she was seeking reassurance she may have found it in my response as I explained how intrigued I was by her experiments with technique. At any rate the experiments continued.

Her next painting, composed just two days later, reflected once again her interest, at that time, in forms of growth.

'Wednesday, March 9th

Yesterday morning Julie came to see me, with Louise. They had finished their writing and felt that they would like, if they could, to find something to work at outside. It was a beautiful day, sunny and warm, and already four or five children were at work on the terrace outside the classroom. Julie and Louise asked if they could go for another walk across the playing fields, looking for seeds or flowers, or things like that. I suggested that they walk down to one of the large trees at the bottom of the field and each make a sketch of the tree, looking carefully at how the branches relate to the trunk and trying to set this down in their drawing. I found them a ring backed notebook to take with them and this novelty had the effect of reinforcing their eagerness to follow my suggestion and to add to it. How about making some bark rubbings too, they suggested. We got paper and wax crayons for the rubbings and then they set off, taking my watch with them so as to be sure to be back, as I had instructed them, by playtime some half hour later. They returned about half way through play, having done all that had been suggested and more. Each of them had a sketch of one of the trees showing, just as I'd hoped, the way in which the branches spread out from the trunk. They had made two bark rubbings in many coloured crayons and explained to me how, as they crayoned, the paper had stuck to the bark so that they didn't have to hold it in place. Louise had found two young plants in among the rubbish at the bottom of the field and had dug them up by the roots; they were her chief delight and by the end of the morning she had carefully potted them. At dinner time she took them home to show her mum. They had also decided to write a list of things they noticed as they walked along, perhaps under the stimulus of the new ring backed notebook, and this they handed to me, cackling and smiling over the opening entry, "old prison dump" (the school).

Julie and Louise stayed in the classroom over playtime, what was left of it, potting the plants and fetching sugar paper on which to paint full scale pictures of trees based on their sketches. And this they did after hymn practice at the end of the morning and start of the afternoon. Neither painting had quite the accuracy or delicacy of the two sketches but on the other hand each represented, as I saw it, a new conviction in the handling of the painting of a tree. [Unfortunately neither the sketches nor the paintings have survived.] This time Julie tried out yet another technique with powder paint (though Stephen told me later that he had seen her using the same sort of technique on part of her painting of "growing things"). She painted the trunk and branches of the tree conventionally enough but then she scattered green powder across the branches and smeared it over them with her fingers to represent the tree in full leaf. Louise meanwhile had stuck to the more straightforward technique, filling in the branches with brown paint but adding no leaves at all to her tree. [As I recall, neither of the original sketches contained leaves.]'

Julie's method of representing leaves had been anticipated in her previous picture. In that work the tree beside the half built house had been given a roughly painted trunk above which the leaves and branches were represented impressionistically by blobs and smears of green and brown paint. In the new picture it was only the leaves themselves that were treated impressionistically in this way, a green haze of colour superimposed on the clearer outlines of branch and trunk. I was fascinated by this way of representing leaves which marked a new approach within the class to a familiar problem. Children often had difficulty deciding what to do about leaves. Sometimes, like Louise in this case, they simply omitted the leaves altogether, especially, it seemed, when they were drawing direct from life. At other times the trunk of a tree would be capped by a simple disc of green, as it was in Paul's painting of his go cart.* When Paul himself made a sketch of a tree in the playing field later in the year** he chose to ignore the leaves until he had returned to the classroom and was enlarging his sketch into a much grander painting. Then he attempted to solve the problem by adding a set of leaves to each large branch of his tree, each leaf erect on its own little stalk, the serried ranks of leaves creating a somewhat incongruous effect against the more natural outlines of branch and trunk. Julie's was an altogether more subtle approach in its attempt to capture the leafiness of trees without drawing or painting in each leaf in turn. The new painting gave added point to her determination to reject the simple colouring in of her drawing in favour of more adventurous techniques — though she frequently returned to the more conventional approach in her later paintings.

The painting of a tree was followed within a week by a third large picture which suggested, alongside the adventurousness of her technique, a new or revived confidence in her painting. On this occasion,

* See above
** See Chapter 5.

Fig. 7

moreover, she chose for her painting a subject that could not have been treated in a three-dimensional form, thereby, whether by accident or design, drawing attention to the distinctiveness of her painting as compared with her modelling.

'Monday, March 14th.

Julie asked for a subject to paint — "something scary" she said. I couldn't think of an appropriate theme and was casting around for an idea when something I said, or something at any rate that had emerged out of our mutual chatter, gave Julie by chance association the kind of idea she sought. She went away to begin the picture and I didn't see her again until the preliminary drawing was finished and the painting itself had begun (see fig. 7). She had drawn and painted a flowering meadow of tall grasses and bright flowers beside a large tree, only a small part of its base visible to the right of the picture. In the grass beside the flowers she had drawn a grasshopper which she painted yellow and green, a word-balloon coming out of its mouth with "eekkk" written on it. Immediately above the grasshopper was a large white hand with yellow nails descending out of a thick black sleeve (later changed to blue) which swept down in a curved line from the top of the paper next to the tree trunk. The tips of the fingers were just about to touch or poke the insect. Beside the sleeve, against the bark of the base of the tree, was a very large and so far unpainted butterfly, a little larger than the hand which in turn was a little larger than the grasshopper. The hand, it turned out, was mine, the sleeve a part of my guernsey sweater. I have no idea whether the subject was entirely Julie's own or whether it harked back to some remembered picture and it is not important to know where the subject came from. I would never have dreamt it up for her myself and I would not have immediately identified it as a "scary" subject, though I think it was. Yet it did seem to have taken our conversation, however desultory — a thinking over and vaguely chatting about possibilities — to bring the idea into her mind. And this seems to happen often. It's not so much that children need you to give them an idea or subject for their painting or writing but that they need you to help them generate the idea or subject for themselves. Thinking together and chatting together, even if the talk is off the point, often seems to do the trick. So I think it was today with Julie.

Julie's painting technique was again highly complex and, as it were, painterly although on this occasion she did not mix her paints quite so thickly or repeat the technique of smearing the paint over the paper with her fingers or by scattering dry powder onto the paper. The flower heads were ornate, richly and delicately coloured, as if she had been using watercolour rather than powder paint. The hand was whitish grey, a somewhat deathly colour, with black veins and yellow nails, the spaces between the fingers marked with white lines. The sleeve was deep black, which Julie later changed to blue, I think because she found the black too severe. Once as I passed by while Julie was painting I noticed a rather messy black patch on the painting below the grasshopper. I asked Julie about it and she explained that she hadn't intended it, she'd made a mistake. I suggested painting it over later, if she could. This afternoon, looking at the painting after school, I noticed that she had found a fine solution to the problem of the messy patch. She had added streaks of orange, yellow and white paint, thick and powdery, across the black patch and beyond it, blending into the green grasses and brightly coloured flowers, transforming her "mistake" into earth and stones across the floor of the meadow.'

The more carefully Stephen Rowland and I inspected this picture the more we admired it. On this occasion Julie's handling of paint rivalled, and even surpassed, the delicacy of her drawing, especially in the treatment of grasses and flowers in the bottom half of the picture. The grasses are painted with light strokes of green, pushing upwards against the tree trunk and into the space beside and above the grasshopper. The flowers are richly varied, in shape, in decoration and in colour — red, yellow, blue, pink, purple, white. In the centre of the petals, which are of several different forms, are yellow, blue or black stamens, sometimes simple circles or blobs of paint but in two places a cluster of tiny yellow dabs. On some of the flower heads the coloured petals are overlaid with contrasting points, dots or circles of black and pink and pale blue. Only a few leaves appear among the pile of flower heads, some of them veined with black or yellow strokes painted on top of the green of the leaf. The flowers are not drawn or painted from life but the impression they create is as lively and as fragile as any cluster of real flowers. The soft white hand with its yellow nails seems to have been influenced to some extent by the delicacy of the flowers which it brushes past, but the dark blue sleeve and the thick, encrusted brown mass of the tree trunk make a powerful contrast with the fragility of the grasshopper's world of grasses and flowers. Only the butterfly, which was painted last and almost as an afterthought, although it had been included in the original drawing, seems to me to be out of place, being too large and too crudely coloured in comparison with the world below it, if not perhaps in comparison with the tree and the arm, between which it lies.

Julie's treatment of scale in her picture is as absorbing as the treatment of colour and form. In a sense the entire picture is an exploration of scale,* of the contrast between two worlds, the miniature world of the meadow floor, seen from the grasshopper's viewpoint, and the intrusive, gigantic world suggested by the descending hand and forearm and the edge of the tree obtruding from the right of the picture. The scale is not strictly accurate, it is true; the grasshopper is a little too large for the hand and the butterfly much

---

* For further exploration of scale, see Chapter 5 and 6.

too large. But the contrast between two different scales is indeed exact, precisely established by the assembling and placing of the particular objects that compose the picture: the grasshopper set among the grasses and flowers; the arm and the tree trunk disappearing beyond the painting, fragments of a huge world which cannot possibly be accommodated within the picture frame but has to infiltrate it from the top and sides of the paper.

As for its emotion, the painting did, after all, live up to Julie's desire to paint a 'scary' picture. The 'real world' of the picture is the grasshopper's world while the world of human scale is giant sized and frightening. Notice the menacing sweep of the arm as it invades the delicate grasses and flowers, reaching down towards the unsuspecting grasshopper — unless the 'eekkk' that he emits is intended to imply that he already senses the threatening hand above him. It was as exciting a painting as any of the year, at once delicate and sinister, the product of a certain thoughtful exuberance and much experiment with paint.

The paintings, drawings and models which I have been examining in this chapter illustrate the expressive skill of eight year old artists. The skill can be observed both in the works themselves and in the manner in which the children composed them. Although Paul, Robert and Julie were among the most ambitious artists in Stephen's class — which is not to say that they were necessarily the most accomplished — they were still, like all the children, only at the beginning of an understanding of the world of art. They knew a little, but only as yet a little, about the possible uses of paint and pencil; their understanding of how to represent objects in space was still in many respects rudimentary. Yet however limited their experience, and however incomplete their mastery of the means of artistic expression, their art already exhibits a pattern of thought that is characteristic of more mature artists. In each of their considered paintings, drawings and models they are consciously striving to use their developing skills for significant artistic purposes.

Thus each of them, as we have seen, paid careful attention to the composition of their pictures: to the use of colour and line, the various effects of paint, the orderly arrangement of forms on the picture surface. Each of them, too, aimed at representation but they represented the world in different ways. Paul interwove realism with fancy, depicting an emblematic world in which reality is intensified or exaggerated or made fantastic. Robert, by contrast, sought to represent, with a certain impassioned precision, the actual world which he saw in front of him as he sketched. Julie portrayed the contrast of scale and of feeling between different worlds, and explored, more self-consciously perhaps than either of the others, the means of representation themselves, particularly in terms of the expressive effects of paint. But whatever the image of life presented by each of the three artists, it was made up of a wealth of particular details intently and often lovingly observed whether the details were real or imaginary: reeds, flower heads, leaves against branches, a swan's outstretched wings, ruffled feathers or arched neck, a ripple or a reflection, a sea bird's beak and eye, a harbour wall, a go cart engine, a sun smoking a pipe.

There is, thus, a close parallel between the character of the children's involvement in art and in literature. I have already suggested that in the best of their stories the children's literary concerns were those of any serious story teller or writer: concern for the form of the story, for presenting a certain view of human life, character and circumstance, and for presenting it through the experience of particular lives, characters and circumstances. From the evidence of the art examined in the present chapter it seems clear that the children's artistic concerns had, at least at times, a similar range and depth. As they laboured, though often playfully, with pencil and paint, Paul, Robert and Julie were at one and the same time exploring the character of pictorial form and making use of it to portray, in vivid detail, the world as each of them interpreted it.

I have considered only one aspect of children's art in this chapter. Many children in Stephen's class displayed in their painting a similar range of concerns as those of Paul, Robert and Julie but the large representational painting, and the sketches associated with it, represent just one of several kinds of art to be found within the class. In discussing children's writing, for instance, I mentioned the use of art as a stimulus for writing, as a decorative accompaniment to the written word, and sometimes as an extension of narrative means. Often, also, art became an independent form of narrative, as indeed it had been in Julie's painting of grasshopper and hand, or a record of personal experience, similar in intention to the autobiographical writing discussed at the start of the last chapter. Further examples of children's representational paintings are discussed in Chapter 5, together with the use of sketches as part of a scientific record. Children's modelling is examined in Chapter 6, which also considers the variety of materials employed by children for pictorial effect, as does the next chapter. Perhaps the most significant aspect of art omitted from this chapter, however, is the love of pattern and pattern making displayed by many of the children over the course of the year. It is to this particular aspect of the children's art that I want to turn in the next chapter, and in particular to the relationship between the children's explorations of pattern and their mathematical, scientific and philosophical thought.

4 The Language of Pattern

All year long Sally was fascinated by patterns. Her absorption and skill found expression in an abundance of abstract and decorative designs, in two and three dimensions: spiral patterns made by drawing pen, crayon or paint brush across paper spinning on a turntable; symmetrical patterns made by blotting paint; tessellations, frameworks and geometrical figures assembled out of stiff white card; mobiles of wire, cotton and fragments of discarded machinery; patterns of elastic bands stretched across a board; patchwork; delicately decorated models in clay and plasticine. Even her relatively infrequent representational paintings seemed to reflect her fondness for abstract design. Consider the stiff, formal elegance of a vase of daffodils painted in the summer term. Six long green stems fan out in close array from a pale mauve vase the rim of which is carefully painted in perspective and disappears behind each separate stem. Yellow flowers perch stiffly upon the stems, daffodil heads with long, frilly trumpets, five of them bending sharply towards the right while the sixth points upwards, relieving the monotony of the rhythm. For all its careful realism, it is the ordered severity of its forms and colours that chiefly distinguishes Sally's painting and in this it presents a striking contrast to the vase painting from which it appeared to derive, a painting of Sarah's completed a day or two earlier and equally engaging although utterly different in style. Sarah's painting is in fact less carefully realistic than Sally's, at least in the treatment of the flowers, but above all it lacks the serene stiffness that characterizes Sally's daffodils. The design is more intricate and subtle, and there is a depth and an impressionistic glow in Sarah's treatment, for example in the manner in which the flower stems are reflected through the design on the side of the apparently translucent vase, which goes beyond anything that Sally attempted and serves to underline, by contrast, the formal severity of Sally's conception.

Sally's fascination with pattern and design reached its climax early in the summer term, in a set of eleven tiny patterns created out of the seemingly unpromising material of a box of sticky red stars, of the kind still used in some primary schools, I dare say, to reward a good piece of written work. They were among the most memorable designs that anyone in the class produced all year, both on account of their intrinsic beauty and as evidence of children's speculative thought and action, of their capacity to pry, or search, into the objects and ideas that catch their attention. It is with these designs, and other patterns of Sally's composed at around the same time, with the circumstances in which they were made and the quality of thought which they displayed, that I want to open an account of pattern making in Stephen's class and of the mathematical, scientific and logical inquiry to which it was related.

One afternoon, at the end of the school day, early in the summer term, Stephen and I began playing with a box of tiny ball bearings which Stephen had brought to school. Stephen wanted to see what happened when he pulled a cluster of ball bearings out of the box with a magnet. In what configurations would they cluster? We also tried placing a small piece of card over the magnet and stacking the ball bearings on the card. The following morning after registration Stephen began to experiment with the ball bearings again and it was then that Sally noticed what he was doing. Stephen described the incident later in his weekly notes:

'Although it was my own playing around with magnets and ball bearings that started Sally off I had very little to do with her discovery. I had been interested in using ball bearings in connection with the packing or stacking of objects, an idea related to the work on capacity and volume with which our first informal maths groups this term have been concerned. I placed a piece of white card over a cylindrical magnet and tried to stack the ball bearings on the card. The ball bearings cling together initially on the card but as more ball bearings are added, others tend to be repelled; with a certain amount of fiddling however the ball bearings will form clusters. I had done no more than begin to form a cluster, with a few ball bearings piled on top of a bottom layer, when Sally saw what I was doing and asked if she and Helen could have a go. I left them to it and returned half an hour later to see the beautiful tetrahedron of ball bearings which they had formed on the card, perfectly regular and held in place by the magnet underneath. This must have been no easy task as I discovered when I started to remove one of the bearings to see how the tetrahedron was constructed. As soon as one bearing was removed the others all shifted, being attracted and repelled in different directions and it took me some time to restore the original shape. Michael found this too when he was trying to get Louise and Gwyneth interested in a similar task later in the week. He had the greatest difficulty in constructing a tetrahedron like Sally's, even after studying her example.

Together the three of us, Sally, Helen and myself, looked closely at the tetrahedron formed by the ball bearings. I asked Sally if she thought it would be possible to construct a second pyramid-like shape but this time using a hexagon as the base rather than a triangle as in the case of her tetrahedron. At my suggestion we made the base layer of ball bearings like this, and Sally began to pile up additional ball bearings with the aim of bringing the shape up into an apex above the centre of the base. She remarked how the new ball bearings always stuck "down into the gaps" between the ball bearings beneath, like this — and not this —

I left her to continue by herself, returning some time later to find that she had indeed brought the shape up into an apex but that it had lost its 'hexagonality'. She said that it hadn't really worked as the balls didn't want to make that shape. This was not of course surprising, given the observation above, since, for the hexagonal pyramid to have been constructed, the ball bearings along the axis of the pyramid would have had to be piled directly on top of each other, like this (in cross section) — Sally appreciated this point.'

On the evening of that day I recorded my own impressions of Sally's work:

'Tuesday, April 26th.

Some time in the late morning Sally came to show me what she had made with the ball bearings, the card and the magnet which she had taken over from Stephen earlier. Her face was alive with pleasure and a kind of inner excitement. I noticed this particularly, because Sally quite often feigns a mild disdain, almost a world weariness, in relation to herself and her activity in the classroom, half mocking but perhaps half serious too. But there was not the slightest trace of that now. She had made a perfect tetrahedron of the ball bearings, held in place by the magnet, a beautiful shape, tiny and precise. In a sense there was nothing else for her to do then that could match the arresting beauty of what she had already achieved and her absorbed delight in it, but the achievement spilled over into whatever else she did. She began getting people to guess how many ball bearings there were in the piled up tetrahedron — I'd asked her that earlier myself; she tried out other configurations of ball bearings, at Stephen's suggestion; she played around with a set of tiny wooden triangles from some Dienes equipment, seeing how they too could be stacked on top of each other. She worked as I have not seen her work for some time, wholly absorbed in a single minded intellectual pursuit (for that is what it seemed to be) and wholly relaxed in her work in a way which has seemed quite rare with Sally recently.'

Sally's absorption in the ball bearings and the magnet seemed all the more significant to Stephen and myself in view of the dissatisfaction which Stephen had expressed only a day or two before in regard to the progress of his maths groups that term. He had decided to introduce the children, group by group, to ideas relating to capacity and volume and they had begun by experimenting with different ways of measuring the capacity of particular objects in the class-room. Despite the ingenuity and variety of some of their experiments Stephen was doubtful whether the children's activity would amount to much in the end. The precision in measurement at which he wanted them to aim appeared to him to have no clear purpose to sustain it and he began to suspect that he was paying too much attention to the concepts which he wanted the children to acquire and too little to the materials which he hoped they might explore. He outlined the problem in his notes:

'Just a few general points on the children's activity (the measuring experiments related to our work on capacity). While there was quite a lot of free experimenting with the materials, this work seemed to provide no clear goal for the children. I could easily structure their activity — indeed I did — giving them the task of measuring this or that. But measurement of things does not in itself seem enough. In life one measures *for a purpose* — in order to make something, to find out how much something will cost, and so on. The children's work, while it might be carried out satisfactorily enough, seemed to lack this purpose. There was nothing concrete to show for it. At the 'play', or 'free-experimenting', stage the doing itself may be sufficient. But when we want to develop precision — accuracy of measurement in this instance — there needs to be some reason for being precise. If the reason is not "to get the right answer", as it is in text-book sums for example, then it must be "in order to make it work" or "in order to make it look good".

While most of the children in the maths groups seemed to gain some insight into the concepts involved — capacity, volume, density — I don't somehow think that this work will catch on and spread around the class like the construction activities of last term. Perhaps the reason for this is that I was concentrating on the concepts I wanted to put across rather than the materials themselves.'

This was the tentative conclusion which Stephen had drawn from the children's earliest investigations of capacity — between April 18th and April 25th. It was the following day that Sally constructed the tetrahedron out of ball bearings piled on a magnet. It seemed to both of us that her activity, which was only indirectly related to the work of the maths groups, exhibited the very qualities that we suspected to have been missing from much of the children's previous work on capacity. The ideas, or concepts, which she began to examine once she had completed the tetrahedron — ideas relating to the form and structure of stacked objects — arose directly out of her own reflective exploration of a particular material. Although it was Stephen who helped her, by his conversation, to formulate these ideas, they were determined not by his own preconception as to the outcome of her investigation of the ball bearings but by the character of the investigation itself, by the form of her exploratory play.

Yet there was no conflict between playfulness and precision in Sally's thought and action. On the contrary, the form of her playful investigation required precision and gave purpose to precision. It was not on this occasion a matter of making exact measurements but of fixing the exact position of each ball bearing in relation to the others. To achieve the effect which she sought demanded a steady hand, a keen eye, and a nice judgement of the formal properties of the emerging shape. Without precision Sally would have found it hard to conceive, let alone to complete, the task. As to the purpose or goal of precision, that was provided by the romance of exploration itself, by the delight and excitement which Sally felt in the intricate perfection of the created object and in the act of creating it, and by her compelling desire, as Stephen had put it, 'to make it look good'. Precision was the condition for satisfying her sense of romance.

But Sally's absorption depended upon two further vital elements besides the romance and precision of the task which she had set herself. The first was her readiness to experiment. Although neither Stephen nor I had watched her as she set about constructing the tetrahedron we both felt sure, justifiably, it seemed, in the light of what happened the next day, that there was about her activity an element of conscious experiment, an intention to take up an idea and follow it through in order to see where it led. She did not know that her construction would turn out to be a tetrahedron; she did know how she intended to set about constructing it. Later on, in her attempt to construct a pyramid on a hexagonal base, her experimental attitude became more explicit. She accepted the hypothesis proposed to her by Stephen, she tested it, and she found it wanting, or at least unsatisfactory. It was at this point that another vital element in her absorption became apparent: its speculative character. It was evident in the self-conscious way in which she examined the behaviour of the ball bearings, remarking how they always 'stuck down into the gaps'; still more so in the theory which finally she offered in explanation of the partial failure of Stephen's hypothesis: 'the balls didn't want to make that shape'. There was nothing fanciful in her imaginative personification of the ball bearings. It was a resourceful and persuasive way of representing and interpreting the forces operating on the ball bearings, as it seemed to her when she pored over the model and sought to account for its failure to conform to her intentions.

A fascination with materials, precision, linked to a sense of romance, in exploring them, a readiness to experiment and to speculate: these then were the qualities that made up Sally's absorption and delight as she set about investigating the stacking of ball bearings above a magnet that day. The following day the same qualities were displayed still more conspicuously in her investigation of an apparently less adventurous and promising material: a box of sticky red stars.

'**Wednesday, April 27th.** [These notes were in fact written on April 28th, but April 27th is the day to which they refer.]

On Tuesday night, as I was looking for various containers, and objects with which to fill them, to take to school in connection with our work on capacity, I came across a box of gummed red stars. Remembering the work that Sally had done that day, using the ball bearings and the magnet, I thought I would give them to her the next morning to see if, by sticking them down in any patterned formations she chose, she might be able to explore further the kinds of patterning which she had been investigating that day with the ball bearings. However, when I showed Sally the stars first thing on Wednesday morning, I had no particular sequence of activity or investigation in mind, and I had not looked closely at the stars themselves; in particular, I had not noticed that they were five-pointed stars. I simply handed the box over to Sally and Helen and suggested that they might like to try arranging them in patterns on paper, reminding them of what they had done the day before with the ball bearings. They

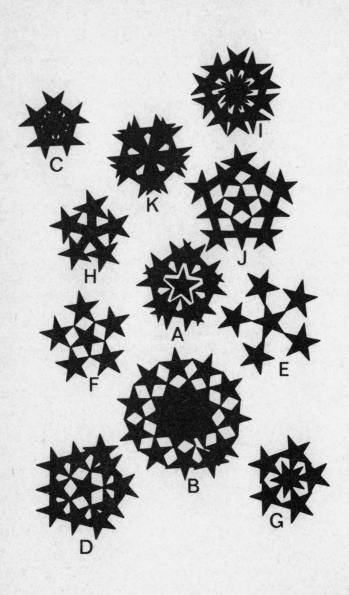

took the box away, into a secluded nook which they had created at the entrance to the classroom by arranging a small screen against the wall. There they stayed virtually all morning, missing the hymn practice after morning play, at work on the stars. Sally took the lead and it was her own enthusiasm about pattern making, so clear the previous day, that dominated their common activity.

She began with a single pattern, stuck in the middle of a page of ordinary lined exercise paper: a star in the centre surrounded by a close grouping of other stars which she carefully overlaid, one across another, all around the central star (see illustration, A). I watched her, off and on, as she developed this pattern. She was very systematic in her placing of each star in relation to the central star, making sure that the pattern was regular and concentrating as much, it seemed, on the spaces between the stars as on the shapes created by overlapping stars, as I could observe by the way in which she re-arranged the stars as she proceeded so that the spaces were as regular in pattern as the stars themselves. Thus she deliberately created a sort of white frame around the central star and, at each inner point of the frame, a tiny, white, kite-shaped space. She also seemed to be paying close attention to the regularity of the protruding points of the stars around the outside of the pattern. She had, incidentally, no hesitation in superimposing stars on each other; it didn't occur to her to make patterns only by juxtaposing stars rather than by overlapping them, as I imagine it might have occurred to children who were less adventurously involved in the medium.

Once the first pattern was complete she began a different one below it: a cluster of stars in the middle this time, surrounded by a ring of touching stars (see illustration, B). After this she and Helen asked for plain paper in place of the lined paper they had used at first and Sally spent the rest of the morning recreating her first two patterns on the plain paper and then surrounding them with nine more patterns, all but one of them to her own design, the last one picking up a hint of mine. Once, she asked me whether I could suggest another possible pattern but I had much less idea how to proceed than Sally herself and it was only at the very end, as I looked at the eight patterns she had already created, that I could spot a variation which she seemed to have missed (although I had also at one point, I think, suggested to her the possibility of making a ten point star by carefully placing one star on top of another as in illustration , I).

Sally was keenly aware of the occasional flaws in the execution of her designs and pointed them out to me: especially the weakness at one point in her second design (see illustration, B), and again in one of the later designs (see illustration, D). There was not the slightest doubt that each design was the product of conscious and deliberate choice, although the implications and subtleties of the various patterns only emerged in the course of their creation or when we looked back together over the finished

Looking at them in the staffroom at dinner time, and again now, this evening, what astonishes me is the virtuosity they reveal. The pentagon appears all over the place throughout the designs. I asked Sally and Helen if they noticed how often you'd get a pentagon inside a pentagon, the points of one opposite the midpoints of the sides of the other. In some patterns Sally has arranged the stars so that only their points are touching, achieving this in three completely different ways (see illustration, E, F, G). In other patterns one star is laid along the line of another, as in the remarkable example (see illustration, H). Elsewhere touching points and touching lines are combined (see illustration, I, J). Only in the first pattern (see illustration, A) is the central star touched by no other star, swimming in its own space. Five of the patterns superimpose stars, while in the remaining six there is no intentional overlapping. The only universal feature is the central star itself, with which each of Sally's patterns began.

At the end of the morning, holding up to the light the paper on which the stars were stuck, Sally and I both noticed the intriguing patterns created by the shadowed overlapping areas in the patterns which superimposed stars. [This discovery was to come into its own a little later (see below).]

Helen also produced a page of patterns but on the whole hers were less successful, although she did create a beautiful fifteen-point star. Perhaps Helen is, as one says, "less good at this sort of thing". But what does this really mean? No more, perhaps, than that for Helen pattern making is not, at present, or was not on this particular occasion, as exciting a prospect as it so plainly is, and was, for Sally. At any rate, Helen was happy to go along with Sally in her activity, partly because she and Sally normally go along together, and partly, I think, because she was genuinely pleased by Sally's delight. She also appreciated the richness of Sally's designs. But she didn't feel so personally committed as Sally, and so it was, I suspect, that her own patterns were less carefully deliberated and executed even if in her exploitation of the ten-pointed and fifteen-pointed stars she went beyond what Sally had attempted.

Throughout the morning Sally, her face, manner and movement, assumed the same expression of unforced delight that I had noticed the day before. Tuesday's mood was sustained.

[When she read this entry in my notes, Mary Brown was able to confirm my impression of Sally's changed mood. She wrote alongside this passage: "Amazingly I had noted a very real change in Sally's 'about school' attitude these last few days — a new 'open' attitude is about the only way I can express it. Has she perhaps come to a new awareness of her own potential as a 'learner', in these activities, and therefore of herself?"]'

I had hoped that Sally would find in the box of stars a way of extending her investigation of patterns and pattern making, and so she had, beyond my expectations. Her pattern making, that morning, confirmed the impression which I had already formed from her previous day's activity. There was the same dexterity and precision of hand, eye and mind, and the same delight, playful and deeply serious, in the logical, orderly construction of forms and patterns. In working out each new design she appeared to be setting herself a test, devising a rule for the formation of that particular pattern and seeing what happened as she followed it through. Once it became clear to her just how a pattern would turn out, its individual parts, the separate stars, could be readjusted to remove inaccuracies and the whole was then the proper object of contemplation and examination. As before, with the ball bearings, Sally seemed to be equally absorbed in each part of the enterprise.

I am inclined, now, to regard the first pattern that Sally made — the most complex of all in some respects — as initially a kind of sketch. It was a way of discovering what the pattern making potential of the stars might be, a tentative prying or searching into the properties of the new material. It was in this pattern, and in the next, that Sally established the formula to which all her subsequent designs conformed: the regular grouping of stars around a central star or a central cluster of stars. The second pattern may even have been a way of testing the variety inherent in this formula, seeing how different a pattern might be contrived within its limits. Certainly the second pattern was in strong contrast with the first; it was the only pattern, in the event, that made use of a cluster of stars for its central core. Perhaps Sally was deterred from repeating this particular experiment by the difficulty of executing the pattern; it turned out to be the most seriously flawed of all her designs, as she herself acknowledged at the end.

The first two patterns showed Sally how to proceed further. She began to appreciate how precise she would have to be in placing each separate star and how carefully she must arrange and rearrange the stars in order to preserve the consistency and regularity of her designs. She noticed that it was important to pay as much attention to the spaces between the stars as to the stars themselves since each space had its own distinct and regular shape, as exact as the shape of a star. She worked out her method of procedure for generating new patterns: invent a rule, and submit it to a test.

Having satisfied herself as to the richness of the new material, Sally was ready to start again, this time, as it were, for real. The first two patterns were reassembled on a more appropriate paper, plain rather than lined, and what followed was, in effect, a set of variations, as in music, around a common theme, the theme represented by the formula established in the first two patterns. It was these successive variations on a theme that constituted, on this occasion, Sally's speculative thought and action. They can properly be seen, I think, as an extended examination and exploitation of the pattern making properties of the five pointed star. Sally's aim was to see just what she could do with her chosen theme, how many different patterns she could create out of it; her method was one of self conscious experiment, rather than casual trial and error. In the end I think that she was as surprised as anybody how various and entrancing the results turned out to be.

At the end of her set of variations Sally returned, at Stephen's instigation, to her point of departure. Stephen had suggested that she might like to draw and paint a greatly enlarged version of her original design, which was still the one she liked the best, making a template of a five pointed star out of cardboard first so as to help her draw the stars accurately. Sally agreed and she and Helen set to work on the task together, with Stephen's help. The enlarged design became a kind of emblem of her achievement, a final expression of her skill, and, in a way, of Helen's too, for Sally was very particular about telling me that this was Helen's work as much as her own. (So was Helen.) It was also, more incidentally but no less significantly, an occasion for purposeful measurement of the kind which had seemed to be missing from the children's experiments with capacity a few days earlier.

Stephen explained in his notes how he had helped Sally to make the cardboard template.

'I gave Sally some help in making the template. I suggested she first drew a circle onto paper, which she did, tracing round the base of a bucket. I then said that if we could mark off five points equally spaced around this circle, these could be the points of the star. Sally measured around the circle using a piece of string. It measured 60 cm and Sally immediately told me that each point should be 12 cm further around the circle. I checked Sally's measurement, feeling that a mistake in making the template could waste a lot of time, and made it 62 cm, showing Sally. She said that each point would have to be 12 and a bit cm apart, showing me how big the "bit" should be. We measured, starting at A and measuring around the circle, marking off the points, and, sure enough, the last space (EA) was the

same length as the others. I then asked Sally how we should proceed. After examining a star closely with me, she said we could join A with C and D; then B with D and E; then C with E. Sally then cut out this paper star, and traced around it onto stiff cardboard, while I cut out the final template from the cardboard which was too thick for Sally herself to work.'

Although I knew about the enlarged version of Sally's original design on which she and Helen were working I did not see it properly until two days later when they came to me with an urgent request for equipment.

'Friday, April 29th.

Sally came to me to ask if I'd approach Paul Merrison [another teacher, with a class of eleven year olds] for one of his really thin paint brushes so that she and Helen could tidy up the edges of the stars in their large painting, the edges being a little uneven and fuzzy because they had only had thickish paint brushes. The picture itself had worked out well. The drawing and placing of the stars, using Sally's template, had been very accurate. I was quite impressed because when I had glanced at the drawing earlier, while Sally was working with the template, I had noticed what a confusing array of lines there were, making up the overlapping stars, and I had wondered whether she would be able to paint the stars without getting into a muddle. They had painted the encircling stars alternately yellow and blue, following a suggestion of Stephen's, so that where the stars overlapped the colour was green. The effect was the same as we had observed on Wednesday when we held the paper of red star designs up to the light, as Sally pointed out to me. Appropriately enough, they had decided that the central star ought to be painted green too, or rather blue on yellow like the overlapping areas. The original pattern appeared in a more complex form than when it had been made of uniformly red shiny stars.

I fetched the thin brushes and Sally and Helen touched up the edges of their pattern. Then they decided to cut the whole shape out and mount it on black paper. I helped them cut it out; it was hard to do because the inner kite shaped spaces had to be cut out as well as the outside edge of the pattern. In the end I finished the cutting myself, during morning play. After play, pleased with the new effect, they stuck the whole pattern onto black paper; I found myself worrying, as I was working with other children in the class, whether they would stick the pattern carefully enough, a silly anxiety in view of all the precision Sally has shown this past few days. But the sticking went well, and during the dinner break I pinned the picture up on a display board outside our classroom where it looks superb, especially from a distance as you turn the corridor from the library area. Later this afternoon Helen said to me "We didn't know you'd put our picture up". She sounded satisfied.'

Before the close of the year there was to be an interesting sequel to Sally's patterns of stars. It was the last occasion in the year on which Sally had an opportunity to practise her skill and invention in pattern making and it gave us a final, decisive, glimpse of her aims and methods, which on this occasion were tinged with a certain end of year frivolity.

'Thursday, June 23rd.

Sally was wanting a suggestion this morning. Having been thinking about her stars again recently, and having to hand some coloured gummed paper, I suggested cutting out shapes and playing around with them. I suppose I was interested to see how far the skill which Sally had shown earlier in the term would recur. I also guessed that she would like the idea. She did.

We borrowed a couple of stencils from Paul Merrison and I began by cutting out for her a number of small pentagons in red and blue paper, the colours which she had chosen after telling me that she was no good at choosing colours. She began to group the shapes together and stick them down. I left her to it and on my return a few minutes later she had completed her first design. She had arranged the pentagons into two interlocking rings of different colour (see illustration, a).

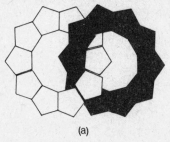

(a)

The same precision in placing each shape, and in rearranging the shapes to ensure the accuracy of the completed pattern, which had been so apparent in the making of her star patterns, was displayed once more. She said that she had not intended the pattern that emerged inasmuch as she had not known in advance what it was going to look like. What she had done was to place a red and a blue pentagon alongside each other and then add pentagons of the same colour to each of the two original shapes until she had completed the two interlocking circles. I don't think she had realised at first that her procedure would lead to two circles of pentagons, nor had she foreseen the possibility of interlocking them. The potential of her procedure became clear only as she proceeded. She showed me how she had set about it, having a little difficulty at first in reproducing her procedure but finally succeeding. There could not have been a clearer demonstration of the point made by Stephen in relation to her star patterns. Without a doubt she had devised a rule and submitted it to a test. The pattern was the result. [When it came to interlocking the two circles she had had to reconsider her procedure which had not taken into account this possibility. Several pentagons had to be unstuck and rearranged to create the desired effect.]

There were six pentagons left when she had completed this first pattern, two red and four blue. These she arranged in a circle, their bases touching, and then with the scraps of coloured paper

that had been left over after cutting out othe pentagons, she
turned the shape into the figure of a man, a kind of dancing
cossack with a quaint hat and baggy trousers (see illustration, b).

(b)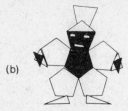

Six more designs followed, using different shapes cut from the
same stencil. Two of them were constructed out of rounded

shapes, like this — — which Sally arranged into two strongly
contrasted designs, one of them diamond shaped, the other in the
form of a cross, both perfectly regular. Two more were made of

T shapes, like this — 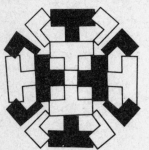 — and one of these was especially
noteworthy for the way in which it shows how Sally combines
aesthetic and logical elements in her patterns. The fundamental
pattern here is cross shaped and follows a clear and simple rule,
as to both colour and shape,
but Sally has added T shapes
between the arms of the cross,
turning it into an eight-sided
figure. For these diagonals
however she has split each T in
half and placed a half T of one
colour next to a half T of the
other (the colours being pale
pink and deep brown) leaving
a small space between the two
halves of each T. The effect is both to animate the pattern and
to preserve the symmetry of its colour contrasts. As regards the
second of these effects, it is another instance of the paramount
importance of rule in Sally's pattern making, the split Ts being
strictly necessary in order to preserve the rule that each shape
must be adjacent to a shape of the opposite colour. Sally herself
pointed out to me what she had done, later in the day. Even
two designs which she described to me as just "playing around",

"putting the shapes down anyhow", exhibited a strong sense of symmetry and balance. It seemed that Sally saw herself as putting the shapes down "anyhow" whenever she was not consciously observing a rule which she had selected for generating a pattern.

Later in the morning Michelle joined Sally in pattern making but she used the shapes to make figures with, like Sally's cossack, rather than to create patterns. Many children later said they especially liked the quaint pig-like face which Michelle had made with pointed and wing-like ears. Gwyneth later followed Michelle's example, making a clown with a funny top hat, while Debbie constructed a pattern in Sally's manner, somewhat complex in plan, as did Louise. Meanwhile Sally rounded off her morning's pattern making by taking over the pin board, across which Michelle had been stretching elastic bands, and demonstrating her equal skill at manipulating elastic bands into elaborate and strong designs. It had been quite a morning for her.'

The speculative and experimental power that was so evident in Sally's pattern making, a quality of thought at once inventive and analytical, can be traced through many other investigations of pattern, shape and structure carried out in Stephen's class over the course of the year. These investigations, which seemed to partake equally of art and of science, often had their origin in the work of the regular small group sessions devoted to mathematics, which Stephen held about once a week during the autumn and spring terms. I want to consider three of these group sessions as Stephen described them in his notes. Each of them led to investigations which, in one way or another, shared something of the spirit and quality of Sally's experiments with ball bearings, stars and stencils. Together they serve to indicate the range, variety and style of the children's invention and speculation.

I think it was probably the playing of a group of children with coloured pegs on a large peg board that first alerted Stephen and myself to the prying, searching quality of the children's explorations of shape, pattern and design. Stephen had decided one morning half way through the Autumn Term to introduce into the classroom a number of new mathematics materials for the children to examine and play with, 'hoping', as he put it, 'that with only slight intervention they would begin to see greater possibilities in their use'. Among the materials, which he assembled on two large tables in the middle of the classroom, was a large sheet of peg board, approximately 4 foot long by 2 foot wide, part of an old screen, together with a very large bag of pegs in assorted colours. It was some while later in the morning that he first visited the group of boys who had chosen to examine the peg board.

'Wednesday, October 13th (Stephen's notes).

Julian, Philip, Paul and Neil had made pictures on the board, using the pegs. [The capacity of children in the class to create pictures out of any material that came to hand never ceased to surprise us.] Paul had made what he originally thought of as a car and trailer. Then Neil said "No, it's an old fashioned plane". Paul seemed even more satisfied with this interpretation. Many of the other pictures were also very elaborate considering the limitations of the apparatus. However, there was no regard to colour.

After the "painting" had been going on for some forty minutes I began to feel that the enthusiasm was at, or past, its peak. I said I was going to join them and make a pattern. I put down some pegs as follows:-

```
      G
    Y G   (Here and elsewhere letters represent
  B Y G   different colours of peg: green, yellow, brown, etc.)
```

Philip said "That's a triangle". I said "Would you like to carry on with it?" He seemed very enthusiastic so I left him to it for ten minutes or so. On returning I found he had completed something like this:-

```
            Bl
          R Bl R
        O R Bl R O
      G O R Bl R O G
    Y G O R Bl R O G Y
  B Y G O R Bl R O G Y B
M M M M M M M M M M M M M M
M                           M
M M M M M M M M M M M M M M
```

His pattern showed due regard for symmetry. He said "That's a yacht. Can you write 'yacht' underneath it because I can't spell it?"

His interpretation reminded me of the picture poems which some of the children wrote last week. This time it was a mathematical idea which had been incorporated into a picture just as before it had been words which had been made into pictures.

After playtime I returned to the board to play. I started like this:-

```
        G
      R G
    B R G
    B R G
      R G
        G
```

Robbie seemed interested and I pointed out my rule that I add two pegs each time. He continued this. Paul then came up to watch and I asked him if he could make a similar pattern going up in threes (much more of a problem if you want to retain symmetry). Without any help he made this pattern:-

```
Y Y Y Y Y Y Y Y Y Y Y Y Y Y Y
  W W W W W W W W W W W W W
    R R R R R R R R R
      B B B B B B
        G G G
```

He pointed out that 'B' goes two to the right and one to the left of 'G'; so 'R' has to go two to the left and one to the right of 'B'; so 'W' has to go two to the right and one to the left of 'R'; and so on. At no time had I drawn his or Robbie's attention to the idea of symmetry and I did not hear them talk about it. Nevertheless Paul had devised for himself a rule which would maintain a kind of overall symmetry in his pattern.

By now it was time for swimming so we left the peg board.'

Stephen was impressed by the manner in which the children had exploited the pictorial possibilities of the peg board and had begun to explore ideas of symmetry and balance. The board itself had attracted more attention and enthusiasm than any of the other apparatus he had introduced that morning, partly perhaps by virtue of its enormous size and the number and variety of colours of pegs. It seemed that the board could be applied to many branches of mathematics — to the study of shape, symmetry, multiplication, sets, graphs — as well as to making pictures, devising games, and creating patterns of many kinds. So at the end of the day, while Stephen returned to the maths cupboard most of the other apparatus he had introduced, to be brought out again on a future occasion, he left the peg board and pegs in the classroom where, in the event, they remained all year.

In the days that followed most of the class, at one time or another, had their turn on the peg board. Fresh pictures and patterns appeared on it daily while the boys who had explored it on the first morning contrived later to turn it into an elaborate computer control panel for a space adventure they were enacting. One week after his first notes on the use of the peg board Stephen returned to the theme.

'Tuesday, October 19th (Stephen's notes).

Work on the pegboard again.

Debbie and Debra had said they would like to use the peg board and bearing in mind the current interest in circles and spirals which has stemmed from experiments with the old gramophone turntable, I suggested they try to make a spiral on the board. Straight away Debra replied that this would not be possible since the peg holes were all in straight lines and there weren't any curves on it. I suggested she should still have a go and see what she could produce. I left the two girls at this stage. On returning about half an hour later I found that they had produced an enormous configuration like this:

The pattern was carefully and symmetrically positioned on the board and the finished effect was most satisfying. They immediately pointed out to me how the two outside spirals went in different directions. Later they proudly showed their work to the rest of the children in their maths group. The response of most children was to follow round the spiral with their fingers. It seemed as if they were checking to see if you really could start in the middle and progress to the outside.

After talking about the peg board spiral in the maths group we collected a number of spiral objects to examine further: spirals made on the turntable, snail shells, clock springs, conical and cylindrical springs, and a model of a spider's web. Mina compared a clock spring with a conical spring. She came to show me that if she pushed out the middle of the flat clock spring she could change it into a shape just like the other one, the conical spring. She was very excited about this and wanted to find a stick so that she could secure the clock spring in its transformed, conical state.

Meanwhile Mark, who had been very impressed by Debbie and Debra's square spiral, decided, after examining the spiral closely, to withdraw alternate pegs counting round the spiral and see what happened. The effect was as follows:

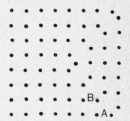

I did not observe this activity in detail but afterwards I noticed a bunch of children arguing as to whether or not this really was a spiral. Mark was explaining how he had made it and how it was indeed a spiral, following round it with his fingers. Someone else pointed out that it was not really a spiral because you could "cross the lines" (e.g. from A to B on the diagram) through the gaps between the pegs.

The following morning Mark was at the peg board again and when I approached him he had set out some pegs as follows:

I interpreted this as an attempt to make a disc shape and asked him if he could make any other circles. After a while he came up with a variety of shapes:

He said that the last one was the best and nearly was a circle. I asked him whether, since he had made a shape that was so nearly a circle, he could also make a curved spiral, as opposed to the square spiral that Debbie and Debra had constructed. He seemed satisfied that this should be possible so I left him to it. I returned half an hour later to find he had finished, having produced an octagonal spiral like this:

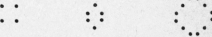

Again the children crowded round to follow the spiral around with their fingers.

Mark was followed on the peg board by Gail and Louise Ann. They had been interested in the previous day's ideas as to the "path" of a spiral and "not being allowed to cross the lines" and it was this I think that led them now to make a maze. The maze covered the entire board, all 2 feet by 4 feet of it, and was extremely intricate. Several of us tried to solve it and failed. At one point Mary Brown came into the room and she tried too, without success. After still more attempts a certain ambiguity in the rules arose. Obviously one was not permitted to cross a horizontal or vertical row of pegs

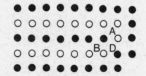

but was this move allowed?

• = pegs
o = open holes
Paths have to follow the lines
of open holes but can they cross
a diagonal, e.g. A to B?

We discussed this point and Louise Ann, agreeing that a move from A to B should not be allowed, swiftly adjusted the maze by removing the peg at D, and other similarly placed pegs elsewhere on the board. Even with this adjustment the puzzle was still very difficult, and seemed to have only one solution.

The mathematical character of the apparatus impressed me a great deal. It seems as though almost any activity on the peg board involves a mathematical aspect. The structure of the board and pegs, both in its opportunities and in its limitations, seems to impose its mathematical character on whatever the board is used for.'

The success of the peg board did much to determine our later attitudes towards the children's patterns, models and constructions. We had both been surprised as well as encouraged by the children's enthusiasm for the peg board, by the variety of uses to which they put it, the ingenuity of their constructions and experiments, the problems, questions and arguments to which the board gave rise, the ubiquitous mathematics involved in making peg board patterns, pictures and games. At the close of the Autumn Term we observed the same richness and variety in the model making on which a large group of children were then engaged, using thin white card,

oddments of wood, metal and plastic, and a light glue or paste.*
During the Christmas holiday Stephen decided that in the Spring
Term he would try to relate as much of the class's mathematical
activity as possible to the children's obvious interest in making
patterns and constructing models, presenting them with materials
and encouraging them to experiment. He began with a study of
shape, firstly of triangles.

'Tuesday, 18th January (Stephen's notes).

My broad aim in maths for the first part of this term is to draw the
children's attention to simple shapes (at first, triangles, squares and
rectangles), relating this to their models, patterns and designs. I also
hope to introduce them to two- and three-dimensional frameworks
and tessellations, and to simple ideas about angles, symmetry and
rotation.

As during last term, the work will be based around a weekly group
meeting, but I envisage a greater emphasis on individual children
following the ideas introduced in the group sessions in a variety of
ways according to their various interests and abilities. The work will
be largely practical and related to scientific and artistic ideas. I hope
that in this way maths may form a centre for much of the art, craft
and science in the classroom and not be seen as a narrowly defined
area of the curriculum.

I started the first group session by asking all the children to draw a
triangle. Typical results were:

Almost without exception, the triangles drawn were approximations
to an equilateral triangle with horizontal base. This may have been
due to the fact that all the children were very familiar with the
Logiblocs in which the triangle is this shape. When we compared
drawings, many children said that the ones nearest to 2 were "the
best".

I then asked the children to draw another triangle which was very
different from their first one. Several children drew triangles that
were similar but enlarged or reduced in size. Others drew:

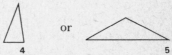

* See Chapter 6.

There was unanimous agreement that these were still triangles, but Elizabeth was hesitant and thought that they were "not so good". The children seemed to have a Platonic idea of a triangle.

Next I drew this: 6

In the first group of children, all except one said that this was not a triangle! (And this even though 6 is identical to 5, above, merely rotated.) This apparent difficulty in dealing with 6, whereas 5 was no problem, is, I think, of some significance. How do children come across triangles? Houses, mountains, their own models of buildings — in all these cases the triangle is similar to 4 or 5, but not to 6. In 4 or

5, or , the non-horizontal sides offer some support to each other, whereas 6, being unstable, does not appear as often in nature.

I now asked the group what a triangle is. "A shape." "It's flat." "It can be any size." "It can be any colour." I asked, "Can you tell me something which all triangles have?" "Three points", said Debra, "and three sides."

After a little more discussion, and after turning around triangle 6, we decided that this was, after all, a triangle.

We then went on a tour of the school looking for triangles. The children seemed very alert and I was bombarded with examples. Someone found triangles between books leaning together on a shelf:

There were triangles in pictures on the walls. Peter found them in the shape of a spider-plant leaf; someone else in the markings on a bee. In all of these cases the children traced around the whole triangle with their fingers. Then Philip said, "On this tile (pointing to the floor) if you had a line here (pointing from A to B) you'd have one."

Other children took up Philip's idea and continued to make triangles out of all the angles they could find, by imagining another line like AB.

The initial meetings of the other three maths groups followed a similar pattern: an introductory discussion first and then a look around the school, before the setting of the first practical task. Many of the problems and questions which had arisen with the first group came up again but there were new problems too which are worth noting.

With the second group of children, after they had drawn and discussed their triangles, I asked them to draw a square or oblong (i.e. a rectangle). No difficulty here. I then said, "Can you draw another line which will change your shape into two triangles?" Several children did this:

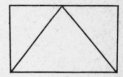

Most of them then realised that they had three triangles, although someone thought there was only one triangle. (Perhaps, again, she was trying to make "the best" (that is, equilateral) triangle from her oblong.)

About half the group soon saw that they had to bisect the rectangle with a diagonal

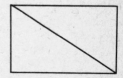

and when this was done, everyone agreed that this was "the answer".

With the third group we went a bit further in defining the triangle. I drew these:

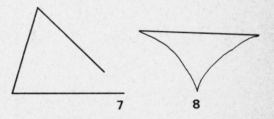

7   8

I asked if they were triangles. All the children agreed that 7 was not, "because there's a gap" as Mina said. Debra said that it had to be closed. However, they weren't quite sure about 8, though eventually all agreed that the lines would have to be straight for it to be a triangle. "So we shall have to use rulers."

Going around the group, we produced some kind of definition of a triangle: 1) it must have three "points" or "corners" (I introduced the word "angle" later); 2) it must have three sides; 3) the sides must be straight; 4) it must be closed.

At the end of each group's tour of the school in search of triangles I asked everyone in the group to cut a triangle out of cardboard, trace around it, and cut around the tracing to produce a second triangle identical with the first. They were to cut out a number of identical triangles in this way and use them, as I put it, "to tile a bathroom floor", the "floor" being another piece of white cardboard onto which they would stick their triangles after colouring them. From this point on their work was to proceed individually.

The task "to tile a bathroom floor" was open to different interpretations. It could mean either "cover the whole floor space with tiles so that there are no gaps" (that is, tessellating the tiles), or "make a design, out of the tiles, which you would like to have on your bathroom floor" (without regard to the problem of spaces between or around the tiles). Many children preferred the second interpretation which left more room for design and was less constricting. Either intepretation was, I felt, acceptable.

Philip's procedure harked back to his discovery that any tile could be transformed into a triangle by imagining a diagonal drawn across it. Remembering that a triangle could be half a rectangle he cut a corner off his piece of card, thus and found that when he

had cut a second, identical piece and put the two together, sure enough he had a rectangle. The problem, as he saw it, was now simple enough; he just had to cover his floor with these rectangles. He wanted however to preserve the appearance of triangles on his floor so he coloured adjacent triangles in different colours:

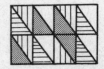

In selecting his colours he seemed to have in mind some kind of rule, but when he had painstakingly finished the task he realised that his colours had "gone wrong" and that the sequence of colours was not regular, as he had intended it should be. The following day, wanting to try again, he asked if he could use rectangles instead of triangles, explaining why he was dissatisfied with the previous day's efforts. What mattered to him now was the regular sequencing of colours, rather than the tessellating of triangles, hence his choosing to work with rectangles. By the end of the morning he had completed the following design:

G = green
Y = yellow
R = red

Y	G	R	Y	G
R	Y	G	R	Y
G	R	Y	G	R
Y	G	R	Y	G

He had done this by careful stages: (1) cutting out rectangles, (2) placing them on the "floor", (3) marking each rectangle with the appropriate colour letter, (4) collecting all the rectangles together and painting them, (5) sticking the "tiles" onto the "floor". His pattern, and the deliberation with which he assembled it, reminded me of some of the patterns we had made on the peg board last term in connection with "rhythm" and "tables".

A problem which soon emerged in many children's work was that of manual skills. The task of cutting small triangles accurately from card so that they were all identical in shape, using blunt school scissors, was not simple. At first I thought that the physical intricacy of the task would detract from its mathematical value. Now I think I was wrong. It seemed from observing the children and coping with their problems, that the manual difficulty of the task led to new mathematical possibilities, above all, perhaps, in the development of Julie's work over the week. Her first triangle was like this: She attempted to cut out more of the same shape but it was clear from her pattern that she had cut inaccurately. She ended up with a pattern like this:

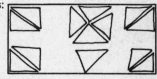

She had already decided not to tessellate the whole floor; she had hoped, however, that the middle part would look more "even" than this and not have any gaps in it. Feeling rather dissatisfied, Julie asked me to help her do another pattern. After some discussion about obtuse-angled triangles (related to the discussion of the first group mentioned earlier), she cut out a triangle like this:

After carefully tracing around this on her card she cut out eight or ten similar triangles. We compared them for size in pairs, and after she had done a little trimming, she was satisfied that they were all very nearly the same. (They were, in fact, much more accurate than those of her previous pattern.)

We then discussed how we could "put together" two of these triangles. Out of the many possible ways of doing this we decided that since we were going to try to tessellate this time, it might be best to place together sides of equal length, thus eliminating bits of sides "sticking out". There were three possible ways of doing this:

a

b

c

Julie thought that the arrows (b and c) looked more interesting and proceeded to put all her triangles into pairs to make up "sharp arrows" (b). I then asked her if she could put these arrows together to make a tile pattern without any gaps. I left her to work away at this. When I returned after ten or fifteen minutes she had produced this:

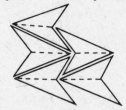

She said that she had left a gap between each arrow "just to show that they were arrows". (The dotted lines on the diagram represent the triangles she had put butting up against each other.) I asked Julie what she thought would happen if we moved the triangles slightly so that the small gaps appeared elsewhere. We fiddled around a bit and then suddenly saw the following pattern emerge, having moved only a few triangles very slightly:

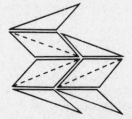

What had been a tessellation of five arrows had now become three parallelograms (we discussed this word) with four odd triangles awaiting their "other halves".

At this point we had to finish. Julie, who is normally very anxious about maths but has considerable artistic talent, seemed quite excited by it all. (It would be nice, somehow, to get across this "movement" of the shapes by using colour.)'

For several days the classroom was dominated by the task which Stephen had set and the various interpretations which different children put upon it. The sequence of activity in constructing a particular pattern appeared to have a strong appeal to many of the children: cutting out the shapes, painting them, organizing them into a pattern, sticking them down. [The order of events varied from child to child.] A large quantity of multicoloured tessellations and designs appeared: rectangular configurations composed of triangles, rectangles and squares, as Stephen had originally anticipated, together with configurations of other kinds — arrows, stars, polygons. Sally, for example, using triangles similar in shape to those used by Julie for her arrow patterns, produced a pattern like this:

She had laid her triangles together in pairs with the longest sides matched (as in example a above), unlike Julie, but like Julie she had been confronted with the problem that no two triangles were identical. She therefore laid out her pattern with a space around each separate triangle, manipulating the triangles with great precision so as to ensure the regularity of each element in the design, its triangular segments and the spaces betwen them. It was her own decision that the diamond should be truncated on two sides; she thought it looked better like that. Her design had the same severe elegance that was to prove so characteristic of her pattern making later in the year. At first she decided that she would not colour the white triangles. Instead, she mounted the pattern on black paper, rather than white card, to great effect. In this form the pattern remained on the classroom wall for several days until one morning, finding a canister of gold spray paint in the classroom, Sally decided to spray the triangles with the paint. She felt, to my own regret, that the gold spray improved the pattern.

Although many of the children had reinterpreted the task set by Stephen to suit their own conception or convenience, most of them had at least observed the principle of tiling, laying their shapes alongside rather than on top of each other. Sarah however chose to disregard this constraint, and in flouting the rules of tiling, created a novel design of her own: a collage made up of two triangles of white card, one painted yellow, the other green, superimposed one upon the other, yellow on green, on a wooden board which was also painted, the top half green, the bottom yellow. The finished piece looked like this:

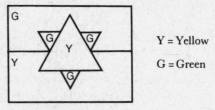

I was struck by the formal clarity of her design, the rhythmic counterpoint of colour and shape. Although she had, perhaps unwittingly, abandoned any pretence of tiling, her construction was clearly related in intention to the work of other children; there was the same interest in colour sequence and in the various shapes, or figures, that could be created out of the small, cut-out triangles. In this instance, however, the six pointed star was achieved by superimposing rather than juxtaposing triangles, a procedural shift which seems to anticipate some of the experiments that Sally and Helen were to make in the summer with the box of sticky red stars.

The investigation of triangles and other shapes led two of the children, Debra and Philip, back to the peg board. Stephen recorded

Debra's new peg board construction as follows, in a note written a few days after the event.

21st to 28th January (Stephen's notes).

'Debra began by making a simple isosceles triangle using sixteen pegs of one colour:

She remembered how, during the tiling work, she had made triangles into rectangles by tesselating them. She wanted to make more of these peg board triangles so that they too tessellated. Using different coloured pegs for each successive triangle she got so far:

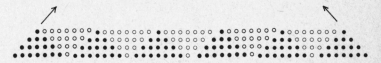

She then remarked that this whole strip was perhaps just the bottom of a larger triangle (its sides extending in the direction indicated by the arrows in the diagram). While I was with her she traced out this larger, complete triangle with her fingers and said that she would try to make it out of the small sixteen peg triangles.

As with much of her previous work, it was quite a grand task which she had set herself, and she completed it with only very occasional intervention from me — a peg "wrong" here or there. The finished triangle consisted of thirty-six smaller triangles, each triangle made up of pegs of a single colour, and it took up a large part of the peg board screen. After Debra had shown her triangle to the rest of the class, to Mary Brown and to Paul Merrison (the school's mathematics specialist), she asked me how many pegs she had used altogether. I did not help her with this problem. She started to add sixteens together but, after adding a dozen or so, she found it rather a strenuous task. She carefully took home a piece of paper for her father to see. He showed her "a quick way" to add together thirty-six sixteens; she produced the answer they arrived at: 576 pegs.'

On the day that Debra made her triangle Stephen had had the class to himself; I was away from school that day. On my return the following morning Debra told me about her triangle with the same enthusiasm and astonishment with which, the previous term, she had described picking mushrooms with her uncle.

'Tuesday, January 18th.

When I arrived this morning Debra was keen to show me the vast triangle of triangles which she had constructed on the peg board yesterday. She was very excited about it and how she had shown it to Mr Merrison and how her dad had shown her how to find out, by multiplication, the precise number of pegs in it, which she herself had proposed to do by writing 16 down 36 times and adding. I was interested in her fondness for the grand design. In its size and elaboration the triangle reminded me of her huge peg board number base diagram of last term, later transferred onto graph paper. I think she finds much pleasure in amassing.'

It was this evident delight in mass which dominated the brief description of her triangle that Debra wrote later:

'My triangle.

My triangle is made of 36 little ones. There are 5 light greens, 4 reds, 3 browns, 4 light blues, 4 dark blues, 2 whites, 4 oranges, 4 yellows, 3 blacks.* My triangle is made out of 576 pegs.'

The sheer size of her triangle was certainly of the utmost importance to her, yet I think that her excitement about the triangle of triangles also owed something to the process by which she had constructed it. The finished triangle represented the successful demonstration of her own hypothesis, the insight she had had into the potential of the growing design. Her first small triangle had led to the desire to tessellate, turning triangles into rectangles; but once she had completed a row or tesellating triangles it had occurred to her that this was not so much a rectangle as the base of a much larger triangle. She had demonstrated her hypothesis in principle by tracing for Stephen the outline of this larger triangle. Then she began the test: she would see if she could construct the larger triangle by continuing her tessellation of small triangles within the outline she had traced with her finger. It worked.

Debra's procedure had a decidedly scientific character and the same could be said of the way in which, following on from Debra, Philip now took up the investigation of triangles and other shapes on the peg board, as Stephen explained.

'21st to 28th January (Stephen's notes).

'Philip too, returned to the pegboard. At first he made a triangle like this:

---
* Debra's numbers add up to 33, not 36. Neither she nor Stephen nor myself seem to have spotted the error.

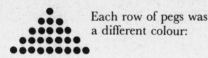

Each row of pegs was
a different colour:

```
        R
       Y Y Y
      G G G G G
   B B B B B B B B B
  P P P P P P P P P P P
```

He remarked on how the rows got bigger. I suggested that he write down the number of pegs in each row. He wrote, correctly, 1, 3, 5, 7, 9, 11. When I asked him if he noticed anything about the numbers he said, "They go up in twos". I asked him why this happened. His explanation and demonstration were quite clear. He explained how each row was just like the previous row but had two extra pegs, one at each end of the row.

He then asked what he should do on the pegboard. I suggested he make another triangle, this time colouring each successive perimeter with a different colour. It took a little explaining to get across my intention. He soon understood what I meant, however, and after a few minutes produced the following:

O = Orange

P = Pink

W = White

Y = Yellow

R = Red

B = Blue

G = Green

```
                     O
                    O P O
                   O P W P O
                  O P W Y W P O
                 O P W Y R Y W P O
                O P W Y R B R Y W P O
               O P W Y R B G B R Y W P O
              O P W Y R B B B B R Y W P O
             O P W Y R R R R R R R R Y W P O
            O P W Y Y Y Y Y Y Y Y Y Y Y W P O
           O P W W W W W W W W W W W W W W P O
          O P P P P P P P P P P P P P P P P P O
         O O O O O O O O O O O O O O O O O O O O O
```

I then suggested he count how many pegs there were in each successive triangle and write down the numbers. He wrote:

1, 8, 16, 24, 32, 40, 48.

When I asked him if he noticed anything special about these numbers he said, "Well, thirty-two is two sixteens". We considered eight and sixteen, and sixteen and twenty-four, and he soon said, "They go up in eights". I then showed him a way to record this:

```
1     8     16     24     32     40     48
 \   / \   /  \   /  \   /  \   /  \   /
  7      8      8      8      8      8
```

Philip was very pleased with this result and, when I asked him, said that the next triangle would have fifty-six pegs in it. He then put in the next triangle and was delighted that his prediction turned out to be correct.

We wondered why this difference of eight should recur, but after some consideration came to no very satisfactory conclusion. So we tried the same idea using a square instead of a triangle. Philip soon came up to me with the completed square and its corresponding set of perimeter peg numbers and peg differences:

```
O O O O O O O O O O O O O O
O P P P P P P P P P P P P O
O P W W W W W W W W W W P O
O P W Y Y Y Y Y Y Y W P O
O P W Y B B B B B Y W P O
O P W Y B G G G B Y W P O
O P W Y B G R G B Y W P O
O P W Y B G G G B Y W P O
O P W Y B B B B B Y W P O
O P W Y Y Y Y Y Y Y W P O
O P W W W W W W W W W W P O
O P P P P P P P P P P P P O
O O O O O O O O O O O O O O
```

```
1     8    16    24    32    40    48
 \   / \  / \   / \   / \   / \   /
  \ /   \/   \ /   \ /   \ /   \ /
   7    8    8    8    8    8
```

By a process of matching the green and blue pegs

```
 B   B   B   B   B
 |   ↑   ↑   ↑   |
 B   G   G   G   B

 B←G           G→B

 B   G   G   G   B
 |   ↓   ↓   ↓   |
 B   B   B   B   B
```

he found out where the extra eight pegs came from.

I asked Philip if he thought this difference of eight would occur whatever shape he started with. He was not sure, but was very keen to try a different shape to see if it would. He suggested a diamond and constructed this:

```
       W
      W Y W
     W Y B Y W
    W Y B G B Y W
   W Y B G R G B Y W
    W Y B G B Y W
     W Y B Y W
      W Y W
       W
```

The corresponding number series was:

```
1     4     8    12    16
 \   / \   / \   / \   /
  \ /   \ /   \ /   \ /
   3    4    4    4
```

Philip was surprised at this result, especially when he noticed that this shape was also a square, tilted at an angle, or standing on its corner.

[Some days later, after Philip had constructed an arrow head shape on the pegboard and written down its corresponding number series in the same way, Michael asked him why the difference between the first peg and the second set of pegs was not the same as the difference between all the other successive sets of pegs. Philip said he thought it was because the first, or central, peg was a "point" and not a "shape". This idea seemed to be confirmed when we constructed a square which, instead of having a single peg at the centre, had a central, four peg square:

```
W W W W W W W W
W Y Y Y Y Y Y W
W Y B B B B Y W
W Y B G G B Y W
W Y B G G B Y W
W Y B B B B Y W
W Y Y Y Y Y Y W
W W W W W W W W
```

The corresponding number series was:

The discrepancy between the first two numbers and the rest of the series had disappeared.]

By now it was the end of Friday afternoon. Philip had spent three quarters of the day working with the peg board and was still enthusiastic to continue. The following Monday he immediately returned to this work and continued for the whole day. At the outset Philip's task had appeared comparatively simple. But he was soon able to see problems and raise questions which the work had suggested. He then went on to make hypotheses about the solutions to these problems and to test them. The sequence of events was as follows:

practical
task

↓

additional
problems
and questions

↓

hypotheses
to test

↓

tests

↓

more hypotheses

Such a sequence is characteristic of scientific procedure and fundamental to scientific and mathematical awareness. It seems that it was carrying out this process that was of particular value to Philip in these investigations on the pegboard.'

While Philip was completing his peg board investigations, Stephen had moved on to his second series of group sessions for the term. This time the subject was two-dimensional frameworks and once again Stephen intended to base the work on the exploration of a particular kind of material. In many of the children's subsequent inquiries we could observe the same sequence of events as in Debra's and Philip's investigations of triangles: the practical task leading to problems and questions, thence to hypotheses and tests, and finally back to new problems and new tasks. The group sessions themselves began, as before, with a preliminary discussion, preceding the first task, in which certain general questions could be aired, this time concerning angles.

'21st to 28th January (Stephen's notes).

The aim of the second series of group sessions for this term was to show the children how to construct frameworks out of cardboard strips (1 cm. wide) and split pins. I hoped to use the frameworks to develop ideas about rigidity and flexibility and about angles and polygons.

Before starting to cut up strips of card we talked a bit about angles. During the study of triangles and other shapes I had done no work on rotation or on the measurement of angles; I had pointed out only that what the children were calling the "points" or "corners" of their shapes were in effect "angles". Now, however, I made an angle with two rulers, like this and asked each group how I could make this angle bigger. In one group, Mina placed the rulers in this position,

moving each ruler in the direction indicated by the arrow. However, she was not satisfied. Assuming that she wanted to make the whole shape larger, rather than the angle, I gave her two one metre rules in place of the 30 cm. rules which I had used and she put them together as above, with the same angle but a larger shape, as I had expected. A few of the group disagreed with Mina's way of trying to enlarge the angle and before long, without further intervention from me, the group had decided that the way to make the angle larger was to rotate the right hand ruler clockwise. (No-one thought of rotating the left hand ruler anti-clockwise.)

I now moved the rulers through these positions:

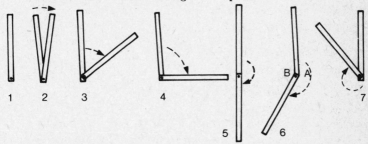

While I was moving the ruler I asked if the angle was getting larger. In each group everyone said that the angle was getting larger between position (1) and position (5), but smaller between position (5) and position (7). There was unanimous agreement that position (5), or, rather, almost but not quite (5), was "the largest possible angle". "Angle" was clearly being understood in terms of shape rather than as a measurement of rotation. There seemed nothing wrong with their conception, or misconception, as applied to shape but I thought that, in order to avoid future confusion when they come to deal with rotation, the matter ought to be clarified now. This was done by discussing how far the ruler moves to get from position (1) right through to position (7) and by getting the children themselves to turn through angles of varying degrees. No particular problems emerged here.

In one of the groups, after we had got so far, Louise Ann remarked that with the rulers in position (6) there were really two angles, A and B. The rest of the group agreed, some of them without a great deal of conviction. However I did not want to take this question further, being anxious, rather, to get down to the process of construction.

The children each had identical sheets of stiff white card, approximately 20 cm x 10 cm, together with ruler, scissors, pencil, compasses (to make holes in the card), and split pins. I helped them cut the card lengthwise into 1 cm strips, pierce holes in the end, and join them up with the pins. Nearly everyone constructed a triangle first and then a square but from there on the work proceeded individually.

Most children remarked on how the square framework could be pulled into a diamond shape:

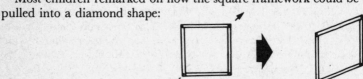

We talked about how the square was flexible whereas the triangular framework had been rigid. Of course, since the card itself was flexible, none of the shapes was truly rigid — one could easily bend them — but this caused no confusion.*

I asked Robbie if he could make his square rigid. With little pause for reflection, he introduced a diagonal strut, as follows —

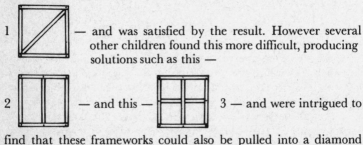

1 — and was satisfied by the result. However several other children found this more difficult, producing solutions such as this —

2 — and this — 3 — and were intrigued to

find that these frameworks could also be pulled into a diamond shape,

4 Paul showed me his shape which was like (3). When I

---

* A friend, reading over this note, suggested to Stephen and myself that the children's lack of confusion showed that they were already familiar, implicitly, with the idea of 'experimental error'. Or it may be that they had abstracted, from the work which they had already done, the rule that, for this set of purposes, one had to consider only flexibility in a plane.

asked him if he could make it rigid, he said he thought he would find this difficult, although he did seem to know what I had meant. After giving the problem some consideration he decided to weave struts together into a square mesh:

His idea was inspired I think by Sally, whose own proposed solution was at the time being displayed on the classroom wall. She had made this:

and was very excited to find that the shape could still be pulled (as indicated by the arrows). I suggested a way of displaying her idea, by attaching further strips at the bottom corners so that the framework could be pulled thus:

Later on in the week Robbie took up this idea of making a framework with several parallel struts which could still be distorted. He then decided to make a completely different shape and, without, as far as I know, any help from others, produced this to show me — saying how it was rigid. He was one of the few children who had actually used strips of card of differing lengths. Most of the children up to that point had stuck to the 1 cm by 20 cm strips which they had used for the first triangle and square.

One of the others who *did* experiment with strips of differing lengths was Michelle. Unfortunately I was not around when she was working on her construction but the result was most imaginative. She had created a shape within a shape, two diamonds joined together by short strips of card at two opposite corners, thus:

The shape was not rigid but as it was pulled the inner and outer diamonds moved in parallel, within the limits imposed by the two small struts. It was the harnessing of the shapes which was perhaps of chief interest to Michelle. The inner diamond was made of strips carefully cut so as to be slightly shorter than the strips of the outer diamond while two of the scraps of strip left over from the cutting were used to join the inner and outer shapes together.

Robert perhaps got more out of this work than anyone else. Having made a triangle and then a square or diamond, he wanted to make polygons of all sorts. He was fascinated by the different ways in which you could pull them. He showed me how a hexagon could be pulled into an oblong:

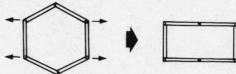

After a brief chat to ascertain that he knew the difference between an oblong and a square (which he did) I asked him if he could make his hexagon into a square. He began to pull it in different directions and then, after a few seconds, suddenly stopped his trial, and said, emphatically, "no". When I asked him how he was so sure he replied it was because the hexagon had six sides.

Later he made an octagon, transforming this into a variety of shapes by pulling:

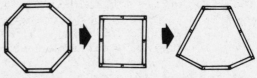

However he was much more enthusiastic with his next stage, a decagon which, he found, after carefully organising the sides, could be transformed into a five-pointed star:

A group of us talked about this and discussed how we might make the star rigid, if for no other reason than that it was such a job trying to get it to look right. Robert has decided to introduce extra struts AB,

BC, CD, DE, and EA. Someone else reckoned that an extra piece such as EB would be needed to ensure rigidity. I'm not sure; we shall see. [Later, however, Robert abandoned the search for greater rigidity in his construction in favour of making it more dramatic, following a similar technique to that used by Michelle. He introduced small struts at A, B, C, D, E, and used them to support a second five-point star positioned within the first:

It was even more difficult to organise this extremely flexible construction into the exact shape required but Robert was delighted by the effect when he had succeeded in getting it right. By that time he decided to add no more to the design, partly perhaps because he had run out of patience and partly because he felt it might spoil the aesthetic effect.]

Sally, too, spent much time and care on the construction of polygons. I have already mentioned her interest in the pulling of squares even when they were made up of several interwoven strands. After this she began work on a hexagon, thinking at first of putting spokes across it like this:

(Similar patterns had been made with triangular tiles the previous week.) However she said she did not like to put a central pin through all the spokes. She thought that this would make the framework weak. So she suggested, instead, putting in a central hub of card from which the spokes would radiate thus . This she did but when she had completed this hub, and attached spokes to it, she found it difficult to connect up the other end of the spokes to the joints of the hexagon. Then she asked me to help and we saw why; she had seven spokes! But if we were simply to remove one spoke the others would be unequally distributed around the central hub. Sally suggested moving all the spokes a little, having removed the seventh, so that the remaining six would be evenly distributed around the hub. I said I thought it would be easier to introduce an extra piece into the hexagon, making it seven-sided rather than six. This plan was embarked upon but it was soon found that now Sally's spokes were not long enough. (Of course I should have realised this; the spokes of a hexagon are the same length as the sides but this is not true of any other polygon.) Michael helped Sally lengthen the spokes and at last the heptagon was completed, to everyone's satisfaction.

Sally is still enthusiastic about this work and is now working with other ways of making polygonal structures rigid. In particular she is experimenting with this idea:

Paul, incidentally, has now finally solved the problem of how to make a square shape rigid, having failed to solve it by weaving. He ingeniously placed two pins in each joint, thus effectively preventing the struts from rotating around the joint: As far as I know he was not assisted in this discovery.   What a brilliant

idea! In terms of technology it was both simpler and more economical on materials than the method I had suggested. He had successfully transformed the nature of the problem and its solution.

Jemma also transformed the nature of the problem but in a different way. She started by making a shape like this:

As soon as it was finished she wanted to bend the whole shape in half so that A and C, and B and D, were pinned together. Her construction then looked like this:

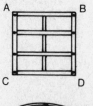

She had thus got away altogether from the idea of frameworks being flat and had gone into three dimensions. It was something which I had myself planned to do in our group sessions — next week!

These were only a few of many interesting frameworks constructed after the group sessions. There has been the same variety of constructions, and of interpretations of the original task, as during the previous work on tiling. And the same inventiveness.'

As Stephen implied in his notes, the next group sessions in mathematics were devoted to three-dimensional shapes: to the construction and examination of cubes, cuboids, prisms, pyramids, tetrahedra and the like; and to the making of models: houses, towers, lamp shades, boxes, toys.* The investigations followed a similar course to that of previous inquiries, exhibiting the same range and variety. Thereafter the weekly maths groups were devoted to other concerns than pattern making and the construction of models, but the fascination with pattern persisted, to emerge again and again during the rest of the school year in such incidents as Sally's explorations with ball bearings or red gummed stars.

I want to conclude this chapter with a brief review of the argument presented in the past three chapters. I have been trying to demonstrate, by means of examples drawn from the life and work of a class of eight year olds, something of the character and quality of children's early intellectual investigations, in writing and literature, in art, and in certain aspects of mathematics and science. I have suggested that a predominant feature of these investigations is their expressive purpose. When children write stories, poems and anecdotes, when they draw and paint, when they experiment and speculate with pattern, they are not only acquiring fundamental skills; they are also appropriating knowledge. Children's intellectual concerns are not dissimilar in this respect to those of more mature thinkers. From their earliest acquaintance with the various traditions of human thought, with literature, art, mathematics, science and the like, they struggle to make use of these several traditions, of the constraints which they impose as well as the opportunities which they present, to examine, extend and express in a fitting form their own experience and understanding. I hope it is clear from my examples that such acts of appropriation are not to be interpreted as mere spontaneity, an inexplicable or innate flowering independent of context. They emerge, rather, out of children's absorption in subject matter, and that depends, as far as school life is

* See Chapter 6.

concerned, upon the quality of environment which a teacher prepares and sustains within the classroom: upon the materials, ideas, relationships, techniques, and forms of knowledge which children encounter there and which in turn become the objects of their scrutiny.

There is a passage in one of Coleridge's essays which defines this development, with great force and eloquence, in terms of the "germinal power" of the human mind. To excite this power is for Coleridge, as he claims it was for Plato, the only proper object of an education of the intellect:

> "We see, that to open anew a well of springing water, not to cleanse the stagnant tank, or fill, bucket by bucket, the leaden cistern; that the Education of the intellect, by awakening the principle and *method* of self-development, was his proposed object, not any specific information that can be *conveyed into it* from without: not to assist in storing the passive mind with the various sorts of knowledge most in request, as if the human soul were a mere repository or banqueting-room, but to place it in such relations of circumstance as should gradually excite the germinal power that craves no knowledge but what it can take up into itself, what it can appropriate, and re-produce in fruits of its own."

In the thought and action of the children whose work I have described in the last three chapters I believe that it is possible to discern already the early excitement of their own germinal powers and the first fruits of their own appropriations.

5 The Practice of Art and the Growth of Understanding

"Without unceasing practice nothing can be done. Practice is Art. If you leave off you are lost." William Blake inscribed these words among the aphorisms and assertions with which he surrounded an engraving of the Laocoon, drawn towards the end of his life. Practice, in a sense akin to Blake's motto, is the theme of this chapter: not practice in the sense of drill or training, as in practising a piece of music in order technically to perfect it, but practice as the sustained exercise of skill, judgement and imagination in successive intellectual tasks.

In previous chapters I have tried to show that it makes good sense to interpret the thought and action of eight year old children — their early writing, art and mathematics — as an appropriation of knowledge. Now I will argue, as a corollary, that intellectual growth can properly be seen as a product or consequence of children's successive attempts at appropriation, from task to task, over the course of weeks, months and years. My argument takes the form of a single illustrative sketch, drawn from the life of Stephen Rowland's class during the summer term. I will describe one particular episode in the life of one particular child, although of a kind that found its parallel in the lives of many children during the course of the year: a thread of activity, stretching over several weeks, in which it is possible to discern the growth of understanding and competence that comes from sustained intellectual scrutiny. The episode that I have chosen revolves around the scrutiny of the natural world, to the observation and recording of which a large part of the summer term was devoted. Of all the children in Stephen's class none was more continually absorbed in that scrutiny than Paul. I have already described a number of Paul's writings, drawings and paintings during the autumn and winter of the school year. Now I want to follow his progress through the late spring and early summer as he struggled with growing success, and in spite of the occasional failure, to represent his own particular vision and knowledge, in art and writing.

Paul's last substantial picture of the spring term had been the

Fig. 8

magnificent second painting of his go cart discussed in Chapter Three, a picture which, as we have seen, combined close observation of the cherished object with a decorative and fantastic treatment of the setting in which it was placed. By contrast, his earliest pictures of the summer consisted of two small sketches of water insects, and now for the first time during the year, as far as I know, Paul drew direct from life rather than from memory or from illustrations in books.

It was an important moment in Paul's development. From now until the end of the school year most of his art grew out of similar life studies, however fantastically the life study might be transformed before a particular painting was completed. The decision to draw direct from life introduced a new tension into his work and was the cause of much satisfaction, and not a little dissatisfaction, to him as the term progressed. It was also, as we shall see, a vital source of intellectual growth.

His first two sketches of water insects were drawn on the first Friday of the term, the morning after the first of the class's regular visits to the river, during which Paul had spent his time fishing for water insects with a net and a plastic tank. We brought back our various 'finds' for further observation in the classroom and on Friday morning Paul and Debra settled down on the verandah outside the classroom, with the water tank and inspection jars, to watch the creatures they had collected and then to draw them. Debra drew as many insects as she and I could identify with the aid of a book of pond life, labelling each small drawing and cutting it out to paste onto a larger sheet of paper for later display. Paul, however, concentrated on what seemed to him the two most interesting creatures: a mayfly larva and a water-boatman (see fig. 8). He did not draw them separately as Debra had but placed them together, one above the other, in a watery landscape: blue water, green weeds, and brown, muddy floor. The two insects are a little larger than life size, as were Debra's also; eyes, legs and tail fins are drawn in as well as a few prominent markings: a segmented back on the larva, spotted wings on the waterboatman. I remember Paul staring at the insects in the inspection jar, to which he had transferred them from the tank, and growing irritated that they would not keep still. When he had finished his sketch he found a drawing of a giant diving beetle in our reference book and proceeded to copy that, pleased I think to have discovered a motionless subject. His drawing was an enlarged but otherwise exact copy of the illustration, but once completed he chose to superimpose it again on an imagined landscape of weeds and mud, with two rows of tiny red insects climbing up the tall weeds to the right of the beetle.

These early sketches led to Paul's first large painting of the term, a gigantic blow up of a minute tropical fish (see fig. 9). I saw nothing of this painting until it was finished and then I mistook the weird, almost sinister fish for some huge imaginary shark, remembering how fascinated Paul was by sharks.* (This was the year of *Jaws*.) It was only later that I discovered that the creature was really a tiny tropical fish swimming in a tank. Had I looked more carefully, at the outset, I would have noticed the aerator of the tank which is visible at the right hand edge of the picture, white bubbles rising from it. The fish is black with huge fins, an enormous bright red tail, and a long, slanting eye which is chiefly responsible for the sinister impression the creature conveys. As in the two sketches of water insects, the fish swims among green weeds above a chequered red and green floor representing, as Paul told me later, the mixture of pebbles, sand and weed at the bottom of the tank.

* e.g. the shark placed in the pond above the go cart, Chapter Three.

Fig. 9

I do not know where Paul derived the idea or the model for this picture; he painted it very quickly, for Paul, and I had the impression that he had conceived and executed it more casually than, for example, his go cart of the previous term. In any event, no sooner had he finished painting it than he began to look around for another subject for a picture.

'Wednesday, May 11th (notes covering Tuesday, May 10th as well).

By Tuesday morning Paul had completed his strange fish, having added to it on Monday, and it was up on the wall. He wanted to start another painting but was at a loss for a subject. Feeling that I would like to encourage him to return to direct observation as a source of ideas for painting, and remembering the success of Louise and Julie's trip to the bottom of the playing field to sketch one of the tall trees there, last term,* I asked Paul whether he would be interested in walking across the field with me and selecting a tree to sketch as a model for a larger painting. He liked the idea and we set off at once, accompanied by Wyndham who had overheard us planning the trip and, when we left, slipped out after us with pencil, paper and board, like Paul, to join in.

As we walked across the field, Paul pointed out to me the tree which he wanted to sketch. It was not one of the large trees which I had indicated but a small, young chestnut — he named it himself — with a straightish, slim trunk, rather clearly defined branches and large, scattered, young leaves. As soon as we reached the tree Paul squatted down and began drawing earnestly, taking great care. He concentrated entirely on the trunk and the branches, ignoring the leaves, twigs and smaller branches, ignoring also the comparative width of the various branches (or maybe, in this instance, he was technically unable to be as accurate as he might have wished), concentrating almost entirely on the twisting and turning line of the branches and their relationship to the trunk. He kept on staring at the tree, trying to get the angle of a branch drawn just right, and looking again. The sketch made the tree look taller than it really was, less widespread at the top, apparently much larger and older. The angling of trunk and branches, however, was relatively accurate. I asked Paul whether he was going to add leaves to his sketch but he said no, he would do that back in the classroom. As we were leaving the tree Paul said to me "When I grow up I'm going to be a drawer and make things up. Yes, cartoons and things, I mean."

Back in the classroom Paul set to work to turn his sketch into a large painting (see fig. 10) and this task has occupied most of his time until the end of this afternoon. The picture is still unfinished but the tree itself has been completed, with a little help from David whom Paul persuaded to help paint the leaves with their browny pink twigs.

The time Paul has taken to get so far with the painting is a matter of some importance. He has to live with his paintings, just as certain other children in the class have to live with their stories. I first noticed this just before Christmas and I have noticed it again now. He works very slowly, as if every part of the work requires the utmost patience; he broods over the picture

*See Chapter 3

Fig. 10

as he works at it, adding a little at a time, leaning back to look with a quizzical air, never quite sure if he is satisfied or not, alternately grumbling and smiling. While a picture is being painted he has little patience for anything else; he prefers to carry slowly on for two or three days if need be, until the painting is done. Paul is like the hedgehog, not the fox: interested in one big thing at a time.

Paul began by making an enlarged drawing of his sketch on a sheet of brown sugar paper. He carefully copied the tree, its trunk and branches, from the sketch, reproducing the accurate angling of the branches and their inaccurate girth. The newly drawn tree was in effect a line by line blow up of the original sketch. Then came the problem of the unsketched leaves. Paul tackled it by assembling individual leaves along each branch like a row of figures, every leaf sticking rigidly up, or very occasionally down, from its branch, poised upon its own little twig. The result was slightly incongruous; stiff, formalised leaves against relatively naturalistic branches. And yet in a way these curious leaves did resemble the "large, scattered, young leaves" of the real tree. When it came to painting the leaves Paul, who had by now persuaded David to help him, decided that it would be too difficult to paint in each leaf accurately and resorted to a series of green blobs and splodges over each drawn leaf, which had the effect of softening a little the rigidity of the drawing.*

Paul prepared the colour he intended for the trunk and branches with some care; it was a dark, greyish, uneven brown, which he mixed for himself, and closely resembled the colour of the real tree. While he was painting the trunk and branches, which he chose to paint first, before beginning on the leaves, he told me that he would like to return to the tree sometime to look at the "moss" which he had noticed on its trunk and which he wished to represent. It took him the whole of this morning to paint just the trunk and the branches and this afternoon, with occasional impatience and a little help from David, he completed the leaves. Finally, at the end of the day, he added a little more drawing to his picture: a fence behind the tree and a standing figure, myself it transpired, leaning against it. These additions still remain to be painted and I will then be interested to see whether or not he decides to paint in the brown paper

* Compare Julie's treatment of leaves, Chapter Three.

background as a blue sky, as he used to earlier in the year.*'

The next day Paul set to work to revise and complete his picture.

'Friday, May 13th.

Paul finished his painting on Thursday. He rubbed out the figure of a man — me — leaning up against the tree, replacing it by a rope ladder ascending to the first thick branch. He added a brown path leading up to the tree across a strip of grass. (The fence remains but has not been painted.) High up the tree he added a brown tree house, with a slatted window, green door and black roof, and a pencilled but unpainted ladder leading to it from the branch beneath. Above the house in a nook between two branches there is something that looks like a bird's nest and above that a rather striking bird with yellow head and neck, an orange beak and a brown body (although the body could possibly be a nest with the bird peering out of it). At the top left hand corner of the painting he has painted, as I had earlier thought he might, the ubiquitous corner cupboard sun with its two eyes, mouth, and yellow rays. (By comparison with earlier suns of Paul's, however, this one is almost cursory.) But he decided against painting in the brown paper background. I asked him at one point if the picture was finished or if he intended to paint in the rest of the paper and he then confirmed that it was finished. I imagine he had already realised how hard it would have been to add a painted background now, even had he wanted to, and when I spoke to him he didn't seem to feel that it was necessary to do so, as he has often felt before.'

I was intrigued by the change that had come over Paul's painting but it was not until the following Monday that I discovered its full significance. At first I thought that Paul had simply decided to turn his tree from the simple playing field chestnut into some grand tree of his dreams, a fiction or fantasy. But there was more to it than that.

'Monday, May 16th.

I talked to Paul briefly this morning about his tree picture. Already, early this morning, Stephen had told me that the bird in Paul's tree was intended, so Paul had told him, to be an eagle.

* See Chapter Three.

Perhaps this explains its distinctly haughty pose which recalls Paul's earlier painting of an eagle, just before Christmas.* I began by asking Paul why he had put the eagle into the tree. He merely said that he felt like it. Next I asked him how he had come to rub out the figure leaning against the tree and add the rope ladder, and tree house. It was a question which I had already asked him the previous week when he had replied, as today with regard to the eagle, that he just felt like it. But now he said that he had decided to turn the tree into his own tree — he meant the tree in his garden at home — which, he told me, was a huge tree. He didn't say that the painted tree had reminded him of his own home tree but I am pretty sure that this was how it had happened, the painted tree looking so large that it no longer resembled the small tree he had sketched at the bottom of the playing field but a great old tree — his own. Hence, he continued, the rope ladder and the tree house, which belonged to the tree in his garden. The ladder like contraption immediately below the tree house was what he used in order to swing himself up into the tree house, while the "nest" just above the roof of the tree house was really a camouflaged back entrance or exit in case he was spotted from the front. A row of dots up the tree trunk, which last week I thought might be accidental, represented nails in the bark on the far side of the trunk to take him up from the house to the camouflaged nook. All this he explained to me with his usual eagerness, that same oddly Buster Keaton like manner which I have commented on before, half surprised and half indulgent. He added, though, that the tree house in his own home tree had collapsed, so that what he had printed was a recreation of this original.'

The origin of Paul's transformation of his picture probably lay in the character of his original sketch. As I have said, even this first drawing made the tree seem larger and older than it was, chiefly on account of the disproportionate width of its sketched branches. The enlargement of his sketch which Paul drew and painted back in the classroom accentuated this effect so that his final, painted tree looked decidedly full grown and imposing. By this time Paul had thrown away his sketch from life and the painted tree, one might say, had begun to assume a life of its own. Paul no longer felt bound by the appearance of the playing field tree he had originally chosen to draw; his mind dwelt now on the painted tree before him. It reminded him

* See Chapter Three

of his own home tree, the tree of his play and of his fantasy, and that is
how he chose to reinterpet it, adding the rope, the tree house, and the
concealed entrance, and in the process restoring the tree house to its
original form (as, earlier, he had restored his go cart to its original
grandeur in his second painting of it). As a final touch he added one
of his favourite birds, the eagle, subject of one of his earliest artistic
successes of the year. The finished picture was thus, after all, in its
way, the tree of Paul's dreams though closely modelled on the tree in
his garden. All that was left to remind one of the young chestnut at
the bottom of the playing field was the rubbed out drawing of his
teacher still faintly visible behind the rope ladder.

His painting finished, Paul began his first substantial piece of
writing of the term, a brief personal recollection entitled The Bull. In
their own way Paul's summer narratives reflected the same interest
in direct experience as had already become evident in his art.
Although he would occasionally, as now, express a desire to write
stories about imaginary characters, most of his writing in the summer
term turned, in the end, on his own past experience: some accident,
surprise, or memorable event which he would struggle to describe as
vividly as he could in words on the page, within the constraints of his
as yet very limited technique. As I have already suggested in Chapter
Two, Paul was one of the least advanced writers, technically, in
Stephen's class. He could barely spell the simplest words and he
found it hard to manage the physical act of writing, for all his
dexterity when it came to drawing. To write a single short page could
take him as much as a morning, or more. As the year went on he
progressed from the stage of copying out the words he had dictated to
a teacher to the stage of writing everything for himself, but progress
was slow and hesitant and his writing never displayed the self-
confidence of his art. Yet in the best, and the most serious, of his
writings he was no less concerned to put his ideas into appropriate
form than in his drawings and paintings and it is in this respect that
we may compare his tentative summer narratives with the much
more ambitious and advanced pictures.

I described how Paul came to write The Bull in my notes for
Monday, May 16th, the day on which I had asked him about the
transformation of his painting of the playing field chestnut.

'Monday, May 16th.

Questioning Paul about his tree led on to other things. He told
me he wanted to write something today but he didn't quite know

what, except that he wanted to write an adventure. I began by suggesting to him an adventure that involved his tree but no, he wanted it to be grander than that and not about himself. He began to think aloud — and what he spoke about, despite his protestation that he did not want to write about himself, was his own adventures. He mentioned an incident that had happened to him at the seaside. How about that as a theme, I suggested. Again he rejected it, and then, at once, he was recalling another adventure, triggered in his memory perhaps by the seaside incident, when he and a friend had been flying a kite in a field and were chased by a bull, as they thought. There and then he decided that this was the story he would write. He spent a good deal of the day writing it and when I first went over to see what he had written he had just screwed it up and thrown it away. He had begun the story as it had happened to him but then he had turned it into a fictional account and he was displeased with the result; it hadn't seemed to make sense. I suggested that he return to what had actually happened and I wrote out the opening of the story for him again, copying the words he had himself written at the start of the piece he had just thrown away. Paul carried on with it and by the time I saw it next he had reached the moment at which he saw the bull. I hoped that he would continue the story of the chase itself as graphically as he had dealt with the kite flying that led up to it. I expected him to include in his account the various details which he had mentioned to me when he was first retelling the adventure: how in leaping over the fence to escape the bull he had missed his footing and fallen head first into the mud. But as it happened he brought the story to a sudden end with a single brief sentence. The story ran thus.

"The Bull.

One day me and my friend Bobby were flying a kite in a field next to my house and I said 'Now, Bobby'. Bobby said 'it goes well, 'cos I am flying it.' 'I could do better' I said. 'No you couldn't do better.' 'Don't crash it Bobby. There is a bull behind you Bobby, turn around.' Bobby said 'no there isn't.' 'Why has the cow got horns?' Bobby said 'it is a bull, run for your life.' Me and Bobby ran home." '

At first I was disappointed by the blandness of the ending, which I was inclined to attribute to Paul's technical difficulties. I supposed that it had been so hard for him to write down what he wanted to write that by the time he had described the circumstances leading to the chase he had already written as much as he felt he could manage. Later, however, the ending of the story disappointed me less and I became less certain that it was Paul's technical limitations which had forced it upon him. I was struck, rather, by the animated way in which he described the occasion, using nothing but dialogue: the excited banter between the two boys as the kite becomes airborne and the sudden transition from mockery to headlong flight. In talking about his adventure Paul had said nothing about the dialogue between himself and Bobby but a great deal about the actual chase. In his reconstruction of the adventure in written form, on the other hand, it is the circumstances surrounding the chase that have become, as it were, the adventure, rather than the action of the chase itself. Each account captured in its own way the memorableness of the event.

Yet Paul did not in the end ignore completely the details of the chase, as my notes went on to explain.

'Monday, May 16th.

Later in the day, Stephen had suggested to Paul that he should try to improve on some of his spellings and he had gone over the writing with him, pointing out the more serious mistakes. Later still I asked Paul if he would like me to type out a corrected copy of his piece on the jumbo typewriter. We made a first typed version but Paul didn't like the way the type was crowded towards the top of the page and since I had also made several typing errors I said I would try again, spacing the piece out better. I explained to Paul, as far as I could, the use of inverted commas and asked him where one speech began and another ended and where the full stops should come, since I wanted to make sure I had understood his piece alright. He was able to tell me, though only after puzzling it out for himself. After I had typed the final sentence, "Me and Bobby ran home", he told me not to stop there but to add the words "and then we had tea and went to bed". It seemed to me that he had felt the ending to be too curt and had sensed the need for a quieter and more relaxed conclusion, which the conventional coda provided for him. It was a formal consideration, then, that appeared to have determined his decision to add this last clause.

There was still a space of almost half a page beneath the typed story and at first Paul suggested my cutting the paper, but when I expressed reluctance, I cannot now think for what reason, he changed his mind and decided to draw a picture in the space that was left, to illustrate his text: on this occasion entirely his own idea. It was late afternoon by now and I assumed that the promised picture would have to wait until tomorrow, but Paul didn't want to join in the game of 'mathematical ladders' with which Stephen was ending the day so he sat just outside the classroom and drew his picture. He drew the field, the fence, the bull, Bobby crying "help", his hair on end, and himself falling head first into the mud. There is also a tree beside the fence with a bird in a nest among the green of the tree top and an un-recognisable squirrel, which he pointed out to me, on the trunk. A larger bird is flying nearby but there is no sign of the kite, discarded of course at this point of the narrative. In the right-hand corner is that old smiling sun while across the sky roars a multi-coloured jet. I asked Paul what the aeroplane was doing there, assuming that he had added it for his own amusement, like the eagle in his tree painting. I was wrong. He explained to me that a plane had really flown over at that moment; it was this, he said, that had distracted him as he was clambering over the fence to escape the bull and had caused him to fall on his head in the mud.

So the sketch is in effect an extension of the narrative, adding elements and incidents which Paul had not had occasion, whether because of the struggle of writing or whether because he had felt no need, to include in the written piece. The drawing itself is extremely rough for Paul, hardly more than a scribble, but it is packed with meaning. When he coloured it in he scribbled across the sky with red and purple crayon. On showing the picture to me he explained that this was not a "scribble", the word he used himself, but the sunset, for, as he told me later, the sun had just been setting at the time. Here then is a story in words and pictures, the drawing complementing and extending the written narrative. [I can recall several similar examples earlier in the year. Consider how Sarah, for example, had elaborated her story of Peter and Sally and the rabbit in the box by drawing a picture of seven boxes in a row, with the rabbit jumping out of the last and smallest.]'

The story of the bull marked the beginning of a period of some two weeks that proved to be the climax of Paul's whole year's work. During this time his study of the natural world, and in particular his various attempts to record, and sometimes to transcend, his observation of nature in drawing and painting, led first to a momentary crisis in his work and then, through the successful resolution of the crisis, to a new sense of mastery and a new level of skill.

On the Wednesday after his story Paul spent most of the day at work on a model car which he had decided to make out of the offcuts of wood which Stephen Rowland kept in a box in the classroom for just such a purpose. It was the most ambitious model he had yet made and he did not finish it until the next morning. The model was a considerable triumph of invention in Paul's eyes, as indeed in Stephen's and mine, and he was still basking in his success on the Thursday afternoon when, with a dozen other children, he returned to the river for further observation of its life. He had intended to continue his observation back in the classroom on the Friday morning but as it happened his attention was then diverted to his model car again so that it was not until the following Monday that he found time to look more closely at the insects which he had found in the river and had brought back in a tank to the classroom. That Monday however was not to be a success.

'Monday, May 23rd.

After his varied successes of last week, today was a somewhat frustrating day for Paul. He arrived late, brought by his mother, having overslept. The family had spent yesterday, surely the warmest day of the year, at Skegness and had been late returning. Paul came over to have a look at the water tank, having caught most of its inhabitants himself on Thursday, and I suggested to him that he begin the day by studying the tank and by recording the life within it.

Thirteen of us had gone down to the river on Thursday afternoon, each person, on this occasion, with a clear aim in view. It had been a pleasant afternoon of relaxed inquiry. Some had been drawing or writing, others making bark rubbings, or looking for wood insects, or reading. Paul and Debra had gone in search of water creatures again. Paul was keen to catch more mayfly larvae so that he could try, among other things, to draw them again as he had done after our first trip to the river. Debra lost interest in fishing quite soon and wandered off but Paul stuck in one spot, just across the bridge, almost all afternoon, staring into the water and fishing with his net for whatever water creatures he could find. He caught mayfly larvae, as he had hoped, together with snails, prawns, water boatmen, and shiny black bettles that chased each other madly across the water among the lily leaves, as later they did across the surface of the water tank. Towards the end of the afternoon, as Debra and I, followed by Sarah, Louise and Gwyneth, were exploring the meadow across the river, we looked back towards the bridge to see Paul stretched out in the sun by the river, dozing.

Paul was pleased with his catch and with the afternoon and chatted away as I helped him carry the tank, full of weeds and insects, back to school. He had planned to study his catch on Friday morning and perhaps to draw the mayfly larva again, but on Friday he had become engrossed in the trailer he had made at home to go with his model car or jeep and in the excitement of adding to it and painting it the water tank was ignored. I didn't feel like pushing it into his attention; it could as well wait till Monday.

So today I was keen that Paul should study the tank — he had already on Friday stared into it from time to time. I had looked into the tank myself, first thing in the morning, and had noticed what seemed to be a dead fly on the bottom. I pointed it out to Paul who immediately exclaimed that it was not a fly but one of the waterboatmen. At first I thought he must be wrong but a closer look confirmed his judgement. Not that Paul himself had ever doubted it; but to me, with its wings apart and its body apparently smaller, the creature was unrecognisable as one of the waterboatmen caught on Thursday afternoon. We fished it out and put it under the microscope, detaching one of its wings and focussing on that. Paul was impressed by the mottled and streaked black and white image he could see through the microscope and he began to draw it, but after a minute or two he realised how hard this would be and gave up. Perhaps it was this small and unimportant failure that affected the rest of his day; at any rate, little seemed to go right with his drawing thereafter. First he drew one of the beetles and that was quite successful, he felt, but then he tried to draw the mayfly larva and he just couldn't get it right, not to his own satisfaction. We had placed the mayfly larva in an inspection jar so that Paul could study it more closely. Each time he began to draw it some particular detail defeated him: the legs, the head, the length of the body, the overall proportions. He stayed in the classroom after morning play while everyone else was at service, so as to continue his attempt to draw the larva, but his dissatisfaction only increased and by the end of the morning he had torn up every attempted sketch.

Perhaps it would have been better for us simply to have stared into the tank and talked about whatever we noticed, without bothering to draw or record, or even to identify by name the creatures we saw. I suspect that I myself was aiming at a spurious precision in the study of the tank, as if I were reluctant to accept that looking and talking was learning enough — as if drawing the creatures in the tank was the proper way to add precision to the romance of looking. If so I was being foolish. On the other hand, despite his own sense of failure, perhaps Paul had been helped to look more carefully by trying to draw what he saw. At any rate his dissatisfaction itself showed how well he appreciated what he saw. For all his disappointment with them, the drawings he threw away were much more accurate than, for example, the drawing of a waterboatman which Michelle had made on Friday and which both she and I had been quite pleased with. Indeed his drawings today were for the most part more accurate, and certainly more detailed, than those he himself had made after our first river trip. It seems that prolonged observation of the water insects themselves has lessened his satisfaction in his attempts to draw them, making him more self-conscious than before about the difference between what he draws and what he sees.

After dinner Paul stopped working on the water tank and turned his attention to writing. He returned to his drawings towards the end of the afternoon, partly at my instigation. I was anxious that he should achieve at least some success in his effort to draw the mayfly larva. By clearing up time he had finally managed to complete a drawing of the larva (see fig. 11) though he was still not really pleased with it.

(Dissatisfied though Paul was with it, this drawing, like the drawing of the beetle, is quite plainly the product of close observation. The larva's back is spotted and segmented; its wings are folded over below its head; the three tail feathers are carefully detailed; the gills are included at either side of the long body;

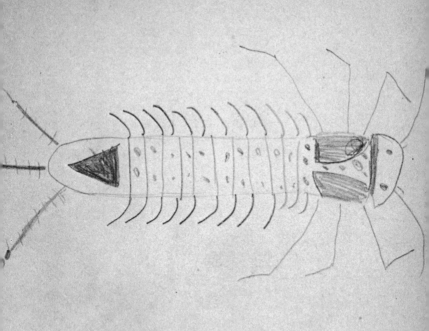

Fig. 11

two sets of feelers are indicated above the head. Paul persistently refused to add the legs, however, complaining that he couldn't make out their proper shape and position; in the end I had to draw them for him myself. The chief inaccuracy lies in the proportions of the larva's body. Incidentally, like the beetle in his earlier sketch of the day, but unlike his first insect sketches of the term, the larva is much enlarged, occupying the greater part of a sheet of A5 paper, and establishing, as it transpired, a pattern followed in all his subsequent drawings of insects.)

Meanwhile, the writing to which Paul had turned his attention immediately after dinner had satisfied him no more than his drawing. He had wanted to write "something exciting" but then we had begun talking about Skegness and he had told me about the stone which he had found yesterday and what a fine skimmer it had been. He decided to write about "The magic stone" and I thought he had in mind a story, based on his skimmer, in which the skimmer would turn out to be more than a mere stone. But he wrote only about the real stone and when I asked him if that was all he had intended to write about he said it was. It seemed he had intended the word magic in its colloquial sense of "wonderful" or "extraordinary", a simple superlative. When I read the story I couldn't make out the end because the spelling was so odd. Paul took it off me and read it to me but when he reached the end he too couldn't make it out and in his irritation he began to cross out the incomprehensible words. But before the whole piece was destroyed he suddenly remembered the crucial word — 'crab' (he'd spelt it "krod") — so the piece was preserved. Even so I think he was now displeased with it; when I asked him if he would like me to type it out, as I had typed out The Bull, the two of us correcting the spelling mistakes as we went through it, he said no, he didn't feel like having this story typed out. The story ran as follows:

"The Magic Stone.

One day I was at the sea and I saw a stone and I picked it up and I said 'it could be a skimmer'. I got a ruler and picked up the stone and threw the stone and the stone jumped a metre and 4 inches and I picked up the stone and a crab bit my toe and I went home."

The story is a brief summary of what Paul had told me at the start of the afternoon. Apart from its worse than usual spelling, even for Paul, it seemed to me a nice enough piece in its plain, straightforward way. Paul however felt it to be less than his best, and I think he was right. It is interesting to observe how far he has come this year: in the autumn and early spring I think he would have been more than pleased with himself for completing a story and two sketches in one day; now his own conception of himself and of his achievement demands something more. I don't want to give the impression that he was totally dissatisfied with his day's work; I don't think he was. He was simply less pleased with himself than he would have liked to be; indeed he complained to me about other aspects of the day besides his work, saying that he had had irritations in the playground too. Perhaps it was the penalty of oversleeping!'

The next day Paul arrived at school determined to prove himself.

'Tuesday, May 24th.

Today Paul achieved the very success that had eluded him yesterday. On entering the classroom he'd glanced again at the water tank, noting that most of its creatures were indeed still alive. I teased him about whether he shouldn't try drawing them again. "Not likely," he answered, in mock horror. As soon as our morning P.E. session was over he announced that he was going to draw a rabbit skull which he has had at school for some days now, wrapped up in tissue paper in his tray. I recalled, then, that he'd already declared his intention to draw this skull yesterday, towards the end of the day, after his dissatisfaction with that day's drawing and writing. He'd declared himself then as if in determination to recover his equanimity concerning his art work, as if to demonstrate again his prowess, under threat after his relative disappointments with the water creatures, as if to say "I'll do this one okay, anyway." Allied to this determination, perhaps, there was a sense that the skull was something chosen entirely by himself for drawing, a prized possession worthy of drawing rather than an exercise, an aspect of "water creature study," though I wouldn't want to make too much of this. [It is also worth noting that a skull, unlike a live insect, can be kept still. Remember how in the first week of term Paul had followed up his first sketch of live water insects with a grander drawing of a Great Diving Beetle modelled on a still photograph.] At any rate, he arrived at school this morning with the intention very much in the forefront of his mind and he had no hesitation about what he should do from the moment he got changed from P.E.

Paul had brought the skeleton of the skull of a rabbit to school one day last week. He'd come up to show it to me first thing, carefully unwrapping it from its tissue paper and proudly displaying it, pointing out its large, curved front teeth and how they could be taken out and put back in, explaining that it was a young rabbit, a "brer rabbit" as he called it. I think perhaps he meant that it was a buck rabbit; all he would say, however, was that it certainly was a brer rabbit though he didn't know why he called it that.

He'd wanted to draw the skull the day he brought it and had intended to, but he'd got taken up with other things and the skull had been left in his drawer. I'd forgotten he still had it at school until yesterday when he mentioned his intention again.

We fetched a large piece of green sugar paper which Paul chose himself, saying it was his favourite colour, and he carefully unwrapped his brer rabbit skull once more and placed it in front of him on the table. Soon after, he came to me to ask for glue so that he could stick the teeth in properly. I was a little reluctant to give it him, fearing that later he might want to extract the teeth and find that he couldn't, but it was extremely important for Paul that those two front teeth should be precisely the right length and when he pulled them out to the right length they just wouldn't stay put, but fell out altogether. (When, last week, he had first showed me the skull, he had pointed out that these front teeth should really stick further out but that they tended to slip back into the skull and thus to seem less prominent than they really were. I don't know how he had come to this conclusion — perhaps he had been told at home — but he had. He plainly felt it to be a matter of some importance and as I looked at the splendid boldness of the two curved fangs I could well appreciate his concern.) I could perhaps have said to Paul that he could always slip the teeth in just for a moment when he was actually drawing that part of the skull but I could see that this wouldn't do. He had propped the skull up on a small plastic jar in front of him and it was vital to him to have the skull posed there, motionless, like an artist's model, so that he could draw it just as it was, teeth correctly aligned and all. So with a dab of Marvin glue we stuck the front teeth in, propped the skull up delicately, and the drawing began.

Paul drew with very special care, as carefully as I'd ever seen him draw, looking and studying and copying what he saw (see fig. 12). At one point he asked me for help in getting the rough-shaped hole alongside the nose correctly drawn, but the rest he drew for himself, rubbing out occasionally but not often, working slowly in his accustomed manner, with many pauses for reflection, rest, or a momentary diversion, but always returning after a brief pause to the task at hand, which, I've no doubt, demanded just such a long-drawn-out effort, regularly interrupted and regularly revived. He drew the skull larger than life-size and yet not very large in comparison with the size of the sugar paper. First he drew a two-stepped plinth on which to mount or place the drawn skull — an imagined plinth, more grandiose than the plastic jar the skull was actually resting on — and on top of that the skull itself. The skull was drawn from one

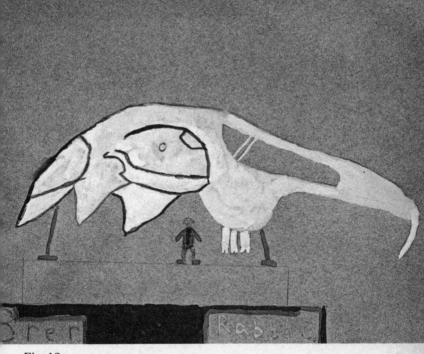

Fig. 12

side and Paul included in his drawing only what could be seen from this particular point of view. He was careful to show the pin-shaped hole which he could see in the opposite eye socket, and the small piece of bone crossing the nose bone on the opposite side of the skull but revealed through the gap in the side he was looking at. He drew, with due precision, the one front tooth he could see as he looked in front of him, and the three side teeth. Not only were the details exact but the proportions too, the chief flaw being the overlarge protuberance beaneath the eye socket.

Up to this point, except for the plinth, Paul's drawing had been an exact copy of what he saw before him. Then, towards the end of the morning, a transformation took place. It began with Paul adding at either end of his drawn skull two struts which served as supports, propping it up on its plinth. Next, right underneath the skull's hollowed eye, he drew a tiny figure, a little man. I was surprised, to say the least, by this sudden development and

asked Paul whether it was indeed a man he had drawn under
the skull. It was. The skull had become suddenly monstrous.
Later Paul explained his developing intention to Stephen. He
had drawn the skull at first, he said, the right size, and then had
enlarged it, made it into a monster. Stephen pointed out that he
hadn't drawn it the right size because the skull as drawn was
already much larger than the real skull. Ah yes, Paul explained,
but it was the size it would have been if it had been the skull of
a fully grown rabbit rather than a young one. In fact it was a
good deal bigger than that, but at least relatively the scale was
still realistic, as if drawn just a little larger than life-size. And
then, having drawn a little-larger-than-life-size skull, Paul had
suddenly, it seemed, perceived it as monstrous in size and added
the tiny figure underneath in confirmation of its monstrosity. The
midget figure utterly transforms the scale of the picture. I
wouldn't want to explain the cause of this development, which
I'm fairly sure was not part of Paul's original intention, but it's
true that when you look at the skull on its plinth with its two
struts, it's easy, even without the little figure, to read it as a huge
sculpture; and I suspect that with the little figure it's impossible
not to read it in these terms.

In the afternoon, Paul painted his drawing, asking me to find for
him an especially thin small brush, and painting precisely and
delicately, the skull white, edged in black to pick out the lines,
the teeth cream-coloured. He asked me to help him mix the
colours for the teeth and kept on protesting that I wasn't getting
the colour absolutely exact. Finally he asked me to put a blob of
paint on the teeth themselves to see if the colour matched. I
thought it did. Paul wasn't sure, or perhaps he was just making a
point of disagreeing, since he went on to use it anyway. The
struts supporting the skull he painted red, and the bottom of the
plinth blue with the name "Brer Rabbit" written along it. The
little man had a buttoned sweater, red and black, with green
trousers and red shoes. By that time, mid-afternoon, Paul had
done as much as he wanted for the day. He told me I could cut
part of the rest of the sugar paper off and put the picture up on
the wall. But it wasn't finished, he said, and he'd probably add
more figures to it tomorrow. (He didn't, in fact, do anything
more to it the following day.) As it is now, the painting matches
the drawing in its clarity and precision and the whole picture has
a delicacy and refinement that is a new development for Paul

though foreshadowed in the picture of his go-cart and the shark-infested pond of last term. Note how the task took up the greater part of the day. It demanded no less, either in the time it took or in the continuous and more or less singleminded attention it called for, together with the many pauses. It required both space and continuity to be completed.'

In the course of the year Paul had subjected many of his paintings to various kinds and degrees of transformation but never as sensationally as on this occasion. The tiny skull turned monstrous surpassed, as much in its daring as in its delicacy, any of his previous pictures: either the Autumn Term's paintings of birds, the Spring Term's go cart, or the tree he had painted a week or two earlier in the Summer Term. There was an economy of means and a degree of calculation about this particular painting that none of the earlier pictures possessed to such a degree. As I looked at the painting on the evening of the day on which he had painted it, I felt that it summed up a whole year's work, and at the end of my notes that evening I described my impression in words which still seem appropriate, even if in the excitement of the moment I was tempted to exaggerate: 'I find in the combination of careful drawing and fantasy, the monstrous transformation of the precise skull, an image of Paul himself, of the unity of competence and creativity in his art and of the manysidedness of his simultaneous grasp and transformation of reality.'

The painting of the skull had been Paul's response to the relative failure, as he saw it, of his latest attempt to sketch the water insects. Nevertheless the new precision which he achieved in painting the rabbit skull reflected, in part, the value of his earlier life studies, including those of the previous day, however much the latter may have disappointed him at the time. Now, in its turn, the conspicuous success of this response encouraged him to return to the study of water insects and to try once more to draw them. As it happened, insect life became a dominant theme in many children's classroom activity that week. Every day since Paul had brought back from the river the tank full of creatures, there had been children around it, usually one or two at a time, staring into the water for a minute or two and exchanging comments on what they noticed: a previously unspotted creature, an oddity of behaviour, some strange or comic parallel between insect behaviour and human behaviour. Then, on Wednesday, the day after Paul's painting, a mayfly hatched out of its larva at the very moment when a group of us were watching it. It was one of those extraordinary pieces of good fortune that from time to time reward the keen observer. Paul was not one of the group who saw the mayfly emerge, having been engaged on a piece of mathematics at the time, so I called him over.

'Wednesday, May 25th.

At the very beginning of it all, when we first realised that a mayfly had emerged, I called over to Paul to come and look since, after all, the larva had been his catch, and his pleasure and concern this past week. He came, looked and enjoyed but then returned to the number work with which he was struggling and I felt at first that maybe he had decided not to show too much interest, as if he were irritated that it hadn't happened while he himself was looking and determined not to fuss about it. But I think it was just that mathematics was his chief concern there and then and he felt he could afford only a moment's distraction. Later, the satisfaction he felt became clear. He came up to me just before dinner when he could get me on my own to say "this time when we go down" — to the river, he meant — "I'm going to look for all the ones with the humps on," which is how he describes the mayfly larvae. And then this afternoon he looked carefully at the Pond Life book which I showed him, deciding which was the species of mayfly larva he had drawn and making sure that his name was down for returning to the river tomorrow afternoon.'

On the Thursday morning Paul brought a dead bumble bee to school to look at under the microscope. He had already, the previous day, been studying the dead waterboatman again under the microscope and had discovered its remarkable eye, like a microphone head, silvery hexagons in great profusion. But we found it hard to focus on the bee's eye and a little later in the morning Paul left the bee to join a group of four children watching another mayfly larva which had risen to the top of the tank and looked as if it might be about to hatch. They watched for about half an hour, passing occasional comments as before: about the mayfly larva's spasmodic jerks as it seemed to be trying to escape from its casing; about its gills and the loss of one of its legs; about the way in which one of the waterboatmen would rise to the surface of the tank once in a while or clutch at a piece of thin weed or sediment. The larva didn't hatch however and after dinner Paul came to tell me that it was floating on top of the water, dead. We picked it out and put it away for later dissection.

In the afternoon eight of the class returned to the river.

'Thursday, May 26th.

Paul, Debra, Sarah, Louise, Mark, Robert, David and Simon came down to the river with Gilly and me this afternoon. It was even warmer than in the morning despite a stiff breeze and we had a quiet afternoon, fishing, sketching, reading, chatting, writing. Paul and Louise caught three exceptionally large waterboatmen, quite a different species from those which we have netted before. The two which Paul caught appeared to be mating and remained on top of each other in the tank all afternoon. There were also dragonfly nymphs, but the mayfly larvae all seemed to have vanished. (Perhaps they'd all hatched?) So Paul caught no more of the ones with humps though he was more than satisfied with what he had caught, especially the monster waterboatmen.'

It was on the following day that Paul again attempted to draw the water insects.

'Friday, May 27th.

Paul arrived this morning with a plastic water carrier covered in a fringed leather bag, in which he intended to take home the waterboatmen he caught yesterday. I had promised him yesterday that he could take them this evening to put in the pond in his garden. After a general look at the tank which revealed that one of the dragonfly nymphs was already dead, he fished out one of the large waterboatmen and placed it in the small inspection jar. Then, without any suggestion from Stephen or myself, he drew it, considerably enlarged, filling most of a sheet of A5 paper as Monday's drawings had. There could not have been a more striking contrast between the way in which he set to work drawing the waterboatman today and the way in which he had tried to draw the mayfly larva at the start of the week. Today he drew quickly and confidently; nothing was torn up, little rubbed out, and there seemed few problems over the proportions of the drawing or the details of the creature being drawn. He didn't once summon Stephen or myself to his assistance and he was dismissive about my one suggestion,

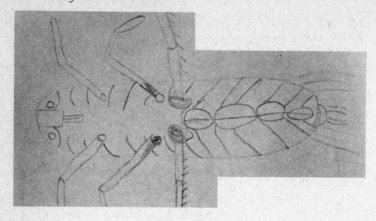

Fig. 13

towards the end of his drawing, not so much because he
disagreed with it — it was about the drawing of the
waterboatman's front legs — as because I was interrupting him
in a process of thought and action which he was perfectly happy
to finish off for himself uninterrupted. By 10 o'clock or
thereabouts the drawing was done: a very rapid piece of work for
Paul.

The drawing (see fig. 13) has a fluency, almost, in places, a
casualness, of line which distinguishes it from all his previous
insect drawings, yet it is at the same time more knowledgeable
and more studied. The waterboatman is viewed from its
underside (this particular species swimming mostly upside down).
Its oars are given the furry fringe or trimming which Paul had
spotted as he inspected them. Both legs and oars are carefully
sectioned and Paul has tried to indicate, a little roughly in
places, how these limbs are connected to the underside of the
body. The body itself is scored with lines representing its various
segments and markings and at its tail Paul has drawn the tiny
hairs around the waterboatman's air bubble. The head too is
carefully marked.

A small sign of how well Paul knew what he was about came
when he glanced at another boy's drawing of the same
waterboatman, and was at once able to show him that he had
placed the legs at the wrong side of the oars. Today there was no
discrepancy between observation and record. As Paul drew he

continued to observe. He was particularly interested in the silvery appearance of the new waterboatman, a point he took up sometime this morning with Stephen. Stephen reports it as follows:

"We were looking at the giant waterboatmen and Paul noticed that they appeared to have silvery blotches on their undersides (which are usually turned uppermost). He wanted to know why this silvery colouring disappears when the creature is out of the water. I fetched a wax crayon and we saw how that also becomes speckled in silver when immersed in water. We also tried spreading or painting water onto the surface of the crayon and saw how the water collects into little blobs. It seemed as though the wax crayon, and also the waterboatman's underside, tried to repel the water. Paul said that this was like trying to paint on plastic. When you paint on paper, he said, the paper 'sucks in' the paint, but when you try to paint on plastic, the plastic 'pushes away' the paint. Paul clearly saw that the observed silvery effect on the waterboatman and on the crayon, and the effect of paint on wax and plastic, were in some way related, though he would not, of course, have been altogether clear about the nature of this relationship." '

In contemplating Paul's achievement during these two weeks in the middle of May I have often been reminded of the following passage from one of David Hawkins' essays in *The Informed Vision**.

'In one of his most important writings on education** (which, incidentally, does not contain the word in its index) John Dewey says this about spontaneity of artistic expression: "Works of art often present to us an air of spontaneity, a lyric quality, as though they were the unpremeditated song of a bird. But man, whether for- tunately or unfortunately, is not a bird. His most spontaneous outbursts, if expressive, are not overflows of momentary internal pressures. The spontaneous in art is complete absorption in subject matter that is fresh, the freshness of which holds and sustains emotion; staleness of matter and obtrusion of calculation are the two enemies of spontaneity of expression."

If one were to try to formulate the quality of any achievement of learning, at its best, one could hardly find a better formulation than "complete absorption in subject matter that is fresh, the freshness of which holds and sustains emotion" — or of the opposite quality, in "staleness of matter and obtrusion of calculation" . . . But we should not forget that *human* expression, for Dewey, is no mere display or

* *The Informed Vision*, David Hawkins, Agathon, N.Y., 1974.
** *Art and Experience*.

outburst; it is a synthesized achievement, compatible, as Dewey goes on to say, "with any amount of labour, provided the results of that labour emerge in complete fusion with an emotion that is fresh." '

It seemed to me at the time, as it still seems now, that Paul's experience illustrated and confirmed this passage. Certainly his achievement was the product of "complete absorption in subject matter that is fresh": the life of the river, the rabbit skull, the love of representation and transformation by means of drawing and painting. But this achievement was only made possible by "any amount of labour", including the apparently fruitless labour of the Monday when nothing seemed to go right. Paul's labour moreover involved a significant degree of calculation, but the calculation was never obtrusive; throughout the fortnight, except perhaps on that Monday, the results of his labour "emerge in complete fusion with an emotion that is fresh".

The new sense of mastery which Paul derived from this achievement could be seen in almost all his remaining work of the summer term. From this time on his drawing acquired a greater freedom, without any loss of control, and in the few weeks of the school year that were left to him he completed a series of further, remarkable sketches of water creatures and of a moth, together with a last large painting. Before describing these final works of his school year, however, I want to return to his writing. On Monday, May 23rd his writing had disappointed him no less than his drawing. He did not write again until the Tuesday of the following week although in the meantime, after sketching the waterboatman on Friday, he had decided that he would, after all, make a neat copy of his short piece of writing *The Magic Stone,* with improved spelling. (This, of course, was after he had already successfully resolved the momentary crisis in his art and it may have been the success of his new sketch that encouraged him to look again, less gloomily, at his previous writing.) I am not sure whether, when he began his next piece of writing, his previous disappointment was still in his mind, but the new story improved upon its predecessor in much the same way as the drawing of the waterboatman had improved upon the drawing of the mayfly nymph, forming an appropriate coda to the fortnight that had just passed.

'Tuesday, May 31st.

We all went down to the hall first thing this morning to rehearse

Gwyneth and Louise's play which we are putting on for the
Thursday morning service . . . Back in the classroom, the
rehearsal over, Paul sat down to write. He asked me for an idea
and we began the usual preliminary conversation: that casting
around for a theme, a plot, an incident, a subject for
composition. Out of the blue Paul suddenly ventured as a theme
his first day at school. Stephen had given this theme to the class,
as a possible subject for writing, at the very beginning of the year
and Paul had at that time dictated to Stephen a somewhat
disjointed account of the first few days he had spent in Stephen's
class. I don't know whether Paul had suddenly remembered the
title of this earlier composition or whether he had simply recalled
his own very first day at Sherard school four years ago. I had
asked him if there were any other dramatic occasions in his own
life, like the bull chase he had written about earlier, which might
serve as a theme; it seemed that his very first day at school was
one such occasion. But did he really remember it, I asked him.
"Yes," he replied, with an expression of ironic wonder, and at
once he began to tell me how he had come into school with his
mum and had looked around him and had asked where the
classrooms were because what he could see looked like halls, not
classrooms. When he finally reached his classroom it was so large
and imposing he started yelling and then walked off, right out of
the school. He told me about his teacher too and the funny
things she used to do.

His conversation was so vivid and impassioned — calmly
impassioned, the events recalled with an excitement rendered
objective and ironic by the passage of time — that I said
something like this: "fine, now try and write that down just as
you've said it." But of course writing is not like that and Paul
couldn't and wouldn't have wanted to write it down as he had
said it. [An aside at this point in my original notes suggests that
it was now that I first began to clarify in my own mind the
essential difference, for children no less than for adult writers,
between the art of writing and that of conversation.*] I watched
Paul as he set about writing and at first I was inclined, as I have
often been, to ascribe the slowness and painfulness of the process
of writing, for him, to his technical problems with spelling,
handwriting, the putting down of words onto the page. But I
think there was more to it than that. The difficulty of writing

* See Chapter Two.

reflected the problem of accommodating a memory which had readily been retold, into an appropriate written form. This problem was complicated and aggravated by Paul's technical limitations but not reducible to them. He was unable, as I now interpreted his actions, merely to write down what he had said; he had first to translate the spoken anecdote into the more self-enclosed and formalised medium of writing.

It took Paul most of the morning and part of the afternoon to finish his piece, with occasional interventions from myself, and also from Stephen, to help him decide how to continue. This is what he wrote:

"One day I was at school. It was my first day at school. Mum was talking to Mrs Brown and I was stroking Sherry [Sherry is the name of the school cat]. Mum came out Mrs Brown's. Mum took my hand and I wouldn't go and I started screaming and I said to Mrs Brown 'there is no classroom so I won't go', so I walked out the school. Mum chased me and caught me and Mrs Brown put me in a classroom."

Every incident in the written account had been included in what Paul had told me or Stephen, but not vice versa. Or rather, on reflection, I think that everything he had told us *is* included in what he wrote but in an attenuated and compressed form. At first glance the compression robs the story of much of the excitement that came across as Paul talked about it; and yet it has a certain excitement of its own, a tension that runs throughout the brief narrative. Consider for example the sequence of tenses, from the imperfect tense at the start where Paul recalls the occasion as if it were a picture, or scene, before his eyes, to the historic tense as the story gathers pace with his mother's emerging from the head's office. Consider, too, the sequence of incident: the stroking of Sherry, the reappearance of mum, the decisive "took my hand", and the climax that follows as Paul refuses to go, for fear of the apparent absence of classrooms, and walks out only to be chased, caught, and sent back. Notice the finality of the concluding sentence with its strong verbs and its air of resignation to the inevitable: "mum chased me and caught me and Mrs Brown put me in a classroom". There was, after all, a classroom, if only by virtue of Mrs Brown's insistence.'

This story of his first day at school was composed in the week before half term. Paul's final drawings and paintings of the year followed shortly after the half term holiday at the beginning of June. On the day the class returned to school after the holiday we made one last visit to the river where Paul continued as before to fish for the water creatures that had so strongly caught his fancy.

'Thursday, June 9th.

This afternoon twelve children went down to the river, with Gilly and me. Paul fished for water insects and snails again. It occurred to me afterwards that perhaps fishing for creatures and observing them was now becoming too simple a formula for Paul, and lacking in precision. But on further reflection I have decided not. To begin with there is his own clear and deep satisfaction in the activity. This morning he told me that if we weren't going down to the river today he wasn't coming to school again. He spoke with mocking tone but serious purpose. This afternoon he knew exactly what he wanted to do. He and I were to carry the water tank back from the classroom to the river to return its creatures, most of whom are still alive, to the water. Then he would fish for more creatures, some of which would be new kinds, he hoped, and we would bring them back in the tank to the classroom for further study.

Once we reached the river Paul went straight across the bridge to his favourite fishing place and spent the whole hour and a quarter of our visit in search of new finds. By now he has become very successful at catching creatures and releasing them from his net into the tank. He discovered yet another species of waterboatman, miniature versions of the large ones, together with a very large shrimp, a strange red-brown beetle or bug, another mayfly larva, snails, and various other minute creatures. The river is murkier now, lower, more weedy; the water lilies are growing fast and spreading out across the water. We caught many more waterboatmen as the afternoon wore on, all of them tiny, and collected weed for them as well as a lily pad to cover the top of the tank. I feel sure, now that I am writing about the day, that for Paul the time for looking, finding, catching and studying is by no means yet past. This afternoon David was his companion, accompanying him more for the pleasure of companionship than out of a shared interest, though he too fished and watched. Looking at the waterboatmen he observed: "they go off like a bomb but when they don't move they *WILL NOT* move, no matter what to do".'

Work on the insects continued in the classroom the following morning but it was not until the Wednesday of the next week that I had occasion to describe this Friday's work in my notes.

'Wednesday, June 15th.

A word or two now about Paul's work last Friday. On Friday morning I suggested to him that he might try to count and list the different kinds of creatures he had in the water tank. I was trying to get him away from the feeling that he had to *draw* the insects in order to record his observation or study of them. The idea of counting them appalled him. He said that they would never keep still long enough, although in reality he had a good idea of just how many of the larger and more conspicuous creatures there were, having identified them all as he caught them down at the river. However he liked the idea of listing the various creatures he could spot in the tank. But he chose to list them by drawing each kind of creature. (So much for my attempt to wean him away from drawing.) So for the early part of the morning he stood by the tank, propping up an improvised writing table alongside it — a box to the side of which he pinned his paper — and proceeded to draw the different kinds of creatures in the tank. He drew them much enlarged, grumbling to himself from time to time about how the beetle would not keep still long enough for him to see it properly or about how some particular insect was really too hard to draw. The scale of enlargement varied considerably since each creature was made roughly the same size. It was the size of the paper that determined the size of enlargement, as it had done with his earlier insect sketches.

Paul drew without hesitation; his pencil strokes are faint but not at all tentative and each creature is presented as a simple, forceful image. He drew the redbrown beetle, seen sideways on; a snail, seen from above, its head and feelers protruding from its shell which was drawn as a simple spiral; a leech, and a minute unidentified creature. Around the first three creatures he drew water weed, decoratively placed to enhance the formal effect of the sketch. Some of the creatures which he noticed in the tank he nevertheless chose not to draw at all; these were the creatures which he had already drawn earlier in the term: the mayfly larva, the waterboatman, and the large black water beetle. He explained to me that because he already had drawings of these creatures he could simply add the old drawings to the new to make up his collection of all the creatures observable in the tank now.

Then, after morning play, he decided to draw the entire tank. He cut out a sheet of sugar paper in the shape of the plastic water tank and began to draw the water weed, the lily pads, and the creatures in the water. The lily pad he drew in perspective as seen from water level looking in at the side of the tank. Alongside the lily pad, and in the same perspective, he drew some of the oddments of weed that floated on the water surface. Lower down he added the strings of weed that lay across the tank down in the water, distributing them across the paper with an eye to formal effect again, it seemed to me, as much as in accordance with what he could see as he looked in. He had moved the water tank to the table at which he painted in order to be able to look at it as he drew the outlines of his picture but once he had completed the lily pad and water weed he largely abandoned direct observation, using, instead, his previous sketches of water creatures as the models for the creatures which he now drew in the water. The chief exceptions were the snails, which he drew clinging to the sides of the drawn tank, as he could observe them doing on the tank itself. It is quite clear, as one looks at his picture, that he has modelled his creatures on his previous drawings rather than on immediate observation, especially in the case of the waterboatman. This procedure helped him to draw without the distraction caused by the rapid and frequent movements of the creatures in the tank itself but at the same time it in turn distracted him from the problem of scale so that the creatures he drew are for the most part much larger than in real life, almost filling the tank. I think it was Sally who pointed this out to Paul. He looked, smiled, and chided, somewhat conventionally, "well it's only a painting": a rare admission for Paul and increasingly uncharacteristic. (Paul has often rearranged reality for his own benefit in his paintings but usually with any amount of subtle interplay between the elements of reality and fancy and with all kinds of explanation to offer. He would not normally want to say, I think, that a painting is just a painting.) I was myself uneasy with the uneven distortions of

scale in his picture and I somehow feel that Paul too considered
it to be one of his less satisfactory pictures once he'd finished
painting it at the end of the morning. For all its ambition — and
perhaps it was simply too ambitious, considering the minuteness
of the creatures relative to the size of the tank — it did not have
the finesse of the early morning sketches that had led up to it. It
did, however, serve to complete Paul's compilation of water
creatures.'

If, on this occasion, Paul's painting failed to live up to the
expectations aroused by his sketches, at the beginning of the
following week painting and drawing were to be combined more
fruitfully, and perhaps with a greater degree of calculation, in his
differing treatment of another insect brought into the classroom for
observation: a moth.

'Tuesday, June 10th.

I was not in school yesterday but Stephen had told me over the
phone last night how Paul had spent part of the day excitedly
engaged on a piece of mathematics and much of the rest of the
day at work on two startling sketches of a moth which he had
brought to school that morning in a jam jar. This morning, when
I arrived late, having had to come by train, Paul came up to
show me his new find. "Here, come and look at this," he insisted,
half-nodding, half-shaking his head. It was a large greyish moth,
veined like a leaf, its wings shading into brown. Paul had put
leaves and grass into the jar alongside the moth but it was only
an ordinary jam jar and the moth was presssed up against the
side. I said that it looked dead — he had left it at school
overnight it seemed — at which he grew indignant, gently poking
it to demonstrate that it was still very much alive. (Later in the
day I looked in various library books to see if we could identify
it, but without success.)

Paul wanted, now, to make a large painting of the moth and I
helped him select a sheet of sugar paper for the purpose. He
chose brown, having wanted but failed to find a pale blue paper.
He sat down at the painting table, set the jam jar beside him,
stared into it and began drawing in pencil the outline he would
later paint, following his usual custom. First he drew the body,
after an unsuccessful early attempt at the moth's wings. He drew
it as he saw it, looking down into the jar: a bird's eye view from

over the moth's back. He made it very large, the body over a foot long and quite thick though not in fact proportionately as thick at the head as on the moth itself. Then he started again on the wings. He sketched in one wing quickly enough but the other proved more difficult. He was anxious to make the wings symmetrical but couldn't seem to manage it, and was in no way reassured by my suggestion that there were probably many minor discrepancies between the creature's two wings. I noticed him using a ruler to try and measure the length of the wing which he had already drawn, so that he could get the other wing exactly right. But even this presented a problem, for it wasn't easy to decide where precisely to measure from. I noticed him trying out various measurements and seeming dissatisfied with each. "I can't get it exact" he kept muttering to himself and at last, after several attempts and several rubbings out, he called me over to help. I helped him draw the outline of the second wing although in fact I was no better, if not indeed rather worse, at it than Paul himself. He waited until I had got the wing more or less right and then said "I'll do it now," taking over from me and further correcting my drawing. The wing was still not as exact as he would have liked but he felt it would do. Then he asked me where he should place the moth's eyes. Looking down at the creature in the jar I felt that the eyes were not visible from the angle from which he had chosen to draw the moth, but Paul insisted, and added an eye, in perspective, at either side of the head: curved crescents that looked immediately convincing once he had sketched them in and became still more effective when he painted them, later.

The painting began towards the end of the morning, after play and morning service, and carried on into the afternoon, remaining unfinished at the end of the day. Paul worked slowly at it, with bouts of disillusion and occasional demands for help, and with a few longish pauses. By clearing up time he had finished painting the body and head, together with one of the wings. I told him that I thought he just had time to paint in the other wing, using up the rest of the paint he had mixed for himself, but by that time he felt that he had had enough of painting for the day so picture and spare paint were set aside for tomorrow. We had had a spot of trouble mixing the colours themselves. The grey of the body was easy enough — I helped Paul mix this — and after painting in the body grey Paul had added two small patches of deep red at the inside edges of the wings, in imitation of the colouring he had observed on the more widely spread of the real moth's wings as he looked into the jar. But neither of us could find the right shade of greyish brown for the main part of the wings. Paul kept on rejecting the various colours I mixed and it was some while before we achieved what he regarded as a rough approximation.

It was only at the end of the morning that I saw the two sketches of his moth which Paul had drawn yesterday. They are completely different from his painting of today and in many ways more daring. One is drawn from the front, looking straight at the moth's head on an eye level with the head. The other is drawn from the side, the moth's wings drawn up. These sketches convey an intensely dramatic image of the moth; the vigorous, rapid drawing stands in marked contrast to the large placidity, the ornamentalism — as of a moth pinned on card — of today's painting. Today, however, Paul himself tended to dismiss them. He pointed to a misleading effect, as of horns, on the first sketch; he seemed to find both of them too casual in treatment. I suspect it was just that today's attempted precision was at stake and the impressionism of yesterday's sketches was therefore temporarily less appealing to him . . .

Wednesday, June 15th.

This morning Paul completed his painting (see fig. 14). He had taken the moth home last night in its jar and had not brought it back this morning. He had let the moth go, he said, but it had stayed in the jar. I asked whether it might be a good idea to take it out of the jar to let it free. He had done so, he replied, but the moth had not moved except to shuffle along. Later in the morning I learnt that he had not found the moth at home as I had assumed; it was his grandad who had found it, while on holiday, and had brought it back home for Paul.

Paul began by completing the painting of the main part of the moth's second wing, using the brown paint mixed yesterday and stored away at the end of yesterday afternoon. He was pleased to find it still in fit condition for use, though I suggested he should thin it down a little. It was typical of him that after finishing the second wing he repainted the yellow veins or lines running down the main part of each wing. He had painted these veins in

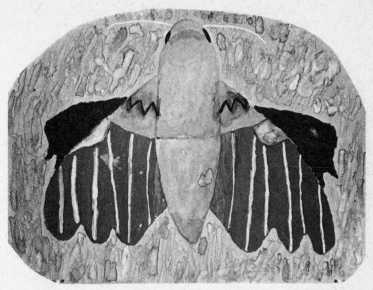

Fig. 14

yellow yesterday, before filling in the rest of the wing in brown, and the yellow veins had been partially obscured by overlapping brown paint. So now he retouched them before sitting back to think about what to paint next. He decided to paint two small patches at the edge of each wing, as yet unpainted, and asked me what colour he should use. We fixed on another shade of grey, mixing white and black with a little brown. But before he filled in these areas he retouched yet another part of the painted wings. Yesterday, before tackling the main part of the wings, he had painted the top of each wing, nearest the moth's head, grey. In so doing he had painted over the V shaped markings which he had pencilled in, at the top of each wing, on his preliminary drawing. Now he picked out these chevrons in black paint. That done, he filled in the two small patches, the right hand one with my assistance, and then he started on the two smaller wings which he had pencilled in behind and above the main wings on either side. He decided to paint these smaller wings black. When I saw them painted I felt that he had treated them less carefully than the rest of his painting, as if he was getting tired of painting, and I noticed that a tiny patch at the tip of one of the wings was still unpainted. I was less happy about his choice of colour on this occasion too, although Paul was decisive about it. On looking at the finished painting however, I noticed that Paul had gone over the smaller wings a second time, adding the missing patch and tidying up the edges of the painting.

In its final colouring the painted moth was less accurate a representation of the real moth than the preliminary drawing had led me to believe it would be. This may have been partly because Paul no longer had the moth itself beside him today, and partly because of the difficulty both he and I had experienced in making up the exact colours he wanted. (Perhaps, in this and certain other respects, Paul could have made good use, on this occasion, of a level of technical expertise which I, at any rate, was unable to offer him. I might well, on reflection, have sought the advice of Janet [the school's art specialist].) But I would tentatively propose that the discrepancy between the painted moth and the real moth was also due to Paul's sense of appropriate colour values — of the blending and contrasting of colours — and to his desire to distinguish, by means of colouring, the different segments and layers of the moth's outstretched wings. In any case, the painted moth was an imposing sight, grand in the manner of the real thing, however lavishly heightened in colour.

But that wasn't the end of the painting, for Paul now asked me how he should treat the background of his picture. I said I would myself be inclined to leave it as it was but Paul wasn't satisfied with that. (I recall the backgrounds he painted on his pictures of birds in the Autumn Term. He is less insistent nowadays on filling every part of the background of his paintings but he still prefers the background not to be entirely empty. The barest of all his backgrounds is that of his painting of the rabbit skull and this is partly explained by the fact that in the end he chose not to complete the picture by adding more tiny figures around the skull as he had at first intended.) He began to paint broad green strokes across the background all around the moth, representing the leaves and grasses against which the moth was placed. I assumed that he had in mind the greenery at the bottom of the jam jar in which the moth had lain but he told me he was thinking of where the moth had been found by his grandad. The grasses finished, he was still not completely satisfied and thought at first of adding trees and a fence, as, he assured me, in the spot where the moth had been found. I tried to persuade him against this however on the grounds that it would look odd to set his greatly enlarged moth among apparently much smaller trees and a minute fence. I'm not sure whether he appreciated the point or indeed whether I was right, but in the end, admittedly after much prompting by me, he discarded the idea of fence and trees and chose instead — for he insisted on adding something else whatever my doubts — to add a number of eggs among the greenery above the moth. (There had been a mass of eggs on the leaves in the jam jar with the moth.) The eggs are yellow, barely visible among the green brush strokes and quite large, very roughly in scale with the moth. Having painted in the eggs he added still more green brush strokes all around the moth till the background of the picture was almost filled with green. Finally he cut the sugar paper into the shape of a shallow arch, thus

As so often in the past, his decision to paint in a background was wholly justified in the event. The moth stood out sharply against the bright green brush strokes, which provided a much livelier setting than the dullish, pale brown sugar paper. The background turned the painted image of a moth into a more complete picture. It broods over the classroom, now, as the rabbit skull did before it.'

The portrait of the moth, and the two sketches that preceeded it, appeared to signify a further development in Paul's conception of art. The impressionism of the two sketches represented, I think, Paul's immediate response to the object and to the task of drawing it. Their success depended in part, I think, on the careful precision of previous drawings; in the freedom and roughness with which he now sketched a moth, Paul recalled and absorbed the lessons he had learnt in several weeks of close study of water insects and how to draw them. But Paul went further. He seemed to regard the sketches, retrospectively at least, as no more than preliminary drawings in the furtherance of a grander design. It was the painting of the moth that was to be his definitive statement, requiring a degree of calculation that would have been inappropriate in the sketches. In the end the painting achieved perhaps only a part, though a major part, of Paul's intentions. His technique was not yet wholly adequate for the task he had set himself and in viewing the process by which he painted his picture we can see him attempting to extend the technical boundaries of his skill. The sketches may therefore have seemed more remarkable than the painting. Yet I think it is most particularly in the inter-relationship of sketches and painting, though Paul himself may have been no more than half conscious of it, that we may perceive the growth of his understanding and the direction in which the sustained practice of his art was leading him.

Paul left school before the end of term to go on holiday with his parents. Only one week remained after his painting of the moth and in that time he began to experiment in a different aspect of art, making patterns in two and three dimensions on the turntable which we had in the classroom and on a small spinning disc. A whole new area of inquiry opened up for him which he barely had time to explore before his own term ended, although his first experiments were full of promise. Thus diverted from his insects, he made no further life studies and the portrait of the moth was thus his last picture of the year, bringing to a fitting conclusion a term of intense inquiry into the natural world and how to represent it in art. Paul's summer studies were, for me, the most appealing of all the examples, within Stephen Rowland's class, of knowledge as appropriation and of the growth of intellect as a consequence of a child's successive attempts to appropriate knowledge through sustained practice, whether in art, science, literature, mathematics or any particular form of thought. When Paul departed for his holiday, on June 24th, I was left regretting only that circumstances would prevent me from following him, and the other children in the class, up into the third year juniors to see what happened next.

6 The Intellectual Life of Play

I spent the greater part of my first day in Stephen's classroom helping or watching Robbie as he constructed a cotton reel tank, of a kind which I used to build and race myself when I was a boy. It was my first experience of model making in a primary school classroom and introduced me to a range of activity and a pattern of thought that came to seem of particular importance in the children's intellectual growth as the year progressed. I had met Robbie for the first time early that morning when I noticed him standing by a woodwork bench which had been set up on the open verandah outside Stephen's classroom, watching three boys who were building model boats. I asked him whether there was anything which he would like to build himself to which he replied that "Mr Rowland" had suggested making something "that worked", only he could not think what. Casting around in my mind for some object that might fulfil the necessary requirement I suddenly remembered how, when I was myself a schoolboy of about Robbie's age, I used to make tanks out of cotton reels powered by elastic and race them. Somewhat sketchily I put my idea to Robbie, and we began. Unfortunately I was soon to discover that I had forgotten rather more than I had remembered about the cotton reel tank; in particular I could no longer recall precisely how its propelling mechanism worked.

As the morning passed I grew more and more anxious. Our first attempts to get our reel moving were total failures and I was afraid that Robbie would lose interest and drift away. So I suggested to him that we should put the tank away until after the weekend when, as I had already promised him, I would get in touch with a friend who, I knew, would remember exactly how a cotton reel tank worked. (We had already asked Stephen for help, but he remembered only a little more than myself.) Robbie seemed pleased by this promise of more complete information but in the meantime he refused to give up. All morning and right through the dinner break he worked on his tank, continually adjusting and revising the propelling mechanism, until at last, by early afternoon, he succeeded in getting the tank to crawl forward smoothly and slowly, as it should. It was only then, as I watched him demonstrate the tank's performance, that at last I remembered clearly how it had been in my own cotton reel tank racing days. Robbie spent the rest of the day confidently experimenting with his own particular something "that worked", testing it out on different surfaces, seeing how far and how long it would run, how much time it took to cross a given area, how steep a slope it could climb, and so on.

At the end of that day I tried to account for Robbie's success, in my daily notes:

'Friday, September 3rd.

In successfully completing his cotton reel tank Robbie has resolved a whole series of mechanical problems, with little help from me, and some of that misleading, except for the initial idea and the one tip which I derived from Stephen. I, indeed, had given up at an early stage and was all for waiting until we could be told by someone else what we were doing wrong and how to put it right. I had shown little confidence in Robbie's own ingenuity. What then had helped him to persist and finally to succeed: his eagerness to get his machine working properly, his own mechanical aptitude, or a series of intuitions, guesses and happy accidents? All of these had helped perhaps, but above all what mattered, I think, was his responsiveness to the materials, to toys and toy making, and to a certain kind of playing, fiddling, experimenting, making do and imagining.'

This was the first occasion in the year when I was impressed by what I propose to call the intellectual life of play in Stephen's classroom. On this occasion I was surprised as much as delighted by Robbie's absorption in perfecting his model, even though my own experience as a parent of young children ought to have prepared me for it. I was struck by the inquisitiveness and inventiveness with which he set about the problem, by his obvious determination to carry the project through to some kind of success despite my own qualms, and by his capacity to direct and control each aspect of his activity for himself, with my occasional, fitful collaboration.

It was not long before I began to appreciate how important play was within the class. The same qualities of experience as had characterized Robbie's early experiments with a cotton reel tank recurred many times in the children's classroom play: in the models they made, the improvised dramas and games they enacted —

offshoots in part of their experience of the Wendy House in earlier years at Sherard School — the way they used bricks, lego, plasticine, water, junk. In the middle of the year I happened to read an article on *The Role of Play* by Maggie Gracie* which neatly summed up what I had by then myself come to feel: that play is one area of classroom activity where children undoubtedly "exercise autonomy" as the author puts it; where they "have few constraints on their power to formulate ideas, experiment with them and evaluate the results".

The intellectual life of play, and the uses to which it is put, forms the subject of the present chapter. In one way this chapter represents a shift of focus in the argument I have presented in previous chapters. In discussing children's writing, art, and mathematics I have been dealing with adult traditions of thought in which children are making their first trials and experiments, early efforts which, if my argument is correct, are none the less distinctively literary, artistic or mathematical for being elementary. The present chapter, by contrast, concerns a tradition of thought which in a sense is native to childhood. In the realm of play, of games, toys and make believe, children are already experts. The intellectual uses to which they put their expertise, in home, school, street and playground, reach out beyond the realm of childhood play, however, to embrace those adult traditions more commonly associated with classroom life, while, in turn, their early experience of literature, art or mathematics infiltrates both the form and content of their play.

I have drawn my examples of play from the children's model making. I would like to have included examples of their play acting also but although I often used to watch the children in the classroom as they set about their improvised dramas, I found it hard to recall their acting in sufficient clarity of action, mime and language to describe it fully in my daily notes. In any case I have no reason to suppose that what appeared to be true of their model making was any less true of their play acting. Most of my examples are taken from two particular periods in the life of the class when for several days on end the entire classroom seemed to be dominated, if not at times overwhelmed, by the children's passion for modelling. It was on these occasions above all others that I came to understand the significance of model making, and of play, in the children's learning.

It was towards Christmas, almost a term after the making of his cotton reel tank, that I next had occasion to work with Robbie on a model. Christmas was a time when a large part of the energies of Stephen's class was consumed by the familiar ritual of the Christmas nativity production which was to be presented to parents a few days

* Published in *FORUM for the Discussion of New Trends in Education:* Vol. 19, No. 3, Summer 1977.

before the end of term. On the day of the dress-rehearsal I remarked in my notes on the sudden and unexpected enthusiasm for model making within the class which had been set in motion by a project begun by Robbie and his close friend Chris the day before.

'Wednesday, December 8th.

The dress rehearsal was over by morning play but the rest of the day, so far from being the anti-climax that I had expected, proved to be exceptionally fertile. It was dominated by certain ideas which had first been mooted within the class yesterday and which absorbed more and more children's attention during the course of today. At dinner time we stopped in the middle of things, leaving work just as it was without clearing anything away. There was an air of expectation in the classroom; most children had already created fresh pools of activity for themselves after the turbulence of the play although one or two were still hopping about as if the excitement had not yet quite worn off. The afternoon began at the very point where the morning had ended, as if without a pause. It seemed pointless to call the class together for a formal registration, still less for an introductory word or plan. Stephen waived such preliminaries. Work had begun before he and I entered the classroom and almost everyone knew what they wanted to do and how. And so it remained for most of the afternoon until clearing up time; an hour and a half of sustained self-direction, mostly centred around model making or painting but with a number of activities, on the fringe, of a more 'sober' kind — reading, writing.

The most influential activity of the day was the modelling which had begun with an idea hatched by Robbie, Chris and myself yesterday morning, after the dress rehearsal for the dress rehearsal, when the two boys had asked me for ideas for a large drawing or painting. We talked things over and I suggested a picture of Robbie's farm which I knew to be familiar to Chris as well as Robbie. (The two of them live right out in the country, not far from each other, and occasionally meet at Robbie's.) They concurred, Robbie adding as a rider that they would draw the farm from above, as if seen from a helicopter or plane. (He said something, which I didn't quite catch, about his dad having shown him how this was done.) I was not particularly keen on this gloss on the idea of a picture of the farm and tentatively demurred but to no effect. A few minutes later the two of them showed me their completed drawing: the farm seen from above, in plan, except for the farm house itself which was drawn in elevation. The sketch seemed to be largely Robbie's work. I noticed how accurate, in general, its scale seemed to be, despite the roughness of the pencilled drawing; as we talked about the sketch and about the farm itself it became clear that the farm house and chicken sheds had been distributed quite precisely across the surface of the picture, with firm indications as to their relative size and position.

[The more I studied this drawing the more I appreciated it. It is a crude enough sketch in many respects and yet there is a deliberation in the detailing of the various objects comprising the picture that suggests a considerable sophistication. The farm house, in front elevation, stands in its yard at the bottom left hand corner of the paper, eleven chicken sheds, in plan, ranged behind and beside it across the picture surface. These sheds are not mere oblongs, as on a map; their asbestos roofs are scribbled in with dark pencil strokes and on each roof there are three or four vents represented by squares enclosing crosses thus — Several of the chicken sheds have hoppers, drawn in plan, beside them while the paths and outlying spaces around the buildings contain a variety of vehicles and farm machinery, also drawn in plan, in some instances with particular care. For example, in front of the topmost chicken shed stands a tractor, its short front wheels and huge back wheels very deliberately drawn in plan, with a trailer attached in which a pile of hay, manure or chicken feed is lying. To the left of the same building stands a bulldozer, equally distinguishable in plan, and beyond it a large haystack, its bales marked out as a series of irregular squares and oblongs across its surface. There are three other, less distinct, vehicles or implements at the back of another chicken shed while in the corner of the path in front of the farm house stands a wheeled cart or trailer containing two reclining matchstick figures: perhaps Robbie and Chris. Other details are less readily interpretable.]

I think it was at this point, though it might have been earlier, that I suggested to Robbie and Chris the possibility of making a model of the farm. A few days before I had been standing in for another teacher and had noticed in his classroom a very fine model of an old mill; it was this that had put the idea for a model farm into my head. I took Robbie and Chris over to Paul Merrison's classroom to see this model mill but they did not immediately seem much impressed by it, nor by my idea. After dinner however they reminded me that I had said we would make a model of the farm — and so it was that we began.

We found a piece of hardboard to serve as a base for the model and some thin white card from which to cut the shapes of the various buildings. I suggested that they use the drawing as a plan to guide them in calculating the size and shape of the various buildings. (On reflection, I think it was as much as anything my disappointment, however unjustified, with Robbie's particular interpretation of the idea of drawing his farm that led me to suggest the model: as if I could only see this rough sketch in plan as the preliminary to a grander and more finished design. But in addition I knew how fond Robbie and Chris were of large scale projects on which to spread their energies; it was the daily routine of class work that they found hard to accommodate.) We began to cut out the first shapes, the three of us together. I showed Robbie, first, how I thought he might make the long chicken sheds, bending the cut rectangles of card this way and that to create the shallow sloped roofs and low walls of the buildings, as Robbie described them to me. Having made the first one for him, minus its two short ends, I left him to get on with the rest while I turned my attention to Chris who had drawn on the white card a simple elevation of the farm house. I showed him how to extend this shape so as to allow for roofs and the opposite wall and, again, how to bend and cut it. When it had been cut out, bent into shape and set down on the hardboard, but without its side walls, Chris and Robbie each exclaimed how like the real farm house it looked, although to me it had seemed too shallow. Next Chris wanted me to show him how to make the side walls of the house and how to stick them on. We experimented, found a method, and I made the first side for him, hoping that he would be able to complete the second for himself. But he found the task too awkward, so he said, and because I was anxious that he should not give up at the first sign of difficulty, as occasionally he is inclined to, I cut out and stuck on the second side panel myself — and there we had the finished farm house. Chris was delighted with it, as was Robbie too. I left him to pencil in its windows and doors and to help Robbie with other parts of the model. Meanwhile I drifted off to another part of the class.

When I returned I was surprised to see how quickly the model had blossomed. Chris and Robbie had developed many new ideas for themselves, Robbie especially demonstrating something of a flair for making a model of this kind. He had completed all the chicken sheds, following the general pattern established in my original cut-out, and they shared the same relative precision of scale that had characterized his drawing. Indeed between drawing and model, once he had set his buildings out on the hardboard for me to see, there was a remarkable correspondence, the one a three dimensional representation of the other. But this was not all, for Robbie had gone on to model a number of objects which I had not previously noticed in his sketch and for the modelling of which I had therefore given him no hint. He had made models of all the food hoppers beside the chicken sheds — tiny cylindrical models, each one resting on even tinier paper stilts and each one with a lid, as it were, on top. These delicate models were nicely balanced so that each stood up on its stilts or legs without support. He had also modelled a tractor out of the white card, equally delicate and quite detailed. I was impressed by the patience and skill of his modelling especially in view of the small scale — the scale being determined by the size of the hardboard base and the quantity and size of white card, and myself worrying whether this wasn't too small a scale for Robbie and Chris to manage. There was a precision of form in Robbie's newly modelled objects that had been wanting in my own roughly built chicken shed. The scale of the hoppers and the tractor was in proportion to the size of the sheds and though the individual objects were minute they displayed a command of volume that reflected the manual and intellectual dexterity that had gone into the making of them.

Chris too had come up with his own ideas. He had insisted, against my "better judgement", on adding a chimney to the farm house roof, slightly lopsided since it was fitted four square onto the sloping roof, but for such a fiddly object quite stoutly constructed. Out of it curled a paper of smoke, a beautifully incongruous touch — the modelled insubstantiality alongside the modelled solid — as wholly in keeping as it was wholly out of keeping, and just the sort of touch, it seemed to me, that an adult mind would not have conceived, though perhaps an imaginative artist or draughtsman might. He had also modelled, on one corner of the farmyard, a tree, a cylinder of paper — not card on

this occasion — out of which rose jaggedly cut and twisted
strands of paper representing branches.

This was as far as Robbie and Chris had taken their model by
the end of yesterday. At the close of the afternoon I had promised
Chris to bring from home a new sheet of hardboard which he
could use as the base for a model of his own house and its
surroundings. Robbie had said that he was going to take the
model farm home when it was finished and now Chris wanted to
have a model to take home too. I forgot the board this morning
but when Chris asked me for it, early in the day, I managed to
find another piece of board in the classroom itself so that after
the dress rehearsal we were able to make a start on his new
model. Chris decided to model his own house and the two houses
that stood nearby, as well as the main road which ran past the
houses and the paths which led up to them. I suggested that he
should again draw a plan or sketch first to guide him, as Robbie
had, and he did, a little reluctantly because really he wanted to
begin modelling at once. The sketch was quickly drawn and
modelling began. Again I had to help with the three houses
themselves, despite my attempts to foist this task back onto Chris
himself, but that apart, the conception and execution of the
model were all his own. First he pasted a paper road onto the
hardboard; next he made the houses with my help; then he had
to move a part of the road which was not quite in the right
place; finally he added swinging cardboard gates and doors
around the property, another grand paper tree, and at the end of
the afternoon, partly at my instigation, some hedges. There was
less detail on the model than on Robbie's and it seemed to be
only half finished but already Chris was asking to take it home. I
dissuaded him, hoping that tomorrow he will add to the model as
well as paint it. He had worked rapidly and less carefully than
Robbie and with rather more direct help from me, yet he had
contributed the more novel ideas himself and the model as it
emerged reflected his own thinking far more than mine. (I would
not have thought of the stuck on road, nor the swinging gates.)

Meantime Robbie had been continuing with the model farm. He
began on it first thing this morning, before registration and
before getting changed for the dress rehearsal. He seemed almost
more interested in the model than the coming rehearsal. After the
rehearsal was over he returned to the model immediately and
spent the whole of the rest of the day working at it — as indeed

did Chris at his model. He cut out side panels for every one of the chicken sheds, a most laborious task, which I had not anticipated that he would attempt, reflecting to myself that it made little difference whether these buildings had their ends filled in or not, a view which, as it turned out, Robbie was far from sharing. At one point he moaned at the length and awkwardness of the job but he stuck at it till every end was in place and all the buildings were solidly four sided. He made haystacks next, thinking at first that he might use Oxo cube boxes for the purpose but then, since none were available among the old shop materials in the classroom, reverting to the white card, scissors and paste. He made more farm machinery and implements, including the family car. By the end of the day the model was almost finished and he had just had time to begin painting the chicken sheds. They were of creosoted wood, he explained to me, with asbestos roofs. We decided to paint the walls brown leaving the white cardboard roofs unpainted.

It was not long before Robbie and Chris's modelling began to attract the attention of other children. Already by the end of yesterday afternoon the first glosses on their idea had appeared and throughout today fresh imitations and extensions were set in train until by the end of the day there were at least a dozen children working on some variety of model making, using all kinds of materials. All of this activity was self-generated; there was no question of Stephen or myself encouraging children to experiment on lines similar to those of Robbie and Chris. On the contrary I was myself a little wary of the idea taking a widespread hold on the class since scissors, glue, card and hardboard were in relatively short supply, as also was teacher assistance should the experiments become bogged down at an early stage, as Chris's modelling had. Yet by the end of the afternoon a variety of models were already nearing completion, others were in mid construction, and few if any had been abandoned.

It was John, I think, who had been the first to take note of Robbie and Chris's idea yesterday and he had promptly redirected it to a quite different end. He had the idea of sticking the white card onto some broken electrical plugs, which Stephen had brought into the classroom several weeks ago, in order to create new-fangled toy machines and vehicles. Today he finished the first of his machines, a flying saucer, and painted it; later he added new parts to it, painting these too. Except for the fact that he had observed Robbie and Chris modelling with thin white card his idea was entirely original, representing, as Stephen pointed out to me during the day, a new use for the bits and pieces of gadgetry which have been lying around the classroom more or less unused since the early part of the term. This transformation of electric plugs into futuristic machines — or into artillery as Neil and Paul attempted later — by the judicious addition of stuck on card represented a small triumph of the eight or nine year olds' constructive imagination. The objects themselves might be derivative of TV films, Action Man paraphernalia, or whatever, but the ingenuity of their construction out of uninspiring bits of plastic was derivative of nothing but the individual fancy.

Paul Anthony, imitating John, also made one or two futuristic machines while Neil and Paul, Simon and David, played variations on John's idea, relating it to Robbie's by building their plastic, card, and metal constructions on cardboard or wooden bases, assembling them into weird scenes and landscapes. Neil and Paul's elaborate scene, like a stage set, included a paper figure swinging wildly from a line stretched between two upended nails like high posts. A balloon of paper was stuck to the head of the figure, with the word "help" inscribed on it, while on the floor beside the swinging man a note named the victim as "Mr Armstrong", a large arrow of white card pointing upwards to the figure just in case anyone hadn't got the message. Simon and David built an eccentric city of the future, a landscape that in its quirky way seemed to be just what one would have expected of them, Simon in particular. Other children stuck more closely to the theme established by Robbie and Chris. Julie and Helen, for example, began a model of a village street while Peter, late in the afternoon, decided to make a model of the large house and grounds in which his family have their flat. Wyndham modelled too, turning the back of an old clock into the body of a horse and adding head, tail and legs of white card.'

The following day the modelling continued in full spate.

'Thursday, December 9th.

This morning more modelling: it was as if it had never stopped. Robbie was already working on his farm as I entered the classroom while Chris, John and Paul Anthony were playing with their flying saucers. Neil, Paul, Simon, David, Peter, they were all busy already with their models, and Julie, who yesterday I had thought to be less involved in her modelling than some of the others, came up to ask me if she could take one of her houses home tonight because she had been telling her dad what she had been doing but he hadn't understood.

The modelling went on all morning but for much of this time I was anxious and depressed about it. Almost everyone had started to paint their models and the early results were discouraging. There was a good deal of repainting, sloppy mixing of paint, splashing and spattering. After all the intensity of yesterday there seemed today to be a lot of idle chatter, too, though really it was no more than the early morning gossip that accompanied today's more relaxed activity of painting and decorating the freshly created images and models. I fussed about, grew irritable, and imagined that yesterday's work was in the process of being ruined.

By the end of the morning however I had cheered up, having observed that in most cases the painting had finally proved successful whatever the intervening mess or confusion. Thus Chris's black road, with its broken white lines down the centre, and the severely brown walls of his houses — all of which I had worried over early in the morning — mellowed into a strikingly realistic effect as the paint dried. A passing teacher picked out the road, which had particularly bothered me while Chris was painting it, as one of the neatest features of the entire model. Robbie's farm, too, looked most convincing once the painting was completed and the paint dry. He had dealt with the paint that had spattered his white asbestos roofs early in the morning by painting the roofs after all, mixing an off white colour which effectively disguised the splashes and in fact gave the roofs a more realistic appearance.

Towards the end of the morning Chris began to remember fresh details to add to his houses or to correct in them. Both he and one or two others also asked Robbie to help them make miniature cars such as Robbie had made for himself. (Several children have commented in passing how fine Robbie's farm was; I think there is widespread agreement that it is the best of all the models.) Meanwhile Peter was slowly adding paper trees around the grounds of his large house, after the manner of Chris, while Julie, with a little help from Helen, had turned her street into a village square with a rather grand church as its centrepiece. The idea of modelling the church originally occurred to her as a way of masking the ill fitting end wall of one of her houses and I rather think that it was this church which had given her the idea of grouping her buildings around a square or green rather than along a street.

As for the fantastic scenes imagined by Paul and Neil, Simon and David, they have been continually destroyed, rebuilt, revised and corrected all day in the light of the stories that their creators have woven around them. These particular models have been conceived far less, I think, as products to be completed than as readily adaptable elements in an extended fiction, the props of an improvised drama. Paul and Neil's model took a gruesome turn this morning. It turned out that the man swinging from the wire had in fact been hung. (I was relieved to discover that the figure was no longer intended to be "Mr Armstrong" whose name had been erased from the base of the model.) Alongside the hanged man Paul has now added the figure of a man being squashed between the plates of a wrecked radio selector, his blood a red stain on the cardboard base. Paul delighted in showing me how the broken radio selector could be turned round, shredding the figure into numerous segments.'

Although there was still more modelling the next day, and again on the following Monday, by then the impetus was fading. It was Robbie and Chris, the inspiration of so many models themselves, who found it hardest to move on to other things and the two of them spent much of Monday designing a cardboard draughts board, with draughts modelled out of tiny squares of white card, their corners turned down so that they stood up on the board. But with that their modelling came to a close and on the Monday evening, having carried their models around to the younger classes to show them off, they finally took them home.

However that was not quite the end of modelling for the term, for at this point Stephen chose to intervene, as he described in a note written on the following Wednesday.

'Wednesday, December 15th (Stephen's notes).

The modelling which Michael has been writing about seemed by Monday to be coming to an end or else to be in need of some extension. Remembering the measuring work carried out in the maths groups towards the beginning of term, I thought it would be a good idea to begin some work on plans, making use of the children's recent experience of modelling. This kind of work could, and perhaps should, have been approached in a formal way, getting the children to make bird's eye pictures of simple objects: tables, cupboards. However, at this stage I thought it better to provide a definite goal to work towards, tackling the problems as they arose. [It is interesting to note how Robbie had already included such bird's eye drawings, some of them anything but simple, in the sketch of his farm from which his subsequent model was derived.]

We had on several occasions talked about how to organise and distribute the classroom furniture and now I suggested that if we were to make a plan of the classroom on a large sheet of paper and then cut out pieces of paper to represent the various tables, bookshelves, screens and such, we could move these pieces around on our plan and so design our classroom on our plans before actually moving the furniture. This way we could discuss the children's different plans, bearing in mind classroom ergodynamics before rearranging the classroom itself.

When I outlined this suggestion to the class as a whole, about ten children were particularly keen to be involved. I discussed the project with this group in more detail. The first question that arose was "how big shall we make the classroom?". This immediately brought up the question of scale — the word first used by Philip. Philip suggested that one square on the large sheet of squared paper which I had brought in should represent one metre on the ground. The children now, individually or in twos, measured the length and breadth of the classroom. After collecting and comparing the different results we eventually agreed on these dimensions. Philip then showed us how this would look on the squared paper (cm squares). It was immediately obvious that this produced a plan which would be much too small to be useful — only 6 cm x 8 cm. 2 cm to represent a metre was then suggested, but it was seen that again it would be too small. Then 10 cm — but now the classroom wouldn't fit on the paper at all. 5 cm, 6 cm and 7 cm were all suggested. At this point I rather strongly suggested 5 cm, seeing the problems with decimetres that would emerge if we chose 6 cm or 7 cm to represent 1 metre. I felt that the reasoning behind my choice was too complex for many of the group to understand and that it would be better to get going than to be bogged down at this stage.

Clearly there would now be many problems in accurately drawing the plan of the classroom with sink, door, openings, fire doors and other relevant permanent fixtures, so I decided that I would act as draughtsman while the children decided on the relevant measurements, doing the measuring, converting these to distances on the plan and showing me where to draw the lines. This task took up the entire half morning session, the children measuring the room with metre rules marked with 1 decimetre divisions but unnumbered. Everyone was quite happy for 1 dm on the ground to be drawn as $\frac{1}{2}$ cm on the plan but the idea of measuring "to the nearest dm" produced one or two problems. Philip solved this in an interesting way. While measuring a cabinet which was 1 m $3\frac{1}{2}$ dm long he started at one end, put his finger on the 2 dm mark and said "one square"; then on the 4 dm mark and said "two squares" and so on up to 1 m, saying "five squares". Moving the rule on, he continued with 1 m 2 dm, saying "six squares". He then placed a finger on the 1 m 4 dm position (which was, of course, off the edge of the cabinet by $\frac{1}{2}$ dm) saying "seven squares". While holding one finger on the "six squares" position, and a finger of the other hand on the "seven squares" position, he said "I can now see that this (the cabinet) is six squares and most of the seventh square long". Thus, rather than scale the object down to the plan, he had scaled the squares on the plan sheet up to the object and produced a visual aid (with fingers) to solve the problem, which did not require any deeper knowledge of approximations or fractions. He was using his own limited experience to maximum effect.

Once the master plan was completed, Simon, David and Philip wanted to make a plan of their own. I suggested that they simply copied mine, itself not an easy task for them, which they did quite accurately. The next job was to make our plan cut-outs of the movable furniture. Square and oblong tables presented few problems apart from those of approximation as before. I felt happy to leave the children at this point.

I returned to this activity the next day to find Philip, Simon, David, Mina and Suzanne working enthusiastically on their tables, carefully cutting out the same number of each as were present in the classroom. On looking at David and Simon's work, I found that they had gone on to cut out a piece labelled "bookshelf". They had produced this by measuring the height as well as the width of the tall freestanding case, ending up with an elevation of it rather than a plan. I said "does this bookcase really take up more space on the floor than a large table?". They both said "no" but that they wanted it to "stand up" on their plan. We talked about plans and models and ants on the ceiling.

They took the point after some discussion but still wanted to keep another elevation which they had made, this time of the folding screen. This took up very little space on the ground, they said, but they felt it was an important piece of furniture when organising the classroom. They said they wanted to make a paper base to their screen so that it would stand up on their plan. In all this they had shown a clear grasp of the point of our activity — an aid to redistributing the classroom furniture — and were not happy to be restricted to my rather narrow idea of a plan, where in some cases a model would be more useful. David went on to suggest making legs for his tables but Simon said there would be no point in that.'

At the end of my year in Stephen's class a friend of mine, Tony Kallet, who was reading the year's notes, commented on this particular passage that "the apparent tension between plan and elevation in David and Simon's plan of the classroom shows a fascinating half way stage to being comfortable with what is really a fairly tricky abstraction — how often do we see the world from above?" I was dissatisfied by this explanation and it set me thinking about the relationship between David and Simon's classroom plan and the sketch which Robbie had drawn of his farm, which was also largely but not wholly drawn in plan. I have already suggested that Robbie's sketch was remarkable for the skill with which he was able to represent even such a complex shape as a tractor as seen from above. Yet one object in his picture, the farm house itself, was drawn in elevation rather than in plan. Why had Robbie selected this particular object, by no means the most complex in shape, for special treatment?

The experience of David and Simon seemed to me, on reflection, to provide a relevant clue. They too had chosen to represent certain objects, on their plan of the classroom, in elevation and stuck to their decision even after Stephen had satisfactorily explained to them its inconsistency. Stephen's interpretation of their action was that they considered the height of the folding screen to be more important in determining where to place it within a redesigned classroom, than its insignificant ground plan implied. Hence the need, as they saw it, to present this object in elevation rather than in plan, standing it up on the plan like a model. Simon, particularly, seemed to recognise the exceptional character of this treatment of the screen — and the same argument might well have been applied to the tall bookcase — by firmly resisting David's suggestion that they put legs on their tables as well, which would have had the effect of turning the entire plan into something more like a model. It is unnecessary therefore to explain

Simon and David's inconsistency in terms of an inability to comprehend the abstraction involved in the concept of a plan. The shift from plan to elevation has a more immediate explanation, and one that is logically impeccable within its own assumptions, in terms of the special importance attached to the height of one object in the plan, which its mere ground plan failed to suggest. As Tony Kallet himself put it in a later comment: "what this suggests to me is that the children, probably fully able to make a straight plan, don't have any felt need for such purity of intent: if a mixed drawing seems to them to convey the information better, then they will make a mixed drawing. To them, it seems, the plan is a kind of ellipsis, a shorthand, which is all right until you reach an object for which the symbolism is inadequate. If you think about this there is a fundamental sense to it: if you were in fact redesigning the room, a thin line for a screen might well not communicate, even to a sophisticated plan reader, the psychological presence of that screen — what it would feel like to be near it."

I think that a similar argument might be applied to Robbie's elevated treatment of the farm house in his sketch. It is not that he found it hard to view the world consistently in plan, nor that he was unable to master the complexities of representing particular objects in plan, but rather that he required some way of drawing attention to the significance of the farm house — in this instance, even more than in the case of the screen, a psychological rather than a physical significance — among the complex of buildings that made up his father's farm. How could he mark the fact that this was the most important place on the farm: his home? In plan it would have been reduced to the level of the chicken sheds; in elevation it can declare itself properly for what it is: the heart of the farm. It calls to mind those tourist maps of famous cities in which the most important buildings rise up incongruously from the street plan, making it difficult at times to spot just where they are supposed to be.

I have dealt at some length with Simon, David and Robbie's treatment of plan and elevation on this occasion because it illustrates the variety of intellectual uses to which young children put their love of drawing, of model making, of playing with models, plans and pictures. Among many other things, children's play is another way of examining the nature of the world and the means of describing and controlling it: in this particular instance a way of beginning to come to terms with problems of representation and of scale. Before looking forward to the next burst of model making within the class I want to draw attention to another aspect of play revealed in Robbie and

Chris's models and their many imitations and extensions in the work and play of other children. I have described play as one area of classroom activity where children undoubtedly exercise autonomy and indeed the autonomy of Stephen's class during these few days at the end of the Autumn Term was very noticeable. Consider the fantastic models initiated by John with his flying saucer of plastic plug and cardboard: idiosyncratic conceptions for all the conventionality of the science fiction that lay behind them. Or consider the way in which Robbie and Chris, and later Simon and David, reinterpreted ideas originally suggested by their teachers: Robbie's decision to draw his farm as seen from above, his and Chris's elaboration of detail in their subsequent models, Simon and David's recension of Stephen's plan of the classroom. Nevertheless it would be a mistake to emphasize the children's autonomy at the expense of the collaboration offered by teachers. This is not simply a matter of the quality of materials or of the enabling environment provided by Stephen within his classroom. Many of the children's inventions and reconstructions might not have emerged at all without Stephen's, or my own, suggestions, hints, explanations, discussions and direct instruction. There is always a danger, in drawing attention to children's potential and actual autonomy, of ignoring the supportive context in which it thrives. In these few days of intense activity one of the critical elements was, I think, the mutuality or reciprocity which, as much perhaps by luck as by judgement, seemed to exist, on this occasion at least, between adults and children within the classroom: the sense, or knowledge, that ideas and plans, both in project and execution, could be freely and sympathetically exchanged between teachers and learners. The experience corroborated what Maggie Gracie writes, in the article cited earlier in this chapter, when she sums up her own experience of classroom play in the following terms: "On reflection it was easy to see what the children and I were learning in conventional terms, some principles about balance, construction and sound, but I think they may have learned more: 1) how to frame and test hypotheses; 2) that an adult can share and contribute in the process, not by cutting off to articulate the concepts but from participating in the learning of the group, and 3) that adults and children can have equal status in the learning process."

Early in February there was a fresh bout of model making in the classroom, partly as a consequence of Stephen's explicit intention to centre the mathematical work of the children during the first half of the Spring Term around their fondness for patterns and models which had become so apparent during the previous term. The first two subjects which he introduced to his weekly maths groups — the tesselation of triangles and other simple shapes and the construction of two dimensional frameworks — have been described in Chapter Four. At the beginning of February he introduced a third subject, the construction of three dimensional solids. As with his earlier maths groups that term, he began by walking around the school with each group in search of the shapes which he had already briefly enumerated: cubes, cuboids, cones, prisms and the like. I overheard Sarah, outside the classroom, pointedly asking whether a particular oblong shaped flower pot was "a cuboid". Afterwards Stephen produced a pile of white card and showed each group how to hinge the card together with short strips or tabs of paper or card, so as to assemble the various solids. With that the modelling began.

By the end of the first week in February everybody seemed to be modelling again.

'Friday, February 4th.

Already, yesterday, the classroom had begun to be dominated by modelling and assembling, in various guises and with a variety of materials. Gail, Jemma and Lisa had made a plasticine playground peopled by figures with speech balloons, fashioned from white card, emerging from their plasticine mouths. Paul Anthony had spent the morning building a model landscape of a snow bound road and hedges, with a model snow plough clearing away a drift, the whole scene constructed out of white card like Robbie's railway track of the previous day which seemed to have been Paul Anthony's inspiration. Paul and Peter had also started work on a model landscape but theirs was of the village where they live. Several children were working on scratch pictures which also made use of white card, having picked up the idea from Peter Burgess's class next door. And then there were the boxes of varied shape — cuboid, cube, prism, tetrahedron — assembled under the stimulus of Stephen's maths groups. Neil had been the first to construct a tetrahedron, having earlier made a prism. He was keen to add new shapes to his collection. Later in the day I had noticed that he was making a cuboid by carefully assembling in front of him on the table a complete lattice of cards, like this:

He hinged the card next, as it lay flat on the table, and then he folded it and stuck it together. I was interested in his procedure because Stephen and I had been discussing earlier the inadvisability of presenting children with prepared lattices so that all they needed to do was to fold and stick them. It seemed a more productive strategy to help them to arrive at the idea of such lattices through their own attempts at construction. And here was Neil already grasping the purpose of a lattice.

By the end of yesterday the modelling, however loosely related the different examples, was beginning to amount to a class obsession. Today, as if without the night's break, the model making continued, most of the class caught up in it in one way or another. I can think of only six or seven children who still seemed relatively unaffected by it all, including, as it happens, Robbie and Chris whom I would have expected to be involved but who spent much of the day writing.

The obsession with model making today had not been planned; it emerged out of a series of incidents, activities and products over this past week, the influence of which has spread through the class as the week has progressed. This diffusion of activity within the class, without prior deliberation or intent, is something which I have often observed in Stephen's class. So too is the overlapping of one day's activity into the next, often with the sense of no intervening pause. So it was, individually, with Philip and his maths at the start of the week;* so now, with the class as a whole.

. . . Of all the models I saw today, it was Paul and Peter's model village that interested me the most. They worked at it together all morning and part of the afternoon. The model began yesterday and was intended to be of the village where both of them live — though Peter has only lived there for a few weeks. Its base was made of four rectangles of card from the pile which Stephen had brought into the classroom at the beginning of the week. The boys had hinged the four cards together, in the way Stephen had demonstrated to his maths groups, forming a larger rectangle. On this base the tiny model buildings were stuck when completed and, later, roads were pencilled in between the buildings.

Paul and Peter began by making a house each — their own houses, they told me. Beside each house they placed a garage in

* See Chapter Four.

the shape of a rough cuboid with one of its ends open for the car.
Paul added beside his garage a long, low, tent shaped tool shed,
longer than the garage or the house, while beside Peter's garage
is a cylindrical dustbin with a handled lid. (This dustbin, though
tiny, is almost as high as the admittedly diminutive garage itself.
But then the whole model village has been constructed without
that close attention to relative proportion which seemed to
characterize Robbie's model farm last term.) They also made
hedges and fences, the fence around Paul's property including a
swinging gate with which Paul was especially pleased. Across the
road from the two houses is a football pitch surrounded by a
fence or wall and dominated by relatively massive goal posts of
white card: they had some difficulty with these, their crossbars
constantly falling off. Towards the middle of the afternoon they
added to their model a high rise block of flats, close to a village
church with an exceptionally tall tower. Paul also made a model
of a contraption rigged up in his own garden at home for him to
swing along, adding a cut out figure of himself clinging to it —
though later this was destroyed. But what I liked best of all were
the two miniscule go carts which the two of them made to keep
in their garages, or the tool shed, and to race around a large dirt
track which they had drawn on the cardboard base, immediately
behind their two houses, and which included on one side a ramp
for jumping the go carts or cars off. These go carts are smaller
than my thumb nail but extraordinarily detailed. The base of the
go cart was made out of a minute scrap of card, rounded at the
front and with tiny protrusions at each corner which were bent
down to form the four wheels:

On top of this base were added a steering column and
wheel, a hand brake or gear stick, and a seat on
which a miniature cut out figure sat driving. The influences
behind these extraordinary go carts included, I am sure, Robbie's
farm vehicles of last term together with Paul Anthony's recent
snow plough, but no one in the class has as yet attempted
anything on quite so minutely detailed a scale.

Both Paul and Peter seemed to derive a great deal of satisfaction
from the extreme miniaturisation which they were attempting, as
indeed had Paul Anthony yesterday. But then the whole business
of modelling the village delighted them. Although I didn't work

with them myself or hear much of their conversation as they worked, it was clear that the model village incorporated, alongside the comparatively realistic details of their home environments, fanciful improvements of their own devising: above all, the race track. (Remember that Paul had been given a go cart for Christmas*.) As for the intrusive block of flats, I am uncertain how it came to be added to the village, late in the day, although it seemed at least in part to be related to the nature of the materials which the boys were using and which could be folded and stuck conveniently and effectively in the shape of a tall tower block. The huge church tower beside the flats also suggests how much they seem to have enjoyed creating tottering heights, on however small a scale, to set against the minutiae of their go carts.

Peter was especially pleased with the model, and with himself. I overheard him say to Paul "this is the bestest thing I've ever done, is it yours?". Paul didn't seem to understand at first but finally said "Oh — yes," in that matter of fact tone he can assume from which it is so hard to tell with what degree of conviction he is assenting to whatever has been asserted (though I am certain that Paul had also enjoyed his work). There are several reasons why Peter might well have been especially pleased, quite apart from the obvious success of the model itself. Last term, of course, he had attempted to build a similar kind of model by himself — of his own house and grounds — but it had not worked out so well. This time I am certain that he had particularly enjoyed the experience of working cooperatively with Paul: the fellow feeling of getting down to the modelling together. I am sure that he also appreciated the miniature realism of the model, which was entirely convincing whatever the incidental oddities of scale. And I imagine that he also enjoyed exploring the prospect, however fanciful, of creating for himself a more adventurous, more self-determined environment than that in which he happens to live. Working at the model with Paul, and making such a success of it, was in some part, I would tentatively suggest, a way of figuring forth a new environment for himself, designed to satisfy rather than to frustrate.'

The following Monday morning, after a weekend's break, Paul and Peter returned to their model.

* See Chapters Two and Three.

'Monday, February 7th.

When everyone came into the classroom this morning Paul and
Peter went straight up to their model village and began looking
at it, admiring it, fiddling with it and planning how to continue
it. I don't know whether they had been discussing it outside but I
suspect not. It was as if they remembered it only on entry into
the classroom or as if they caught sight of it as they entered and
then remembered; it was this sequence of entering, noticing and
remembering which instantly revived their enthusiasm for
carrying it further. While Stephen was collecting dinner money I
chatted to them about the model, asking them how far it was
their own village and how far an invented village. There were
bits of their village about it, Paul explained, but for the most
part it was an invented village, incorporating elements in their
own lives — Paul's go cart most notably — but enlarging their
own environment, as I suggested in yesterday's notes, by
incorporating their dreams, wishes and fancies: Peter's football
pitch, the dirt track, the tower block.

They asked if they could get on with the model immediately but
I suggested they wait till Stephen had had his say. As it
happened, he asked Peter to work with him at some writing,
along with two or three others. Peter was irritated and went off
with dire mutterings, clenching his fist, but it seems that he
settled down to writing readily enough in the end. Meanwhile
Paul was left to continue the model on his own. I suggested to
him that he concentrate on the revisions or improvements to its
existing buildings which the two of them had just been planning,
rather than on adding new buildings, leaving new developments
till Peter's return. Paul agreed but during the first part of the
morning, while Peter was elsewhere, he fell into one of the
gloomy moods in which he feels that everything he does is
"rubbish", a self-mockery which seems however to stop short of
genuine disgust. It was only when Peter rejoined him, after
morning play and service, that he recovered his enthusiasm and
began to chortle once more over the success of the model. It
seemed, then, to require Peter's presence to sustain Paul's interest
in the model. Of course, the model was the pretext for a vivid
conversation between them about their own lives and the lives
they would like to lead and this was certainly one part of what
attracted them to it. Yesterday I wrote that for Peter the
opportunity to work collaboratively with someone else in the class

was a further spur to his enthusiasm. As for Paul, today I sensed that Peter had temporarily assumed, in Paul's eyes, the role of a sympathetic listener and guide, encouraging Paul by praising his skill and reassuring him, through his own enthusiasm and respect for Paul's skill, that his efforts were in no way rubbishy. No teacher could have hoped to do more.

Certainly it has been a most engaging and productive collaboration which lasted, again, all day. I was not in the classroom much this afternoon and scarcely saw anything of Paul and Peter until the end of the day when I asked them how the model had progressed and looked it over. By now the model was painted. The cardboard base was a mass of black roads and squares interspersed with green, and a little brown. Beside Paul's home was a blue pond and behind it the large brown dirt track crossed on one side by a thin green path. The tower block was blue with red windows and a flat red roof and the church beside it was also blue. (Unlike Robbie and Chris last term Peter and Paul had made no attempt to achieve a consistent realism in their colour scheme.) The houses were brown, blue or yellow, their windows and doors picked out again in a contrasting colour. The football posts were unpainted but the pitch itself was dark green, heavily spotted by blobs of brown, making it seem well-worn and muddy. New buildings had been added during the day: more garages including one with a raised working platform on four stilts; a shop; a large old fashioned pub with a miniature sign hinged to it declaring its function — "pub"; a cinema in the shape of a large house with a poster stuck to the front advertising "King Kong". Early this morning Paul had told me that they intended to put a market in the village but they had decided this would be too tricky to make and had chosen to add shops instead. The object which caught my attention more than any other today was, once again, a vehicle: this time a tiny car (see fig. 15), shaped a little like a mini, which Peter had made and which just fitted into his second garage (the first garage containing his go cart). The body of the car was made out of card supported at the base by four minute strips of wood, taken from a matchbox or something of the sort. Four minute cardboard wheels were stuck to this wooden supporting frame at each corner. The car was painted red with blue wheels while on the strip of wood at the front were painted lights and a number plate (though the numbers themselves could not be made out).

Fig. 15

But not every part of the car was painted. Where the front and rear windows would be, Peter had left the white card unpainted except that in each "window" he had painted two silhouettes — the driver and his three passengers. It was a superb reproduction, every bit as good as Paul's go cart yesterday. These miniaturised vehicles fascinate me more and more. They are decidedly the children's own inventions; their own particular gloss perhaps on the dinky toys and matchbox toys which they faintly resemble and which perhaps serve as distant paradigms, although Paul and Peter's vehicles are far smaller.

I said earlier that Peter was annoyed at having to write this morning rather than continue the model. He managed to resolve his disappointment by choosing to write about his model — and came over to tell me. This is what he wrote today (the piece is still not finished, I think). [It never was.]

"My model.

I went to Paul and said 'do you want to make a model?' 'Yes.' 'I will get some cardboard. Then we will do two houses. When we have done the houses we will do two cars. Then after we will do two garages. Then we will add some things to it when we go along doing the model. Then we will do a block of flats and a church and some cars for the road and some shops for the town. (Note that for Peter it is now a 'town'). We will do sweet shops, paper shops and hardware shops and then we will do a racing track and a shed of tools. That is all, let's get started.' Then we had some problems with the cars and the houses and the garages."

The casting of his account into the form of a dialogue is characteristic of Peter's writing at present. It may be this in part which accounts for his apparent reconstruction of events, for he has included within his expressed intentions all his and Paul's subsequent activity. I am certain that most of their buildings and objects were not so precisely planned in advance but came to mind as they went along. Here, though, all has been assimilated into an original grand design. (Compare reports of psychological and educational research.)'

The next day Paul also wrote about the model. Like Peter he had been asked to write by Stephen. At once he had made up his mind to write about his model. Stephen did not see him again until the writing and its accompanying sketch were finished, which in itself was surprising since Paul would normally have asked for a good deal of assistance even over so short a piece.

"My model.

One day I was bored stiff when Mr Armstrong came and said 'do you want to make a model of where we live?' I said 'yes.' I had great fun with it and the next day I made a go cart and I made a go cart for Peter."

The details of Paul's reconstruction of events were once again a matter for dispute. Peter protested that Paul had certainly not made his go cart for him, though I am sure that Paul had been the first to make a go cart. As for his opening remarks, they follow a pattern that was quite common in the class when it came to writing about a particular classroom activity, as if it were only to be expected that anything special should begin in consequence of being bored. For all that, Paul's account may have been correct although it was not how I recalled the origin of the model at the time. As for the writing itself, I noticed how lively it was by comparison with the laboured and disjointed phrases which were often as much as Paul could manage. When I reread his account of the model half a year later I could still hear his voice within its phrasing: 'I was bored stiff', 'I had great fun'. His evident pleasure in the modelling had spilled over into the writing which was perhaps as close to spontaneity as Paul had as yet come that year in regard to his writing, recalling the vigorous account he had written of his go cart on the first day of this same term.

Below the few written lines, Paul had drawn a rough sketch.

Perhaps because of its roughness, I paid little attention to it at first although I did notice that he had drawn the model houses in plan. It was not until much later that I realised that this scribbled sketch was an exact plan of one corner of the model, the corner which included Paul's own house and had been the first part of the model to be built. Paul's house is there, with its garage and tool shed, and at the left hand edge of the sketch is Peter's house too. The two houses and the tool shed, seen from directly above in plan like everything else in the picture, each have a single line drawn across them, representing the crown of their roofs, while the garage, which in the model had a flat roof, is given no such crowning line. The sketch also includes the roads, the football pitch and posts, the dirt track with its raised ramp and crossing path, the pond at the side of Paul's house — a round red scribble, the sketch, like the writing, being in red biro — and a second pond, inside the dirt track, crossed by wavy red lines and containing a minute pencilled fish, thereby anticipating the shark infested pond that Paul was to paint, above his painted go cart, towards the end of the Spring Term. Along the dirt track roars a go cart, a scribble of exhaust pouring out behind it, while between the garage and the race track Paul has pencilled in thick curved lines which seem to represent the scarring or churning up of the pathway, presumably by the go cart on its journey to and from the track. When I began to appreciate the accuracy and consistency of this sketch of a corner of the model, long after it had been drawn, it occurred to me that here was an answer to the question which Tony Kallet had raised in connection with the plans and elevations produced by Robbie, Simon and David just before Christmas. 'How often do we see the world from above?' he had asked. Part of the answer is perhaps that children do indeed see one kind of world quite often from above: the miniature world of their own toys, dolls' houses, model farms and villages.

By Wednesday, February 9th, nearly a week after it had been begun, work on the model village was coming to an end. Already several parts of the model had been destroyed or replaced and although a few new items had begun to appear, including a stumpy spire to the church tower and no fewer than four more tower blocks, one of them, at the very edge of the model, easily its tallest building so far, both Paul and Peter seemed to be getting tired of it. I should have been less surprised than I was, perhaps, when Paul told me on the Wednesday afternoon that he had thought of adding the Empire State Building to the model — it seemed his interests were now elsewhere. But before the two boys finally stopped modelling they discovered a new and somewhat different focus for their inventiveness, and one which strengthened my impression as to the source and strength of their talent for miniaturisation.

'Wednesday, February 9th.

Paul and Peter arrived at school this morning with various dinky toy cars. I have already speculated in my notes as to whether their fascination and skill with miniaturisation might be associated with the tiny model cars, furniture and buildings which they doubtless play with at home. This speculation seemed to be confirmed now by the appearance of just such toys today. It was to these toys and their improvement that the two of them now turned their attention rather than to their village. Peter repainted one of the cars he had brought, added a cardboard wind foil at the back of it, and stuck on two paper headlights at the front and a neatly painted number plate. On another of his cars he mounted cardboard machine guns, though these had disappeared by the end of the day. Then, at the end of the day, Paul showed me the addition which he had made to the dinky car which he had himself brought in. It was a tool box or extra boot which fitted onto the back of the car, behind the rear window and over the existing boot. Inside it he had dropped two small nuts to indicate its purpose. The box was minute, again no more than the length of my thumb nail, with hinged sides, just like the cuboids made in the maths group sessions except that the hinges were placed on the outside of the box giving it the appearance of a tiny trunk, and a hinged lid. At the front of this lid was a tiny cardboard strap which slotted between two raised flaps on the front of the box, pinning the lid down. There could not have been a more beautifully executed box, I thought, nor a finer example of a cuboid object, either in shape or in method of construction. (I asked Paul what shape the box was. "Oblong" he said at first and then, after a pause, when I said I had a different word in mind, "cuboid". Not that I think this interested him much at the time.)

Now that their model village is virtually finished, I have two general comments to make about it.

First, it is important to remember the element of play making in their modelling, which helps to explain the many bits of the model that have been displaced or destroyed as time has passed, as well as such an apparently absurd idea as adding the Empire

State Building. (Perhaps it was the association with *King Kong*, the film being shown in the model cinema, which suggested the Empire State Building. More likely, I suspect, the previous tower blocks, which seemed to be getting higher all the time.) The two of them acted out their model as they built it, as Paul had done last term when he made his gruesome hanging man and body slicing machine with Neil. It was often the case that once a particular object had been figured out, its role in the life and drama of the model was over and it could make way for something else. Not everything was made to last even for a short while. This intimate connection between model making and play acting has been apparent all year: in the puppets that Philip and Neil made last term, for example, when making the puppets seemed to be an equivalent or substitute for acting with them, as also in the science fictions and fantasies modelled just before Christmas.

Second, I believe that the miniature model making is a compelling example of the value of children's play in the classroom as one activity in which their own competence and autonomy is already apparent. Collecting and playing with model cars, and such, is something which most children at Sherard School will have been used to from infancy. By the time they reach school they are already expert appreciators and operators of miniature models, acutely aware of their smallest details and even of the accuracy with which many a given model imitates the real thing. The verisimilitude of models is, I dare say, a matter about which they are more knowledgeable than most adults. It is natural then that they should show such a fondness, and such a talent, for making miniature models of their own. They already know many of the tricks of the trade, they have handled examples of the art over and over again, they have tested them to destruction, pulled them apart and tried to repair or reassemble them. Thus the world of miniatures seems a particularly appropriate world for them to explore in their own making and constructing. There is nothing trivial about this exploration; modelling is one of the fundamental means available to children for exploring reality in many different dimensions. The fact of children's expertise as miniaturisers gives their modelling an added point and value.'

While Paul and Peter had been busy with their model village, other children had been adding to the collection of cuboids, prisms, tetrahedra and the like which by now seemed to have spread across every available space in the classroom. These geometrical solids reached their apogee when David decided to model a cuboid foot. As he told me later, "I saw all these people doing different patterns and I thought I'd like to do something completely different so I decided to do — a foot." David's foot — "Mr Leg" he dubbed it — was the most extreme and extraordinary instance of a kind of intuitive cubism that had attracted the attention of several children in the class ever since Stephen had introduced them to the geometrical solids. David was in fact not quite correct in describing other people's solids as mere "patterns"; cuboids and prisms had already been turned into hanging lanterns, houses, churches, flats, and even whole cities of skyscrapers. And yet a larger than life size foot was, indeed, decidedly "different". It took David many hours, spread over several days, to complete the foot and he would probably not have managed to finish it but for my practical help in cutting and sticking its many parts; the toes proved to be especially irksome to make, being composed of very shallow cuboids. In its final state, nevertheless, painted pink, or "flesh" as David called it, with white cardboard toe nails attached to the top of the long, shallow cuboid toes, it was an imposing sight, like some Andy Warhol sculpture except that it was cubist.

But the true climax to more than a fortnight's sustained modelling came about, just as David was finishing his foot, with the return to model making of Robbie and Chris. Until this moment, as it happened, they had had little to do with the present phase of model making. The circumstance that occasioned their return to model making was Chris's visit to Robbie's farm one Sunday in February, a visit already described in Chapter Two on account of its providing the subject for a piece of writing by Chris which at first seemed likely to fail, only to be revived after the success of his new model. The models which Robbie and Chris made on this occasion brought the previous fortnight's activity into sharper focus, both by virtue of their intrinsic merits, more particularly in the case of Robbie's model, and because they represented two extremes within the class: the model that was thoroughly self-determined and the model that depended for its success, as David's foot had, on sustained collaboration with a teacher.

'Tuesday, February 15th.

At registration time Robbie spoke to me of the superb new tractors — Ploughmasters — he'd inspected on a neighbouring

farm; his dad had borrowed one for shifting chicken manure.
"They're massive," he told me, admiringly; the two larger wheels
were bigger than himself, the cabs were air conditioned, and each
tractor, so he assured me, cost £20,000.

"Not the tractors again," moaned Chris in mock horror as he
overheard us talking. Chris himself had come up to ask me if we
were going to start today on the promised cardboard model of
the barn — a "Dutch barn" as a passing teacher pointed out
during the day, Robbie confirming the name to Chris's initial
disbelief. This was the barn in which, last Sunday, he'd pushed
Robbie off the hay bales onto his head and into the mud. [The
previous day I had told Chris, when he had been disappointed by
his written account of the day he had spent at Robbie's farm,
that I would help him make a model of the barn.]

Chris and Robbie wanted to work in the open area outside the
classroom again, and when I found my way over to them they
had already begun setting themselves up at the same table we'd
worked at yesterday. They began not with the modelling but
with a drawing apiece of the Ploughmaster, and meanwhile I
had a chance to go and see David about finishing his foot. By the
time I returned the drawings were complete, very similar to each
other though with a few subtle differences, and the boys were
ready to begin modelling. By that time Robbie had decided that
he was not going to help Chris model the barn but, instead,
would model the Ploughmaster. It was not intended to go in the
barn either: it was to be an entirely distinct model of his own. As
soon as we had collected cardboard, scissors and paste he began
on it and from that moment on I contributed nothing to his
work.

Chris, by contrast, demanded my help constantly. First there was
the problem of how the barn looked. Eventually, after
questioning Chris and Robbie about it, I persuaded Chris to
sketch me the front of it. We saw how the roof went, rounded,
not pointed; how wide the barn was; how many walls were
blocked in; how there was a panel across the top on the front of
the barn, the rest of the front being exposed; how corner posts
supported the barn inside the two side walls. Next I showed
Chris, who had at first wanted to fasten the walls together
directly, how to hinge them (Robbie and Chris have not yet done
any of the work on cuboids and such with Stephen), and how,

similarly, to hinge card together when making the bales to go into the barn. Finally we discussed the size of the bales relative to the barn as a whole.

Then we began the hinging, cutting, and sticking, and work continued throughout the morning except for the service after morning play. Chris worked at the model right through play and returned to it for a large part of the afternoon. The barn itself was complete before dinner time but the bales took ages to finish and in the end became laborious. Chris began to complain that he had wanted to stick them all together in a solid mass and that this would have been easier. Perhaps, I agreed, but less realistic. He concurred, but by that time half-heartedly.

When the model was finished Chris was able to show me clearly just how they'd played on the bales, how Robbie had got stuck, and how he, Chris, had pulled him up and then pushed him off. [Later that week Chris added cardboard figures of himself and Robbie on the bales, Robbie in the act of falling.] The model was altogether superior to his drawing of yesterday; indeed, it represented a transfiguration of that somewhat inaccurate sketch. It was, to return to a theme of earlier notes, a real figuring forth of the remembered incident, qualitatively more or less the equal of yesterday's conversation about Sunday's adventure in a way which yesterday's writing had not been. But I ought to add, especially in view of the contrast between Robbie's model and Chris's, that the model itself relied a good deal on my assistance in the execution and would quite likely not have been finished without it. It is true that while I was having my mid-morning coffee and Chris was continuing on his own, his modelling was as good as, if not better than, when I was helping or watching him. Nevertheless, he kept appealing to me for help and in a way which seemed not merely a request for adult company but which implied also a need for reassurance and collaboration in the modelling. It seems to me now as if my collaboration led to a certain loss of individuality in Chris's model, but I wouldn't want to press the point. In any case, my help appeared to be a necessary condition of Chris's success.

The contrast between Chris's and Robbie's modelling could not have been sharper. From the moment Robbie began to cut out the cardboard for his model tractor he was wholly independent. From that moment, soon after registration, till well into the

afternoon, he worked solidly and singlemindedly on his tractor.
(Robbie doesn't go out to play at dinner time these days because
of his bad leg.) He cut his own cardboard shapes, working out
the design of the tractor as he went along (without glancing at all
at his drawing, I think), finding a Poleidobloc of the right
circumference to serve as a template for the wheels, cutting the
shapes and assembling them first, then fastening them together,
though without hinges until he came to the trailer. The tractor
was finished by dinner time and by the start of the afternoon a
trailer had been added, hinged so that it could tip backwards,
and filled with bales. The trailer fitted onto the tractor by means
of a neatly fashioned hitching device, which looked efficient
enough, but unfortunately proved incapable of sustaining the
weight of the trailer when attached to the tractor so that the
hitching rod bent and the trailer sank onto the ground. We
talked about how to remedy this but Robbie hasn't yet solved the
problem. [He did solve it, though, by himself, the following day
at dinner time, replacing the original hitching device with a
wider and stronger one.] Once finished, Robbie took the model
and himself back into the classroom, for the first time in two days
deserting the table outside and Chris — another sign of his
singlemindedness. There he painted the model: blue for the
tractor, with a brown exhaust pipe and black wheels; red for the
trailer, which had tiny black wheels balanced somewhat off
centre; yellow for the bales dumped in the back of the trailer.
Everything was finished by mid-afternoon.

Robbie's tractor was as dramatic an image as any I have seen
this year of independent thought and action. He had begun the
day with his mind full of the huge, superb, borrowed tractor. He
had enjoyed finding out how little I knew about it — I thought
that by a Ploughmaster he meant a ploughing attachment, not a
tractor. He relished his awestruck description despite Chris's leg-
pulling. His drawing followed, competent, quite accurate, but too
schematic, suffering from being two-dimensional, missing altogether the grandeur of the real thing. I don't suppose however
that it was a sense of what was missing from the sketch that
drove Robbie on to the model, for he was already by then
committed to modelling with Chris, as indeed he had been even
yesterday. But now that his mind was full of the tractor, he could
see that his own model must be that tractor and that he must
therefore desert Chris as a collaborator to concentrate on his own

idea. [It occurs to me now, rereading my notes, that it was perhaps as much as anything because Chris had lost the direct assistance of Robbie that he demanded it of me.] The third dimension made all the difference. Robbie's model shows an understanding both of modelling skills and principles and of the essential forms of tractor and trailer, their proportions, their various parts, the way they fit together. It also shows, I think, the beauty which he has perceived in the machine, so that in a certain way, for all its precise observation and careful calculation, it is a deeply felt model. Looking at it, I was reminded of some lines of a poem by Auden:

> Love requires an Object,
> But this varies so much,
> Almost, I imagine,
>   Anything will do:
> When I was a child, I
> Loved a pumping-engine,
> Thought it every bit as
>   Beautiful as you.*

But thinking of Robbie's tractor, it's as well also to remember Chris's barn, less independent a model, less self-sufficient, less intense, less complete, less satisfying finally, perhaps, but nevertheless an achievement that is equally important in its implications for learning and teaching, helping as it does, I think, to pick out the tentative and shifting line that runs between intervention and interference, self-direction and teacher guidance.'

Chris's achievement lay as much in what his modelling led to as in the model itself. For it was the making of this model, as I argued in Chapter Two, that helped him to objectify his experience at Robbie's farm and thus to succeed with his written account of the adventure, to which he now returned, where before he had failed. Now the sentences flowed more freely, the tone grew livelier, the content richer. It was the experience of modelling that seemed to have made all the difference. His story finished, Chris continued to add to his model while Robbie, in the flush of his success, modelled two more farm vehicles: a bulldozer first, like the bulldozer drawn in plan on his sketch of the chicken farm, and then a land rover and trailer. With these last vehicles, as confident in treatment as the Ploughmaster itself, the second burst of model making in the class drew to a close.

* W.H. Auden, from "Heavy Date," *Collected Shorter Poems, 1927–1957*, Faber and Faber, 1966.

On Thursday I photographed a group of the latest models, assembling them on a large map chest outside the classroom. On Friday the school broke up for half term, and when the class reassembled, the following Wednesday, it was other interests that began to predominate.

Although most of the models which I have considered in this chapter were constructed out of cardboard and glue, in reality this was only one among many materials that the children used for making models. When modelling next emerged as a preoccupation within the class, in the final week of the Spring Term, the chosen medium was plasticine. I was fascinated to observe the same control over materials, the same power of representation and fondness for miniature scale, reappearing in a new guise. There was a special exuberance in the children's use of plasticine: a quality of imagination that, for some children, went considerably beyond their intellectual range in other media. I recall in particular the plasticine models made by Gail, Jemma and Lisa, three girls whose art was often somewhat constrained yet whose plasticine figures displayed great freedom and boldness.* It was they who inaugurated the craze for plasticine in the last week of the Spring Term by modelling a plasticine picnic. The model began with the making of two large, matronly figures out of plasticine wrapped around glass jars: an idea of Gail's as I recall. The three girls paid special attention to the clothing of their figures, and to their facial expressions; by comparison, arms, legs, hands and feet were treated quite cursorily. Each matron wore a floppy, wide brimmed hat. One of them had open-work plasticine sandals on her feet, the sandal strips carefully looped over the flattish, toeless stumps. The other carried on one stumpy hand an intricately modelled string bag, also of plasticine, while the other hand was raised to her mouth, holding a piece of plasticine bread which she seemed to be chewing. The two matrons were pushing prams, each with a baby inside. Beside the prams, apparently part of the same scene, was a small round plasticine table spread with exquisitely fashioned food: a cake layered in different colours of plasticine like a sponge, stuffed round cobs, biscuits and sweets.

These two imposing matrons with their prams and their picnic were much admired and emulated and at the start of the next term the three girls followed up their success with a further model which in some respects was still more ambitious. This time the subject was "a kindly ogre and his pet", in Gail's words. In front of a large sheet of

---

* For a rather different example of the same quality, compare Julie's plasticine models, discussed in Chapter 3.

blue grey sugar paper stuck to the classroom wall, were placed two free-standing figures made out of different colours of plasticine. The ogre had a blue face, green eyes, a long and very thin hooked nose, red lips, a thick black beard, and a loose brown cap on his head. The head was easily the most expressive part of the figure, presenting a very peculiar and appealing character. Beside him stood his still more peculiar pet, with the fat body and head of a pig, a tiny, protruding, button like mouth, and a huge, white, scaly tail which stuck straight up, almost overbalancing the body. In its mouth the creature carried a newspaper of black plasticine, pitted to represent the print. When I had first caught sight of the model this newspaper had been stuck to the ogre's hand, or rather to the end of his arm since once again the hands had not been fashioned in detail. Gail told me that it was really supposed to be in the pet's mouth, however, and promptly removed it to its rightful place. Behind the two quaint figures, across the sugar paper, were stuck two fluffy white plasticine clouds in low relief, and alongside them was a third cloud, this time crayoned in, rather than modelled out of plasticine. Also stuck against the sugar paper were two trees with flattened, brown trunks, and tree tops which fanned out in multicoloured, predominantly green, plasticine. A brown bird's nest was stuck in one tree top with a fledgling inside it. In the sky, flying towards the nest, was a bird with a worm in its beak. Bird, nest, and fledgling were modelled in higher relief than the trees which in turn were in higher relief than the clouds. In a final revision, plasticine branches were superimposed on the green tree tops, a bush with berries was added alongside, and the flying bird was removed and restuck in the leafy top of the second tree, looking across to the nest. At this stage too the newspaper in the pet's mouth vanished, accidentally squashed by Jemma — one of the disadvantages of plasticine, as Gail remarked later.

It was the virtuosity of this model that caught my attention, no less than its weird fancy. The use of plasticine to paint, as it were, in low relief, on wood, card or paper, had been quite a commonplace technique in Stephen's class but I had not observed before such a buoyant combination of different levels of relief, from the wholly free-standing figures in front of the sugar paper, through the high relief of bird and nest, berries and branches, to the low relief of clouds and thence to the single crayoned cloud: the vanishing point of relief. Gail, Lisa and Jemma seemed, here, to be exploring the formal as well as the expressive possibilities of their chosen medium, and with singular force.

The playfulness, even frivolity, of the three girls' imagination cannot conceal from us the deep seriousness and strenuousness of their activity. In essence, that is the argument of this chapter, the common element in all of the examples of model making which I have described, from Robbie and Chris's cardboard farms to Gail, Lisa and Jemma's plasticine monsters. Play is a dangerous word inasmuch as it implies the contrary of work. We talk of "child's play" as if it were necessarily "a very easy or trifling matter", as the dictionary says. Playful as it was, the model making of children in Stephen's class was far from trifling. Time and again Stephen and I were made aware of the intellectual value of that "responsiveness to materials, to toys and toy making, to a certain kind of playing and fiddling and experimenting and making do" which Robbie's early experience in perfecting his cotton reel tank had first drawn to my attention. It was the precision as well as the romance of the children's models that impressed itself upon us, the rigorous thought that went into their making, the inseparability of the elements of work and play within the whole activity.

The study of play thus brings us back to the central theme of this book. How are we to understand the understanding of children? One way of beginning is to examine, with careful sympathy, the thought and action of the children whom we ourselves are teaching. That is what I have tried to do in this and previous chapters. I believe that a satisfactory "theory of the life of reason from the beginnings of learning" requires many examinations of this kind, alongside the work of other students of human development: psychologists, philosophers, sociologists, historians. In describing the intellectual life of a class of eight and nine year old children I have sought to draw attention to one particular feature of the early life of reason which seems to me to be of special consequence for the course of intellectual growth. That feature is the seriousness of purpose in children's thought and action: their high intent. We can observe it in their early writings, their art, their mathematics and their play: in every activity which absorbs them intellectually and emotionally. It is the quality of mind which acquires knowledge by appropriating knowledge. It is this seriousness of purpose that makes of children's practice a significant performance rather than a course of training; it is this that justifies us in ascribing to children a creative and critical imagination. Ultimately, it is the quality of seriousness that permits us to describe the life of reason as beginning at, or close to, the beginnings of learning.

"Neither Youth nor Childhood is Folly or Incapacity" wrote Blake. Few thinkers have come as close to an understanding of the understanding of children as the early English Romantics. In an earlier chapter I cited Coleridge's image of education as the excitement of the mind's "germinal power" to appropriate knowledge to its own use. I would like to bring this book to a close with a quotation from another of the Romantics, this time from Wordsworth. "Nature has irrevocably decreed, that our prime dependence in all stages of life after Infancy and Childhood have been passed through (nor do I know that this latter ought to be excepted) must be upon our own minds; and that the way to knowledge shall be long, difficult, winding, and often times returning to itself." The children whose life and work have been the subject of my inquiry persuaded me that childhood is indeed no exception to Wordsworth's rule.

Chameleon is an educational series published in association with Writers and Readers Publishing Cooperative. Each book deals with a key and sometimes controversial educational topic. The series is directed as much at the general reader as at those professionally involved in education.

The Chameleon editorial group consists of Myra Barrs, Jonathan Croall, Francesca Greenoak, Richard Mabey and John Maddison.

Working With Words
Literacy beyond school

Jane Mace

Why are 2 million adults in Britain illiterate? Do they lack ability
and application, or has our educational system let them down
somewhere? Why is the adult literacy movement starved of funds
and existing mostly on voluntary labour, while educationally
privileged institutions like universities eat up money?

In Jane Mace's powerfully argued and provocative book she looks
critically at our attitudes to literacy, the complex learning
relationships between tutors and students, and contrasting methods
of literacy work. She backs up her argument by drawing in detail on
the experience, the writing and the opinions of literacy students,
whose voices are so rarely heard in such discussions. Her book
challenges teachers, at school as well as in the adult literacy sphere,
to question many of their traditional assumptions about literacy.

Absent from School
The story of a truancy centre

Rob Grunsell

What can and should be done for children who stay away from school? For Rob Grunsell and his wife, the solution was to set up an informal truancy centre, which could respond directly to the needs of urban children in revolt against conventional schooling.

Absent from School records with compassion and honesty the dramatic successes and failures of their pioneering project.

'No one working with unhappy children could fail to profit from Grunsell's insights . . . some of the stories he has to tell will break any reader's heart' Edward Blishen, *New Society*

'Any degree of success by centres such as that of the Grunsells is a gain for our society' Colin Cross, *Observer*

Out in the Open
The school records debate

Lucy Hodges

Demand is growing for less secrecy in government, and for more access for the public to official documents. In *Out in the Open*?, Lucy Hodges looks at some of the controversial issues concerning the use, and sometimes the abuse, of school records.

Her book examines the situation in Europe, Scandinavia, North America and Australia. It discusses the legal constraints against disclosure in Britain, including the laws of libel and breach of confidence. It also traces the history of the campaign for opening up school records, in the context of demands by civil libertarians and others for access to social services and medical dossiers, and indeed all personal information kept on computer.

Based on extensive research and interviews, the book argues in favour of a statutory right for parents and students over a certain age to see records kept by education authorities.

Fit For Work?
Youth, school and (un)employment
Colin and Mog Ball

The relationship between school and work has suddenly come to the fore as a major educational and political question. This is the first book since the debate began to draw on the views and feelings of young people themselves. Colin and Mog Ball have talked to a wide range of boys and girls — in school, just starting to work, on the dole. They show how schools prepare — or fail to prepare — young people for the world of work, how teachers and employers often differ in their attitude to what such preparation should be, and how young people react to this adult intervention during a key period of their lives.

Colin Ball was involved in the design and implementation of the Holland Report on Young People and Work at the Manpower Services Commission, for whom he is now an adviser. Mog Ball has already published two interview-based books, **Young Volunteers at Work** and **A Woman's Place,** as well as a book for teenagers on **Death**. Both former teachers, they wrote the successful Penguin **Education for a Change: Community Action and the School**.

Positive Image
Towards a multiracial curriculum

Robert Jeffcoate

Robert Jeffcoate was development officer of the Schools Council
Multi-Racial Education Project, whose report has recently been
turned down as too controversial by the Schools Council itself. He
was until recently editor of the journal of the National Association
for Multi-Racial Education.

This much needed book takes up some of the most delicate issues
facing teachers working in a multi-cultural society. Robert Jeffcoate
explores the many facets of racism in schools, in the belief that
teachers must recognise and acknowledge their pupils' prejudices
before trying to construct a genuine multi-cultural curriculum. He
puts forward ideas for change based on his own teaching experience,
first in Africa and later in Birmingham, and on detailed observation
in a Manchester secondary school.

The Monday Report
A child's eye-view of school

edited with an introduction by
Michael Armstrong

Amidst all the heated debates, both great and small, about
education, the voices of the children themselves are rarely heard. In
The Monday Report they file their own story.

Their marvellously detailed and highly illuminating descriptions of
school life were prompted by a competition organised by the *Times
Educational Supplement*. Children of primary school age were invited
to write on two themes: what they did at school on Monday and
what they would like to do. Their replies — there were nearly three
thousand entries — show vividly how most of us have been misled
by the unhelpful generalization of such ideas as 'progressive' and
'traditional', 'basics' and the '3Rs'.

The children write with alarming candour of the narrowness and
monotony of much of their learning experiences. Their collected
thoughts allow us a rare glimpse of what it's like to be on the
receiving end of education.

Finding a Language
Autonomy and learning in school

Peter Medway

We don't all speak the same language about language. The Bullock Report recommended that every school should have a language policy; yet 'language across the curriculum' has simply not got off the ground in most schools.

Peter Medway believes it should entail a major shift in how children learn and — therefore — in how teachers teach. In *Finding a Language* he shows what he thinks some of the major consequences of a coherent language policy are: changed relationships between teacher and taught, increased opportunities for children to work collaboratively and to initiate their own writing, and a more open attitude to what counts as worth learning in school.

The book contains some impressive extracts from students' log books, demonstrating the kind of autonomy working-class pupils can achieve in these conditions. Overall, it shows the real innovation made by progressive English teaching — to have set up a new model of education within the existing system. Peter Medway argues the case for extending that model to other parts of the curriculum.